The Psychology Project Manual

The Psychology Project Manual

FIRST EDITION

Emma Whitt

Stephanie McDonald

Alice Doherty

Kate Bailey

OXFORD
UNIVERSITY PRESS

OXFORD
UNIVERSITY PRESS

Great Clarendon Street, Oxford, OX2 6DP,
United Kingdom

Oxford University Press is a department of the University of Oxford.
It furthers the University's objective of excellence in research, scholarship,
and education by publishing worldwide. Oxford is a registered trade mark of
Oxford University Press in the UK and in certain other countries

© Oxford University Press 2023

The moral rights of the authors have been asserted

Published in the United States of America by Oxford University Press
198 Madison Avenue, New York, NY 10016, United States of America

British Library Cataloguing in Publication Data
Data available

Library of Congress Control Number: 2022951789

ISBN 978-0-19-883206-5

Printed in the UK by
Bell & Bain Ltd., Glasgow

Contents

Detailed Contents

Endorsements

"The book provides a clear guide to students undertaking their final year project. The text covers all aspects of the research process including allocation of a project supervisor, recruitment of participants, and presentation of research findings".

—Gayle Brewer, *University of Liverpool*

"An easy-to-follow, student-centred and practical guide to dissertations, with useful tips and the added bonus of discussing employability".

—Gemma Reynolds, *Middlesex University*

"A very student centred, practical, and reassuring approach is taken. Students' potential anxieties, frustrations and disappointments are authentically and effectively engaged with and well-measured advice is given to support students in reaching their full potential".

—Paul Dickerson, *University of Roehampton*

"A succinct guide for student project work. Clearly gives the core expectations and challenges, and complements the taught aspect of our dissertation module well".

—David Gordon, *University of Chester*

Acknowledgements

We would like to thank all the students who we have supported through their research projects. Your experiences have helped shape our thinking for this book. Thank you to students from the Oxford University Press student panel who very generously contributed hints and tips from their own research experience.

Thank you also to our colleagues who have shared their experiences as a research supervisor. We would also like to thank Sarah Allen, our wonderful Senior Careers Advisor, who offers expert careers advice to all the students she works with and who provided invaluable feedback on the 'Employability' chapter in this book.

Thank you to the anonymous reviewers who provided helpful comments and suggestions on drafts of this book.

Finally, we thank all our editors at Oxford University Press for their unwavering support through the years. Martha Bailes, who helped form the initial ideas for the book; and Sam Ashcroft, Sarah Iles, and Megan Mentuck for getting us to publication!

About this book

We wrote this book to help you to navigate your way through the psychology research project. The project is a core part of any psychology degree and has many different aspects to navigate, some of which will be familiar and some which you may be less familiar with. The idea of this book is that it is a guide that you can dip in and out of and find practical advice. We will take you through all the stages of your research project, from choosing your supervisor, planning and conducting your research, to disseminating your research findings, and reflecting on the skills you've learned and how these will prepare you for future employment. This book is a practical guide and therefore we do not go into detail about research methods and statistics because you will have covered these in your degree and there are many books around already that do a really good job supporting those aspects. What we instead cover are all those things that you might not have been taught, such as how to manage yourself, how to build a constructive relationship with your supervisor, and how to plan for and deal with some of the unexpected situations that might happen during your psychology research project.

The independent research project is an exciting part of every psychology student's academic journey and we have supervised students conducting their research projects over a number of years. We have therefore overseen many students through the highs and lows of completing their research project and have compiled our best hints and tips into this book. We have written from our own experience, but we have also drawn on the experiences of students to make the content of the book accessible, easy to understand, and relevant to different ways of completing the research project.

Look out for the following features; some of the insights offered in these boxes have been provided by recent psychology graduates who have a very good idea of the challenges and opportunities you may be met with during the research project:

Handy Hints are general tips that we think will help you to navigate your research project experience. These may highlight considerations you hadn't thought of, suggest effective ways to approach a task, or offer advice we, and others, wish we had known when we were doing our own research projects!

Smart Solutions highlight common challenges you may face when doing a research project and ways to avoid or manage these to help your project run smoothly. Students often worry about what could go wrong on their project—these tips show you that you can work around whatever happens and can often turn unexpected hurdles into positives.

Future Focus boxes identify links between your research project experience and your future plans. These help you to identify important skills you will develop through carrying out your project and how these might be applied in a professional workplace. Often, these are competences which are highly valued by graduate employers. The final chapter of the book draws some of these ideas together in more depth.

We wish you all the best with conducting your research project. Remember it is a brilliant way to develop and evidence a range of skills and, despite the occasional challenge, it can be great fun too!

Emma, Stephanie, Alice, and Kate

Figures

Tables

Starting Your Research Project

The research project is a fundamental part of any psychology programme, and it helps you to develop a number of skills that your future employers will want to know about. These can include:

- Data literacy
- Project planning
- Working as a team
- Research skills
- Thinking critically

In getting started on the research project you will already employ a number of these skills to narrow down your project area, plan and design your research project, and form a relationship with your supervisor. Although it might feel daunting, the early stages of your project should be an exciting phase in the project life cycle, a time for inspiration and collaboration. In this chapter we provide tips and guidance on how to get your project going and we will take you through the process of choosing your topic, finding alignment with your supervisor's research interests, and designing and refining your research question. We will introduce you to the process of literature searching and will encourage you to start a research diary.

1.1 Making Topic Choices

Identifying an appropriate topic will involve navigating the constraints of the research project and aligning your interests with the interests of your supervisor (once you know them). It is very unlikely that you will be offered a completely free choice of research topic and it is therefore important to keep an open mind and be prepared to make compromises to make your topic work for you. Many students come to the research project with quite fixed ideas about what they want to do and why. Some students might be lucky to be able to conduct their dream research project. However, here are some typical scenarios that can lead to disappointment and some suggestions on how to make the most of your final topic choice if you do find yourself in similar scenarios.

Many students try to find a research project in an area that is of direct relevance to their future career aspirations. Unfortunately, in practice, there are likely to be constraints on the nature and scale of the research that you will be able to conduct as your first independent research project. For example, many students aspire to become a practising clinical psychologist and it can be very tempting to try to use the research project as an opportunity to gain experience working with clinical populations or other vulnerable groups. Similarly, it can be tempting to try to choose topics that relate directly to your lived experience or that may be personally or politically challenging, for example by involving marginalized communities. In reality, the steps that need to be taken to ensure that both you and your participants are protected in these cases can be prohibitively complex. In this case, to gain any practical experience you are seeking, you may need to find other work experience opportunities that offer appropriate training and support. With respect to your research project, you may wish to think more broadly about wider topic areas and questions that might be applied in your chosen field. You can also discuss your career and personal aspirations with your supervisor as you start to get planning for your project under way. They may well be able to help you to shape your project in a particular direction, or to help you to understand the relevance of their expertise with respect to your wider interests.

Another popular basis for making topic choices can be to do with the methodology students hope to use. For example, many students experience some level of statistics anxiety and might feel that they would prefer to do a qualitative research project on the basis that this may be 'easier'. Qualitative research is not any easier than quantitative research and any research project that you conduct is going to have its own unique set of challenges and pitfalls. Similarly, other students may see the research project as an opportunity to gain experience using specialist equipment (e.g. eye-tracking, electroencephalogram (EEG), and so on). In both cases access and demand can be a significant problem. The number of staff who can supervise qualitative research varies quite significantly by department and specialist equipment is often in high demand by other groups (e.g. research staff, postgraduate research students) who will be offered priority access. If you are particularly keen to gain experience using a specific methodology, then it is a good idea not to rely on the research project to gain this experience but to look for alternative opportunities that might arise (for example research internships).

Smart Solution—Dealing with Disappointment

When I was conducting my undergraduate research, I was determined that I wanted to conduct my research project on a very specific topic and with a specific member of staff. I made them my first choice; I came up with my own research question, and I approached the staff member with my ideas. I literally did everything I could think of to demonstrate how keen I was and try to secure my first choice.

Of course, I was allocated a different supervisor and because I'd been so fixated on devising my own research topic (despite clear flaws that had already been pointed out to me) I hadn't really considered any other options. I was disappointed when I found out who my actual supervisor was, and at first, I really could not see how their interests aligned with my own. However, they were supportive and because I did try to remain enthusiastic, they took an active interest in me and my long-term goals. They recommended an idea, but also encouraged me to think independently about my design. The project gave me a lot of scope to be imaginative and I learned a great deal I had not expected which I was able to apply in my later research.

The key to avoiding disappointment at the topic selection stage is to keep an open mind. By all means look for a topic area that will keep you stimulated and engaged but do keep your expectations open and do keep in mind that psychology is an incredibly broad and applied discipline with implications that might not be obvious. You may not immediately see the links between the topic you are working on and your own aspirations but that is not to say that they are not there to be found. See Figure 1.1 for further tips about topic selection.

Plan to keep your ideas broad to start off with and keep an open mind about the direction your project will take until you have spoken with your project supervisor. Think about broad themes that would be of interest and make sure that you are familiar with your supervisor's expertise and any areas of overlap before you meet with them.

Do a preliminary sift of the literature to identify how your areas of interest might have been approached from a psychological perspective. How does your research area draw on psychological theory? What methodological approaches have been used to explore your topic area? Bear in mind that if you are conducting a psychology research project, it will be expected that you will need to demonstrate your ability to use psychological research methods (for example experimental methods, psychometric questionnaires, interviews and focus groups, etc).

Don't be tempted to try to use your research question to prove a point and only choose a topic if you are confident that you will be able to remain critical and open-minded. Empirical research (whether qualitative or quantitative) is not about providing proof. It provides data/evidence which requires interpretation.

Have a back-up plan if you think your topic might be ethically sensitive. Your supervisor will have the final say on whether it is appropriate for you to conduct research that involves vulnerable populations or asks sensitive questions, but it is helpful to have alternative topics of interest in mind. For more information on conducting your research ethically refer to Chapter 5.

Figure 1.1 Tips for Topic Selection

1.2 The Allocation Process

> **Handy Hint**
> The best way to avoid disappointment is to really consider what you do and don't enjoy. Making sure your top favourite supervisors are at the top [of your list of preferred supervisors] but also consider a supervisor who works in a sector you like but don't love. Ultimately your project is much easier when you enjoy it but sometimes research can be surprisingly interesting.
>
> Student, Royal Holloway University of London

To manage student demand, departments will typically have an allocation process in place to match supervisors with students. Every department has some supervisors who are more popular than others. Importantly, that is not necessarily a marker of how good a supervisor they are or what you will get out of the research project. However, this does mean that some students will be allocated their non-preferred choice of supervisor or topic. As we have already highlighted, in these circumstances it is best to keep an open mind and see your allocation as an opportunity. Whoever does supervise you will be a competent and experienced researcher with the expertise to help you to develop a research project that is both current and achievable. If you are willing to run with things it can be an opportunity to work together to devise a piece of research that might be unanticipated and exciting. In research the best ideas are often unexpected.

Some departments may offer you the opportunity to approach academic members of staff with your own ideas and/or to prepare your own mini research proposal. Usually, it would be expected that these conversations had taken place before any formal allocation processes had started. It is very unlikely that you would be able to request to change your supervisor once the allocation process has concluded. The next section ('writing your own research proposal') will provide some tips on how to write your own mini research proposal. However, this guidance comes with a caveat. It takes a great deal of experience and practice to generate new research ideas and you are likely to receive constructive feedback on your research proposal. It may be that you are advised that your research proposal is feasible with changes, or it could be that there are limitations in your design idea which mean that it is not feasible. In addition, although it is likely that members of the academic team may be able to provide you with some advice around your proposed research, they are unlikely to be able to offer any guarantees that they will be available to supervise your research project.

1.3 Writing Your Own Research Proposal

It is not usually an expectation that you write a full research proposal as part of your research project but sometimes you might be asked to write a mini research proposal, if, for example, there is an expressions of interest process that takes place before the formal allocation process. Please be reassured that it will not be an expectation that you have the knowledge and experience to develop a polished research proposal that does not need some adjustment. However, if you are asked to write a mini research proposal, here are some key tips and pointers about how to present your ideas and what to include. You should, of course, also plan to take into consideration any internal guidance that is provided by the department where you are completing your research project.

It is well worth keeping in mind that academics are busy people, and you can help them by keeping your research proposal short and sweet. You will probably only need to provide up to a couple of paragraphs and certainly not more than a page of information for your reader to gain a good understanding of what you intend to do, and why it is interesting. Your research proposal should:

1. Highlight any background reading that you have done: what are the key papers that have informed your idea?

2. Define your research question(s).

3. Provide some detail about your proposed design:

   a. What participants are you planning to work with and how accessible is that population to you? Be sure to highlight any connections or networks that you may have access to.

   b. Provide sufficient detail about the methods, techniques, and measures you are planning to use so that someone can assess whether your design is feasible.

   c. Give an indication of what analysis you expect to use, will it be qualitative or quantitative and what analysis method will be employed (e.g. linear regression, analysis of variance, grounded theory, phenomenology etc.)

   d. Highlight any research papers that have employed a similar methodology: what is your design based on?

4. Don't forget to add the personal element: why is your idea important to you and what makes you uniquely placed to run this research project? Perhaps you have connections to the right cohort of participants, or maybe this is an intervention or technique you have direct experience of.

5. You do not necessarily need to make this explicit, but consider what makes your supervisor well placed to support your work? For example, is your idea related to some of their own research? In this case then be sure to reference that work.

Putting forward an idea in this way takes both inspiration and confidence and you do need to be prepared to receive feedback that your idea is not appropriate and/or feasible. Be prepared to accept any feedback as constructive. There is always something to be learned!

1.4 What Makes a Good Research Question?

Your independent research project is likely to be your first opportunity to conduct your own piece of original research and the marking scale for your research project is very likely to emphasize the originality of your research design. A concern for many students is that their research question and design is not going to be 'different' enough to be considered original. A more helpful definition of originality would be to consider how your research project is going to make a novel contribution to understanding. This could be that you are researching an understudied topic area, it could be that you are using different methods to explore your research question, or it might be the case that you are conducting your research with different populations or samples. It does not mean that you will be expected to come up with a totally new design that no one else has ever considered. In fact, if you take this approach then chances are you could come up with a question that goes well beyond the scope of a student research project.

Handy Hint
An original research question is one whereby there is a fundamental question being proposed that hasn't been before. Similar research will always exist and is even helpful for background literature but ensuring your question hasn't been answered or developed is always a good sign.
Student, Royal Holloway University of London

The trick in identifying a novel or original research question that is of appropriate scale is to conduct a thorough review of the literature. If you under-research your idea it is possible to fall into the trap of assuming that you have identified a novel idea only to find later that not only has your research question already been examined, but there is also plenty of literature to show that what you want to do is not going to work in the way that you might be expecting. Your supervisor will also be able to help you in avoiding this pitfall and for this reason you will be expected to keep in regular contact with them as you work through the process of designing your research project. Together with your supervisor you should work towards making sure that your research question is above PAR.

In other words, it is:

P—ractical: based on methods, populations, and approaches that are clearly defined and accessible to you within the available timescale.

A—nalysable: you know what analysis you will use to test your research question and you have the training and/or support to be able to conduct it.

R—esearch informed: you have conducted a preliminary literature review to check the background literature to find out how related questions have been approached before and (for quantitative studies) you have done sufficient reading that you have a clear idea about what you expect to find.

We will now take you through the steps involved in making sure that you have met these key objectives.

1.5 The Preliminary Literature Review

It is highly unlikely that you will find a topic area that has not been explored before so you will need to conduct a literature review to establish how the topic has been approached previously. This is also a good opportunity to start to look for current or emerging themes in the literature and to identify any gaps that your research project might be able to fill.

Your supervisor is likely to be able to offer a few key references in getting started but they will be expecting that you do your own review of the literature available. You will have an opportunity as part of your supervision to present your key findings from this activity and to receive feedback from your supervisor; for example, you might be asked to provide a brief summary for discussion during a supervision meeting. You may find that you and your supervisor agree to change the direction of your research project as an outcome of your findings at this stage.

In conducting your preliminary literature review you should consider the questions outlined in Figure 1.2.

Handy Hint

Researching similar studies to the one I planned on conducting aided me in further understanding my research topic and question as they not only provided findings that could assist me in producing my literature review but also background information on my research topic.

Student, University of Roehampton

You are advised not to rush your preliminary literature review, but it is also important to be aware that this stage of the research can take a great deal of time, if not managed; you should take a systematic, thorough, and critical approach.

1.5.1 Being Systematic

The full literature review that you conduct for your project report is likely to be one of the widest literature searches that you conduct during your degree programme. It is not going to be possible to read all the relevant material before you start your research project, and it is also worthwhile keeping in mind that you may need to refer to the materials that you collate in this process over a considerable timeframe. For these reasons you may plan to make some changes to the approaches that you have taken to reviewing the literature for your previous essays and reports.

Have a think about your current approach to literature searching. Are you more like Debbie or Irfan?

Debbie skims through the titles and abstracts on library databases until she finds a research paper that looks interesting, then stops to read the paper. She returns to the database later to find her next relevant research paper.

Irfan likes to have dedicated literature searching time where he uses online tools to collate lists of potentially relevant research papers. He later revisits those lists and reviews each paper in detail.

If you talk to other students, you are likely to find that people take different approaches to managing their research time and they all have their advantages and disadvantages. One of the advantages of Debbie's approach is that you get to the literature very quickly, however it is also quite easy to get side-tracked and find yourself overlooking particularly relevant material. On the other hand, if you take Irfan's approach then you can collate lots of material very quickly and track and record what you are reading, but this can quite quickly become overwhelming if you don't prioritize the material that you are reading. Striking some balance

What are the key research papers in your area?
What are the specific research questions that they have addressed?
How do these relate to the ideas that you want to address?

Any papers provided by your supervisor will offer a start, but you should plan to identify other related papers

Based on the research papers that you've reviewed are there any unanswered questions that you might be able to address in your research?

For example, do they provide suggestions for future work that you could follow up in your own research or have you identified any gaps in explanation that you might be able to follow up?

What data collection methods have been used and what methodologies could you employ in your own research?

Are you reading more qualitative or quantitative research papers and what does this tell you about the methods that are likely to be appropriate?

What data analyses have been employed? Are there any studies that might offer a basis for your own design?

Do you recognize the analyses that have been used from your own research methods training? Could you replicate/simplify them?

How are participants recruited? What sampling procedures are typically employed? What sample sizes are you likely to need?

Sampling procedures may include random sampling, stratified sampling, convenience sampling, and purposive sampling. For more details about sampling methods refer to Chapter 4.

What are potential sources of bias?

For quantitative research you will want to consider whether there are any intervening variables (i.e. variables other than the independent variable) that may explain any variation in your dependent variable. Bias might arise if these variables have not been appropriately controlled.

For qualitative research, sources of bias might include interpretive bias, sampling bias, and personal bias. Bias may arise through poor sample selection, poor instrument design (e.g. using closed or leading questions in an interview schedule) and poor research practice (for example by influencing data collection or not addressing subjectivity during analysis).

Figure 1.2 Preliminary Literature Review Questions

between the breadth and depth of your reading is going to be fundamental in developing an effective literature searching strategy. Good record keeping is also likely to pay dividends when you come to writing up your research project and is a good habit to get into from the start of your research project. Making records of your own notes can also protect you against unintentional plagiarism (see the section on 'keeping notes' for more tips on how to use effective record keeping).

It is a good idea not to read research papers in full to start with but to use the abstract and a skim-read of the introduction and conclusions to target and prioritize what research papers you will read first. Once you have identified which are the particularly key research papers for your research project then you will want to give them an in-depth read, focusing particularly on the methods and findings and how these inform your research design.

Handy Hint

Whilst it is tempting to simply accept everything you are told, read the key papers associated with your project with a critical eye. Make sure that you know the flaws in the key research before you even begin to design your own project. For example, it is crucial to know whether the instruments you plan to use, such as a questionnaire, are valid and reliable measures of the construct you are attempting to measure. Knowing the issues in the key research will help you to avoid the same pitfalls and will generate discussion of the limitations of your own design.

Student, Durham University

1.5.2 Being Critical

Reading critically means that you actively engage with the text by asking questions about what you are reading. Reading critically is not simply about finding fault but it does require an understanding that empirical research does not offer confirmatory proof and that a research paper is only as good as a) the evidence it provides; and b) how successfully that evidence is interpreted.

When you read a research paper critically you will want to ask the following questions.

1. Are the methods and analysis appropriate for the research question?
2. Are there any identifiable sources of bias in the paper? Have these been adequately addressed in the paper?
3. Has the evidence been correctly interpreted?

If you engage critically with the background literature then, as well as identifying limitations to avoid in your own research, this can be a good way of identifying gaps that you might be able to design your own research project to address. However, whilst you should trust your own analytic skills which you will have practised throughout your degree, you do not need to rely solely on your own judgement. A good research paper will discuss any shortfalls in the design and provide justification with respect to what conclusions can/cannot be drawn. You can also consider what other researchers have to say about the paper and whether they identify any sources of bias or limitations (see the section on 'being thorough' for more information on how to identify these citing authors).

FUTURE FOCUS Critical Thinking and Decision-Making

Two skills which graduate employers will be eager to hear about are critical thinking and decision-making. A good example of these, which you could refer to in an application form or interview, is how you utilized the background literature to inform evidence-based decisions about your research design. Doing this successfully requires sound reasoning skills, the ability to critically review the work of others, and the capacity to generate and weigh up different options, all of which are likely to be valuable in a professional workplace. Critical thinking can also have much more pervasive benefits across all aspects of your life—from benefitting your interpersonal relationships to supporting effective goal setting and career planning.

1.5.3 Conducting a Thorough Literature Search

As you start your research project, you will usually want to make sure that you have done a thorough search of the literature that has enabled you to identify and read the most relevant articles, particularly for quantitative research projects. For qualitative research projects, you will usually need to do a thorough literature search at the start of your research project unless you are using a grounded theory approach to analyse your data where the in-depth literature review usually comes a bit later in the research cycle.

To ensure that your literature search is thorough and provides good coverage, use a variety of search platforms to conduct your literature searching which may include online search engines (such as Google Scholar) and bibliographic databases (such as Web of Science and American Psychological Association (APA) PsycInfo; see Box 1.1). To ensure that you capture the most reliable sources, you should start with research papers that you can access by subscription through your institutional library. This is because online search tools may

BOX 1.1 Literature Searching Resources

Your department/institution
Refer to your institutional library or academic skills team for refresher training on how to utilize the literature searching tools available to you in your institution.

Websites
Here are the literature searching websites that have been referenced in this section.

- Google Scholar is an online search engine which uses search algorithms to search journals, books, institutional repositories, and other academic sources to identify peer-reviewed articles, grey literature, and other published/unpublished content. https://scholar.google.com
- Web of Science is a bibliographic database which include details of journal articles from all academic subject areas, conference proceedings, and details of book chapter references from selected books. https://clarivate.com/webofsciencegroup/solutions/web-of-science/
- American Psychological Association (APA) PsycInfo is a bibliographic database which includes details of APA published articles, books, and dissertations from the behavioural and social sciences. https://www.apa.org/pubs/databases/psycinfo

link you to grey literature such as preprints, conference papers, and technical reports. On the other hand, bibliographic databases typically only link to sources that your library subscribes to, which means that you can be confident that you are referring to the final, peer-reviewed sources. That is not to say that grey literature will not be relevant as part of your wider literature search, but you will want to start with the most reliable sources.

Different search tools will search the literature in subtly different ways. Online search engines tend to use search algorithms that are most familiar, but the tools they use to constrain searches (known as search limiters) are not as effective at filtering out irrelevant information. Bibliographic databases on the other hand require a bit more practice but they make it much easier to refine your search. At the start of your research project, it is worthwhile taking advantage of any on-demand support materials or refresher training that your library or academic skills department provides to understand how to make the most effective use of the search platforms that are available to you in your own institution.

Unlike search engines, bibliographic databases typically employ keyword searches to identify relevant information. You will be able to search for key words within several different fields (for example the title, topic, author name, journal title, and so on) and will also be able to use these fields to constrain your search. For example, if you wanted to find all articles on 'attachment' that had been published by 'Bowlby' then you could enter these key words into the Topic and Author fields respectively. Where you are using combinations of different key words, you will find that Boolean operators 'AND', 'OR', and 'NOT' are useful to help widen and narrow your search. To maximize your search, keep in mind that different authors may use different key words for the same topic. Therefore, try to think of all the possible different uses of terminology, word variations, and synonyms for your key term. Research papers often provide a list of key words, so this may be one place to look for further key words you could use in your own literature search.

Other useful references can often also come from the research paper itself. Use the reference lists of key research papers that you are reading to see if there are any articles that have been cited that would be valuable for you to review (we call this backwards literature searching). Also remember that many of the literature searching tools that we use offer the opportunity to do what we call a forward literature search. Every database does this slightly differently but watch out for links like 'article citations', 'cited by', or 'times cited'. So if you have a key research paper that you think is fundamental to your design then you can look to see if you can find any other research papers that have cited that paper to see whether they have approached things in a different and more interesting way. This can also be really useful in your critical evaluation of the target paper as it gives you the opportunity to find out what other authors have said about the research and how they might have interpreted the evidence it provides.

1.5.4 Keeping Notes: Your Research Diary

You should plan to continue to review the literature throughout the duration of your research project and there are likely to be papers and ideas that you initially discount that you may wish to return to later. For this reason, it is a good idea to use a notebook or journal (which could be online or paper-based) to record what you have read, and any thoughts and reflections that you have whilst you are reading. For example, you might feel that there is a term or concept that you have not understood, or you might find that there are emerging themes or links between research papers that you want to explore later. A diary-based approach gives you the opportunity to park ideas that may later serve as prompts for lines of enquiry that you may wish to follow up as you get deeper into your research.

Although your research project is an important part of your final degree you will need to ensure that you balance the time that you spend working on the project with other parts of your degree programme. Keeping effective notes as you work through your research project can help you to balance your time as you come to write up your project (for more tips on how to manage your time effectively see Chapter 2). To this end, you can also utilize your diary to record all aspects of your decision-making process, not simply notes from your reading, so that you have a reference guide when you come to write up your research project. It is particularly helpful to make sure that you have a clear record of the meetings that you have with your research project supervisor or your research project group and any other tasks and activities that you complete that inform the methodological and analytical decisions that you are making as you progress through the research project. For example:

- As you are working through your literature review, you identify several different questionnaires that all test emotional intelligence. In a supervision meeting, your supervisor sets you a task to make a list of the strength and weaknesses of the different questionnaires, and you present a summary of your findings at your next meeting. You have a particular recommendation in mind but when you discuss it with your supervisor then you both choose a different questionnaire. An important point to note in your research diary is not only which questionnaire you settled on but also why you made this choice.

- You are using a Likert scaled questionnaire and, after an informal discussion with your project group, you agree make minor changes to the wording of some of the items on your questionnaire. One of your colleagues makes the changes, confirms that they are appropriate with the research project supervisor, and shares them with the rest of the group. Again, make sure to note down what it was that informed the changes to wording. If this was based on research you read, take care to record the reference so you can find it later.

At the time, the reasoning behind these decisions often feels very obvious and clear, and it can be very easy to assume that it will be easy to remember what has been agreed and why. However, in reality we often forget, particularly when working over several months. Giving yourself 10 to 15 minutes at the end of a meeting or research session to record notes (or as soon afterwards as you possibly can) can save a lot of time and headaches when you come to writing up your research project and justifying the decisions you have taken.

FUTURE FOCUS Project Management

Project management is an important skill that employers are interested in, and one which graduates from disciplines outside psychology may have less experience of. As such, this is a great way to set yourself, as a psychology graduate, apart! Keeping effective records and using efficient systems are a key aspect of this in the workplace when you may be expected to project manage complex tasks, set goals and objectives for yourself and others, and record and audit your decision-making processes. A good way to evidence your proficiency in this during the planning process is to talk about how you used your research journal to manage your time effectively as well as keep a track of key decisions in your project life cycle.

1.6 The Design Plan

After you have completed your preliminary literature review the next step in your planning will be to start to think about your own design. It is not recommended to start from the ground up and try to design a completely original study. Nor should you expect that your supervisor will provide you with a fully developed idea that you cannot enhance yourself. A helpful way to conceptualize the design process is to think of it as an iterative process (see Figure 1.3) where you review and refine your design based on the literature and advice from your supervisor (refer to Chapter 3 for more advice on working with your supervisor). This is an important stage in your research project, and you may need a couple of meetings with your supervisor before you have a final plan which you can use to start to develop a more formal application for ethical approval (Chapter 5) should your institution require it.

1.6.1 Quantitative vs Qualitative Research

In formulating your initial design plan the first consideration that you should make is whether your research question would be more appropriate as a quantitative or a qualitative study. It is quite likely to be clear which direction you take. You won't be working completely from the ground up and your allocation of supervisor and their expertise with respect to the topic that you have chosen is highly likely to be a determining factor in whether you use a qualitative or a quantitative design. However, if you do need to make a choice then there are some considerations that should be made in determining what approach is the most appropriate to your research question (see Table 1.1).

It is worth noting that in the field some researchers conduct what is known as a mixed methods design. One example of a mixed methods design might be to start with a qualitative study based on a narrow sample and use this to generate a questionnaire to test your findings in a wider population. You should speak to your supervisor before considering a mixed methods design as this may well be beyond the scope and/or timescale of your research project.

Figure 1.3 The Iterative Design Process

Table 1.1 Considerations for Quantitative and Qualitative Design

Quantitative Design	Qualitative Design
You are interested in patterns or trends that might be captured numerically through questionnaires, surveys, or experimental studies.	You are interested in individual experiences and how individuals make meaning of their experiences that can be captured in a narrative form through e.g. interviews, online forums, diaries, and so on.
You have a good-sized population from which you can draw a random sample.	You may only have a small population that is context bound (i.e. culturally and historically specific).
You are asking a closed question. You have a clear expectation about what the outcome of your study will be (you are able to formulate a clear hypothesis). You can specifically identify the variables that will predict that outcome.	Your question can be broad or quite specific. The approach that you take in your analysis can be exploratory and inductive (where analysis tends to be data-driven and themes developed from the analysis are grounded in the data) or deductive (using existing theory to drive your research). You therefore may or may not have any expectation about the outcome of your study.

Specifying your research question and hypotheses: Quantitative research

Quantitative research seeks to explore patterns or trends that can be captured numerically. Broadly speaking, any quantitative research project will ask one of two types of question. These depend on the nature of your independent or predictor variable.

1. Where you have at least one continuous independent (or predictor) variable: is there a relationship between my independent and dependent variables? Is there a consistent pattern or trend that can be systematically measured?

   Examples of tests that might be employed:

   - correlation
   - regression.

   Example: do ratings on the smooth-talking ability scale and volume of hair gel applied predict number of telephone numbers collected in the first three hours of a night out?

2. Where you have *only* categorical independent variables (or categorical predictor variables): can I detect a difference in the values of my dependent variable when I compare across the groups identified by my independent variable?

   Examples of tests that might be employed:

   - analysis of variance (ANOVA)
   - t-test.

   Example: do language students learning vocabulary items in the library retain more words than students learning in the pub?

Before you fully define your research question you will need to identify the analysis that you intend to run. This will need to be agreed in discussion with your supervisor who will be able to provide advice with respect to the approaches that sit within your expertise to run and within their expertise to oversee. In specifying your research question, you will also need to be able to define:

a. What will your outcome (dependent) variable(s) be?

This is the variable that you are attempting to predict or find a difference in. Most statistical analyses employ a single outcome variable. There are exceptions (e.g. multivariate analysis of variance) but these are quite complex to analyse, and we only recommend that you plan to use such an analysis following discussion with your supervisor. For some designs you might run the same statistical test for multiple outcome variables (for example in reaction time experiments we often test error rate in addition to reaction time).

b. What are your independent variables?

These are variables that you will seek to change or manipulate experimentally.

Handy Hint

You should only design a study where you can describe what variables you will use and how it will be analysed. If you can't then the chances are that you may have made your design too complicated, too unspecific, or both. Don't feel the need to go this alone, it takes practice to design an analysis strategy. Therefore, do speak to your supervisor if you need support in understanding what analysis you will use and why.

For quantitative research, as well as a clearly defined question you should also have a clearly defined hypothesis.

The first step in defining your hypothesis is to make sure that it is testable. In other words, your hypothesis needs to be specific enough that you can provide empirical evidence for or against it. See Table 1.2 for some examples of testable and non-testable hypotheses.

As well as ensuring that you have a testable hypothesis you should be confident that you can justify the patterns (differences/relationships) that you are expecting to find based on the evidence and theory that you have read. Quantitative research depends on a process of significance-testing, by using statistical tests to understand whether findings are likely to be due to chance or to a factor of interest (one of your variables). Demonstrating statistical

Table 1.2 Examples of Testable and Non-Testable Hypotheses

Exposure to loud noise may lead to stress.	Not testable. The pattern that is described suggests that the effect is not consistent.
Reducing contact with nature will harm wellbeing.	Not testable. This hypothesis is not specific enough about what is being measured/manipulated.
Reading times for high frequency words will be shorter than reading times for low frequency words.	This hypothesis is testable.
There will be a relationship between the frequency of singing sessions and scores on the general wellbeing inventory.	This hypothesis is testable, but it is non-directional (i.e. it is two-tailed).

significance means that you have strong evidence that your findings are unlikely to have occurred by chance. If your findings are non-significant, then this does not prove that there is no relationship/difference to be found, it just means that the data collected has not provided strong enough evidence that the relationships/differences are not due to chance. For this reason, it is much harder to account for non-significant results. As you are planning your study, research the literature and identify what similar studies have found before and consider how this translates for your own hypotheses. If you don't think that there is strong empirical or theoretical evidence to expect a significant effect, then you should consider reviewing your research question.

One mistake that students who are new to research often make is to start with the hypothesis and work backwards to formulate the research design. In other words, they use their own intuition to formulate a hypothesis and then seek out the empirical evidence that supports these ideas to inform their research design and question. This is problematic because of the assumption that empirical research is a confirmatory process which provides proof.

To illustrate this with an example: Let's say that you have got the impression that males may have better spatial memory than females and you decide that this would be an interesting basis for a research question. You then selectively look for empirical evidence that confirms these observations and you use this literature to select your measures and formulate your hypotheses. Your results confirm your hypotheses so in your write-up you conclude that your findings prove that males have better spatial memory than females.

The problem with this approach is that at every step you have looked for confirmation of your own intuitions and biases. This has led to the misinterpretation that your theory has been proven. However, all that you can conclude from the statistical tests you have conducted is that your findings are unlikely to have occurred by chance. It could be that there is an alternative reason why males perform better on the task that you have chosen but, because you have not let the theory determine the task that you have chosen, you have overlooked the confounding factor in your research design. It is therefore important that you always start with the evidence and theory first and don't get drawn into the trap of trying to prove your own observations and expectations.

For further guidance on quantitative research see the list of resources in Box 1.2.

BOX 1.2 Further Resources for Quantitative Research

Your department
Don't forget to use any materials or resources from any quantitative methods modules that you have completed. Check reading lists from your department too.

Books
- Bourne, V., James, A. I., and Wilson-Smith, K. (2021). *Understanding Quantitative and Qualitative Research in Psychology: A Practical Guide to Methods, Statistics, and Analysis.* Oxford: Oxford University Press.

Specifying your research question: Qualitative research

Qualitative research focuses on meaning rather than numbers and, unlike quantitative research, it does not provide a single answer. Instead, qualitative analysis provides structure to generate a narrative about the data (usually text, but sometimes images) under analysis. Qualitative research questions tend to ask 'how?', or 'what?', and not 'why?' which implies there is a cause and effect.

Broadly speaking there are two main camps (Reicher, 2000) that ask different questions of the data.

Experiential qualitative research seeks to understand people's experience and actions, using the data as a vehicle to understand people's interpretations, meanings, views, and perspectives.

Example: what are the experiences of care leavers during the transition from sixth form college to university?

Discursive qualitative research, on the other hand, views language as social action which shapes our understanding of the world. Discursive approaches seek to understand the construction of meaning by exploring how language shapes our social reality.

Example: how are female gender norms regarding body weight constructed in teenage magazines?

Even within these two different camps there are several different methodologies and approaches (such as Grounded Theory, Foucauldian Discourse Analysis, Interpretive Phenomenological Analysis) which are underpinned by different assumptions about how we approach reality (we refer to these as ontological assumptions) and what counts as knowledge (we refer to these as epistemological assumptions). Different approaches are suited to different types of question, and your supervisor may well have particular areas of expertise within the qualitative domain. Therefore, as with quantitative research it is important that you define your research questions in conversation with your supervisor.

Unlike quantitative research which generates narrowly defined questions that can be answered with statistical tests, qualitative research asks broad questions where there is not a single right answer. For this reason, you will not be expected to formulate a testable research hypothesis in the same way as we described for a quantitative research project, and you may well not be expected to define any explicit predictions in advance of conducting your research.

For further guidance on qualitative research see the list of resources in Box 1.3.

BOX 1.3 Further Resources for Qualitative Research

Your department

Don't forget to use any materials or resources from any qualitative methods modules that you have completed. Check reading lists from your department too.

Books

- Bourne, V., James, A. I., and Wilson-Smith, K. (2021). *Understanding Quantitative and Qualitative Research in Psychology: A Practical Guide to Methods, Statistics, and Analysis.* Oxford University Press.
- Braun, V. and Clarke, V. (2013). *Successful qualitative research: A practical guide for beginners.* Sage.

Summary

Don't worry about designing your research project alone. The design process is a key part of the research project which your supervisor will support you with. For this reason, be prepared to be flexible and create time to seek and accommodate the advice of your supervisor. It is a good idea to be open-minded about what direction your project will take as it can be very easy to get too ambitious. Keep in mind that a good design should be practical, analysable, and research informed. Be prepared for the design process to take some time and allow for a process of refinement based on the literature and the advice of your supervisor. It is also a good idea to plan to keep a record of your reflections and insights as you engage in the design of your project. You will undoubtedly need to refer to these considerations as you write up your research project and reflect on the implications and limitations of your research findings at the end of the project. Most importantly take the time to enjoy this process. It is an exciting time where ideas take shape as you begin to drive your project forward.

 Go online to access further resources for the text: **www.oup.com/he/whitt1e.**

References

Reicher, S. (2000). Against methodolatry: Some comments on Elliott, Fischer, and Rennie. *British Journal of Clinical Psychology, 39*(1), 1–6. https://doi.org/10.1348/014466500163031

2 Managing Yourself

It is likely that your research project will be the largest scale piece of work you will need to undertake as part of your degree. It will draw on knowledge and skills you have developed throughout your course of study. A key element in helping you to successfully complete your research project is effective project management. This involves identifying what tasks are required and completing these within a specified timeframe. In this chapter you will find some useful tips on things to consider when starting out on your project, such as creating deadlines and prioritizing work, some common pitfalls and ways in which you can avoid these. The second half of this chapter will focus on working in a team for your research project.

2.1 Some Helpful Tips as a Starting Point

The topic of your research project may be one which you have chosen yourself or one that has been suggested by your supervisor. Once you have finalized a topic for your research project and agreed the focus of your project work with your supervisor, what are then the next steps?

- The first step is to divide your project work into smaller, manageable tasks, creating an action plan with all the things you need to do for your research project (see Figure 2.1).
- You can then create a time planner, or timetable, that works for you. Allocate time in your weekly time planner for your project work. Incorporate all the information from your action plan into your time planner, to fit in with other course requirements and any other commitments you may have (see Table 2.1). Research in general often takes longer than anticipated, as we will cover later on in this chapter, so it is important to bear this in mind when developing your time planner.

2.2 Important Steps in the Research Project

At first, starting and completing your research project may feel quite overwhelming. Your project may be undertaken over a short period of time or over a period of several months, if you are on a full-time course, or even longer if you are studying part-time. Irrespective of the length of time you have been allocated for your research project, it is important for you to consider all the steps needed to complete your project and to develop an action plan early in the process. This will help you to keep track of the progress of your project, in terms of activities that have been completed and what remains to be done.

Figure 2.1 outlines typical steps in the research project process once you have started working on your research project. You can use this action plan as a guide and add further steps as relevant to your project.

Your first job is to create a list of tasks you need to complete in the specified timeframe. Important steps in the process include obtaining ethical approval for your study. This is something you will likely discuss with your supervisor in one of your earlier supervision meetings. It could be the case that your supervisor may already have ethical approval as your study may form part of a larger piece of work that your supervisor may be involved in. Alternatively, it could be the case that you may need to prepare and submit an application for a full ethical review. This needs to be planned early as it can cause delays to data collection if the research ethics committee requires any revisions to be made. More information about ethical approval processes involved in research projects can be found in Chapter 5.

Some tasks within your action plan could overlap during the duration of your research project. For example, you can begin reviewing the literature at the start of your project, as this will help you to identify what has previously been done relevant to your area of research and can inform your study design and hypotheses. Engaging with the literature can then

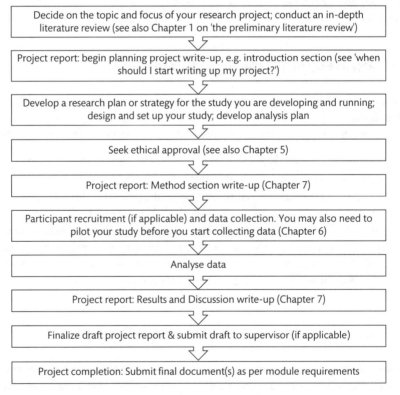

Figure 2.1 Typical Steps or Tasks Involved in a Research Project

be continued alongside other tasks, for example, whilst you are awaiting the decision of the research ethics committee (see Figure 2.2).

The final step typically involves the submission of your research project report and any other activities, such as a presentation of your project for example, as per your course requirements. Once you have created your list of tasks, you can then discuss this with your supervisor as they may be able to advise you based on their experience on research projects.

2.3 Creating an Action Plan that Works for You: Fitting it All In

Once you have created an action plan with key tasks relevant to your research project, you can note down associated deadlines to keep track of the work that you will need to do and when you need to do it. Be sure to check the guidelines provided by your department on key dates relevant to your research project and develop your action plan in relation to these. Creating deadlines and fitting your project in your overall timetable of academic activities and other commitments will give you more confidence in completing the work within the set deadline. It's helpful to start planning from the deadline of project submission backwards. If you are working in a team to complete certain aspects of your project, then there are some additional things you would need to factor into your time planner (see the section on 'Working in a Team' for further information).

An example of an action plan relating to the research project with some of the steps involved in the process can be found in Table 2.1, which you can adapt and use for your project.

It is better to start working on your research project early and to plan your next steps. A common pitfall is leaving certain tasks until quite late in the process, by which time you will probably also have other deadlines approaching. Depending on where you are in the research process (consult the timeline you developed for your project) you can then decide which task to prioritize for that week or for a specific time allocation in your planner.

FUTURE FOCUS Action Planning

Managing your project through action planning is an excellent habit to get into, and one which you could make great use of in a graduate role. Being able to articulate and justify your planning systems to an employer—with reflection on their impact on your productivity and success—could be very persuasive evidence of your capabilities; this is something you may wish to refer to during the recruitment process. Not only is action planning instrumental in professional project management, it can also be very valuable in managing your career. Creating an action plan can help you to set achievable goals and reflect on your progress whether you wish to explore job opportunities, gain work experience, or consider a change in career.

Often not having fixed timetabled classes for your research project may mean that the research project falls towards the end of your to-do list, in comparison to other modules which may have timetabled classes or other activities and coursework submissions. This could cause problems, so creating a time planner where you allocate some time each week to your project, the same way as you would dedicate time for your other modules, can be a helpful way to ensure that you are systematically working on your project throughout the allocated timeframe. You can use a variety of tools to develop your time planner, such as Gantt charts (see Figure 2.2 and Additional Online Resources for some examples).

Table 2.1 Action Plan

Tasks	What resources do I need to complete this task?	Deadline: this task should be completed by . . .
1. Develop plan for study design	Conduct a thorough literature review Note down key aspects of research design (draft plan) to discuss with supervisor Following supervision meeting amend and finalize study design	Discuss some initial ideas with supervisor based on literature review (e.g. next supervision meeting in two weeks' time) Discuss and agree with supervisor a deadline for draft plan based on initial discussion Refine initial ideas and develop draft plan (e.g. X number of weeks) for further discussion with supervisor Anticipated completion date/timeline for finalized study plan: X number of weeks (depending on your overall research project timeframe)
2. Gain ethical approval from relevant research ethics committee for my study	Consult relevant guidelines and resources on obtaining ethical approval Complete relevant forms	Complete relevant documents and forms by X date, send to supervisor for feedback, arrange meeting to discuss Anticipated completion date/timeline: three weeks
3. Set up study (if applicable)	Gain access to relevant software/hardware for study Familiarize myself with how to set up study using chosen software/hardware. Consult relevant help pages or training material Set up study. If working in a group, allocation of specific tasks to group members and collaboration in the setting up of study. Arrange to meet with supervisor to discuss and obtain feedback Pilot study and make amendments if necessary	Consult your supervisor or other relevant individual or resources available in your department for access to relevant software or equipment Setting up the study: X number of weeks, allowing time to familiarize yourself with the software or equipment, and coordinating tasks and group meetings to discuss progress if working with peers on setting up your study Arrange meeting with supervisor to discuss study set-up and obtain feedback by X date Pilot study by Y date Anticipated date/timeline for completion of this task: X weeks

A Gantt chart such as the one shown in Figure 2.2 is a useful tool which you can use to help you manage the several tasks which make up your research project. The tasks to be completed are presented in the left-hand column. The bars show the timeline for each of those tasks: how long you would need to work on each task, how it can overlap with other tasks, and when each task is likely to end. A complete example of this chart, as well as guidelines on how you can create your own Gantt chart for your project, can be found in the Additional Online Resources.

When creating a time planner consider all the steps written down in your action plan and how best to fit these in the allocated time. However, do bear in mind that when conducting research things can take longer than anticipated, so you will need to be flexible in the time that you allocate to complete certain tasks (see also section on 'Risks that May Inhibit Your Research Project'). We often underestimate how long it takes for different tasks in the research project to be completed (Buehler et al., 1994). Once you have developed a draft of your time planner, adding some extra time on each task (e.g. 25% extra time) will likely provide a more accurate reflection of your project timeline. This is something that you can

	October							November							December						January				
	25	26	27	28	29	30	31	1	2	3	4	5	6	7	1	2	3	4	5	6	20	21	22	23	24
Literature review	█	█	█	█	█	█	█	█	█	█	█	█	█	█	█	█	█	█	█	█	█	█	█	█	█
Develop research plan	▒	▒	▒	▒	▒	▒																			
Design & set up study	█	█	█	█	█	█	█	█	█	█	█	█	█	█											
Seek ethical approval	▒	▒	▒	▒	▒	▒	▒																		
Data collection															█	█	█	█	█	█	▒				
Analyse data																						▒	▒	▒	▒
Write up report								█	█	█	█	█	█	█	█	█	█	█	█	█	█	█	█	█	█

Note. This Gantt chart presents example months with selected number of days within each month for illustration purposes. Highlighted bars show the time when a task may start and end.

Figure 2.2 Gantt Chart Illustrating the Research Project Schedule

discuss and agree with your supervisor when discussing your project timeline. You will often find that it may be best to overestimate the time needed rather than to underestimate how long each step of the research process will take. If you find that you have completed certain tasks earlier than what you had originally planned for, you can have an earlier start on other aspects of your project work.

You may also, for example, need to allow time in your time planner to familiarize yourself with or to receive some training on using specialist equipment or software for data collection or data analysis. It is important to develop an action plan that is realistic and flexible, allowing sufficient time for each task in the process. Maintaining flexibility and adaptability are skills which are not only important in any job you may go into, but also important whilst undertaking a research project. Often planning in advance and allowing some time for potential unexpected circumstances can help to keep you on track for completion of the research project within the required timeframe.

You may find it helpful to share your action plan with your supervisor for some advice and feedback. You may also find it useful to speak with other students in your department on how they manage their research projects, as they may be able to provide a student perspective and some useful tips on project management and what to expect from your research project.

Handy Hint

Try to be organized with your work. Have a regular schedule in which you dedicate a set amount of time to your project/dissertation. For example, you might dedicate two hours a day to reading for your project, with the rest of the day left for work for your other modules. It is important not to try to do this all at once and remember that your project is a marathon, not a sprint.

Student, Durham University

Your department may allow you to submit a draft of your research project report or sections of your report to your supervisor for feedback, and they may have a set deadline for you to do this. If you don't have a set deadline for this, then you may want to discuss and negotiate a deadline with your supervisor, to fit in with their commitments, but also for you to have sufficient time to work on the feedback you are provided with.

Handy Hint

Plan to have a draft of your dissertation in early. Your work for your exams will increase after Easter and this can limit the time you have available to work on your dissertation. Get a draft of your dissertation in early to ensure you have plenty of time to act on your feedback.

Student, Durham University

2.4 When should I Start Writing Up My Research Project?

It is never too early to start thinking about and drafting the structure and content of your report. It is better to start early and have some information written down which you can then refine and add to once further information is acquired relevant to the different sections of your report (see Chapter 7 on 'Writing Your Report').

You may find it helpful to start making some notes on relevant literature you come across through your review of the literature, which can then be used to write your introduction. Writing your introduction is something that you can do in the early stages of your research project rather than leaving all the writing until the end. Similarly, once you have designed your study or experiment, you can also start writing the method section of your research project report. You do not need to wait until you have completed your data collection and data analysis to start writing up your project. You can begin drafting your report as information is acquired and fit this in with other project-related tasks in your time planner.

Smart Solution—"I'm Not Sure Where To Start With My Writing"

Getting started on an extended piece of writing often feels daunting! It can be tempting to put it off until near the end of your research; however, there are lots of benefits to drafting sections as you go along. An easy place to start is by mapping out the headings and subheadings you might use—this will give you a structure to work with and breaks your writing up into smaller tasks.

You can use this document to keep notes on any interesting papers you read and start drafting your introduction. A great time to write your 'Method' section is while you are collecting data—it is much easier to describe your recruitment strategy, measures/materials, procedure and so on while you're running the study than it is later! You can also get started early with your 'Results' section by looking at journal articles in a similar area and making a few notes on how they have presented their analyses. Think about the analysis you're likely to be doing and see if you can map out what you'll need to report to address your research questions.

2.5 Risks that May Inhibit Your Research Project

No matter how carefully you plan, it is entirely possible that something could happen to disrupt your plans, and that's when you will realize the benefit of having allowed flexibility and plenty of time in your schedule. Table 2.2 outlines some example circumstances that some students have faced when working on their research project. It would be useful to bear these examples in mind when planning your project as they may shape your action plan and associated deadlines. See Table 2.2 for some suggestions as to how you might overcome these issues or plan ahead to accommodate these in your time planner.

Table 2.2 Action Plan to Address Potential Risks that may Impact Your Research Project

Risks	Addressing the risks
Data collection may take longer than anticipated. For example, participants may not be signing up to do your study, or if you are collecting questionnaire data you may find that you have a large number of incomplete responses. This may also suggest that you could end up having fewer participants than previously planned.	You would typically discuss your sample size with your supervisor in the planning stages of your study. Having fewer participants than previously planned: schedule this as a point to discuss with your supervisor at your next meeting. Is this something that you would need to pursue further (e.g. further recruitment of participants) or would you have a sufficient number of participants, such that you can stop collecting data within the timeframe you have allocated for this specific task in your research project?
You have not previously used the piece of software that you need to set up your study.	Schedule some time in your time planner to familiarize yourself and gain some practice using this software, well ahead of time. Planning this step before you would need to use the software, rather than when you are about to start setting up your study, can help prevent delays in developing your study and, subsequently, data collection. You may find it helpful to consult relevant resources and to speak with your supervisor or other students (e.g. postgraduate students in your department) who may have used this software.
The software you are using to run your study is bringing up an error, which suggests that your study is not working as it should.	When developing your time planner allow some additional time in the setting up and pilot stages of your study, and even in the data collection stage. Allowing this extra time in your time planner can provide some flexibility to deal with such issues (e.g. by discussing this with your supervisor/a postgraduate student, if applicable) without the risk of running out of time in the data collection process. Find out what other sources of information may be available in your department to support you in tackling these issues (e.g. workshops, guides, discussion forums).
You need to use specific tests to analyse your data which you may not feel very confident in using.	Your analysis plan is something that you are likely to discuss with your supervisor in the planning stages of your research project and prior to analysing your data. Take some time to familiarize yourself with the techniques you will be using to analyse your data. Consult relevant sources of information (e.g. notes from teaching sessions, scheduled workshops, textbooks). Also, consider whether taking this time to read and gain some practice with these tests is something you could do whilst collecting your data, rather than waiting until you have collected all your data. Scheduling this task into your action plan and time planner ahead of time will enable you to start analysing your data as soon as your data collection is complete.

(Continued)

Table 2.2 Action Plan to Address Potential Risks that may Impact Your Research Project (*Continued*)

Risks	Addressing the risks
"I can't seem to start writing my report; I'm not sure where or how to begin"	It is often beneficial to spread the writing of your research project report over the course of your research project rather than having this as a single task at the end of your project (see Figure 2.2).
	Students often find the introduction and the discussion the hardest sections to write, and these are often the sections that rely on engaging with relevant literature which can be a bit more time consuming than writing up the method section, for example. Indeed, some people find it easier to begin with the methods section. Once you have set up your study then you can begin to write this up in your report as you will now have all the information necessary to go into the different subsections (e.g. procedure, materials).
	When it comes to your introduction you may find that starting to make notes on relevant literature as you are conducting your literature search can then help you in starting to build the write-up of this section. You can start off with some notes that you can then develop into a larger introduction section. This process often takes time, so you might find it helpful to engage with from the earlier stages of your research project.
	Also, you may find that you are more productive in your writing if you focus on two sections of your report in parallel, rather than waiting until you have finalized one specific section before moving on to the next. For example, can you start making notes which you will use to develop your introduction whilst conducting your literature search? Could you, at the same time, start making some notes on the materials and procedure of your method section, once you have finalized the design of your study? If your department requires you to develop a research proposal, elements of your proposal can potentially be used for your final research project report (be sure to check guidance from your department in relation to this). See also Chapter 7 on writing your report.
"I am sharing a lab with other people so I am restricted in the number of hours I can test participants each week"	Sometimes you may find that you do not have unlimited access to a lab. If this is the case, then you can try and do other tasks in parallel, so you do not feel like you are spending weeks simply waiting to get participants in the lab. Could you, for example, start working on your introduction during the days where you are not collecting data? This can help you to progress through your research project, keeping you on track with your action plan and time planner, without causing any unnecessary delays. Also, it is important to have a conversation with your supervisor or a lab manager, if applicable, and other students using the same lab to develop a fair schedule so as to ensure that all students have equal access to the labs or specialized equipment needed for their research.

As you will have noticed it is often the case that two or more activities in the research process may run in parallel. The Gantt chart in Figure 2.2 presents an example of some instances where this might be the case.

2.6 Looking after Yourself

The research project is a major piece of work, which is likely to be reflected in the weighting given to it by your course and it can be worth as much as a third of the overall mark for the final year. This can result in lots of worry and stress about your project; however, it is important to remember that you (usually) have the entire year to complete your project and your

---

BOX 2.1 Tips for Working when Motivation is Low

- **Structure**—try to bring some structure into your day. Use a daily or weekly timetable to schedule in particular activities. Break activities up into small tasks and they will seem more manageable.

- **Order**—do difficult things at your best time of day. You may work best in the morning so use that time to do the hard tasks.

- **Reward yourself**—just completed 500 words? Fantastic! Watch a TV programme, eat a chocolatey treat, or phone your friend.

---

supervisor is there to support you through it. While it is important to work consistently on your research project you should also make sure you have time for hobbies and activities outside your academic work. It is important to let your supervisor know if you are struggling to manage your project alongside other academic commitments and life events. Life events (such as bereavement, illness, temporary caring responsibilities) do occur when you are studying and often when it is most inconvenient. Your supervisor can help you work out how you can manage your project during difficult times.

Motivation is key to studying. We all experience low points in motivation (even your supervisor) so be prepared for this (see Box 2.1) and concentrate on using time effectively when you do feel motivated. Setting particular goals with deadlines may help overcome dips in motivation. Try to think about what you want to get out of the research project. Most students do find conducting a research project quite satisfying and are invested in the research: we could say their intrinsic motivation is high. Other students perhaps are more motivated by getting a good mark and just getting the research project done: we could say these students' extrinsic motivation is high. Lots of students will have a combination of both types. Whatever your motivation around your project, you will benefit more if you actively involve yourself and push yourself to do things.

It is important that you try and keep on track with your research project work and ensure that you are engaging with it throughout. It is also important to try and recognize what your strengths and weaknesses might be in relation to time management and keeping on track and how you can mitigate those challenges. For example, if you are finding that you are procrastinating in making a start with your report writing, then often breaking this task in smaller components and setting some concrete goals can help you in this process. You could, for example, try using the Pomodoro technique, where you set aside a time where you create a to-do list for a specific task you are working on, set a timer where you can really focus on the task at hand and have regular timed breaks to reward yourself for all your progress on the task (Cirillo, 2006). Often seeing the progress you are making can help with maintaining motivation on working through your project. Different techniques may work better for different people, so it is important to pick a strategy that works for you.

2.7 Having a Support Network

A research project often may not require attending classes or interacting with peers in the same way as the other aspects of your course, so it can feel like an isolating activity. Some students find it helpful to develop a support network which provides an opportunity to discuss the progress of the research project with others, and thoughts, feelings, or challenges faced throughout this process. This could be your peers working on the same project, if applicable, it could be your tutor group, or a group of friends with shared experiences. It is also important to discuss worries or challenges you may experience in your research project with your supervisor, and to keep them in the loop throughout your project as they can advise and support you through this process.

Doing a research project may not always be straightforward and at times this process may feel overwhelming. For example, some aspects of your project may take longer than expected to complete, you may come across some unexpected circumstances that may change your original research plan and you may find that you need to adapt or revise this plan. If things don't always go to plan, or if things appear to be going wrong, then remember that you can arrange a meeting with your supervisor to discuss these issues, and together, you will be able to make amendments to your original action plan, with appropriate deadlines. Similarly, you may come across some unexpected findings which you may need to spend a bit more time on in terms of reading through relevant literature to help you understand these findings and their implications, or you may need to conduct further analyses on your data.

It is important to keep in mind that this is the nature of research, and it would be good to have open communication channels with your supervisor to discuss your thoughts and how best to deal with any unexpected circumstances (see also Chapter 3). Try not to compare your research project work and where you are in the process with other people's research projects. It may seem that others are ahead of you as they may already be analysing data, whilst you may still be collecting your data. Each research project is different, and different projects may have different requirements in terms of the steps needed to complete the work. The best person to discuss the progress of your project would be your supervisor.

2.8 Working in a Team

Some research projects require individuals to work in teams in order to complete certain tasks. For example, your supervisor may pair you with another student in order to design your study or experiment and to collect data. It could also be the case that you will be working in a larger team of individuals, some of whom could be postgraduate students, and you may be working with them to develop your study and to test participants. This can be particularly helpful in terms of dividing the tasks required to set up your study but also working with others to recruit and test participants, if relevant to your research project. It is likely that you will be working in a team for certain aspects of your project, but the write-up of your project remains an independent piece of work (see Chapter 7).

FUTURE FOCUS Teamwork

The ability to work well as part of a team is a fundamental skill sought by the majority of graduate employers. Effective teamworking during your project will itself demand a whole range of skills and attributes, including communicating tactfully, giving and receiving feedback, dealing with conflict, influencing, leading, motivating, and more. It isn't always easy but gaining experience in these areas that you can put to practise in the future will put you in a strong position in a professional workplace. These are skills which can also help just as much in your personal life, so are worth the effort you put into them.

2.8.1 **What Constitutes Effective Teamwork?**

"My project partner has not contributed to the research project that we had previously agreed, so I ended up doing the majority of the work to avoid unnecessary delays to the project".

A common concern for individuals working on a project together is ensuring that everyone works on agreed tasks and completes these within a specified deadline. For example, you may find that your project partner is not delivering the work agreed due to some circumstances outside or even within their control (e.g. lack of time management). It is important for everyone to deliver the work they have agreed to do, so that the research project runs smoothly.

Here are a few tips that will help towards developing and maintaining effective teamwork:

1. If you are working in a team, in addition to your own personal project action plan, it is also important to create a shared or group action plan with specified deadlines for each task. This will help you keep track and monitor progress on key tasks that need to be completed as a group so that you can progress to the next stage of your research project.

2. During your initial meeting(s) with the group, it is important that tasks are allocated to each member so as to ensure everyone contributes equally to the project work. Set deadlines within your action plan and stick to these. Communicate with others if the original plan needs to be revised or certain tasks rescheduled if you need longer to complete tasks, as this will impact others' work and progress on their research project. Communicate this information as early as possible.

3. It is important to communicate frequently with other members of your group and to agree the means by which you will do this. This could be weekly emails, for example, reporting on progress and any issues encountered. You may also find it helpful to use an online platform to collaborate with others in your group, such as Microsoft Planner or Trello. You can share resources online, communicate information and ideas, as well as keep track of tasks that need to be completed. Include all relevant individuals in any correspondence relevant to the project work so that everyone is up to speed with the progress of the work. Similarly, you can create a wiki to manage group tasks (see Additional Online Resources on creating and using wikis for project management).

4. Try to schedule group meetings in advance, as each individual in the group may have a different schedule and other commitments, so finding a mutually convenient time may be tricky if left until the last minute. It could be the case that you all need to meet in a specific room, such as a lab, in order to develop your study. Arranging this meeting and making any relevant room booking well ahead of time (e.g. through an online calendar invitation), will help to avoid delays in scheduling meetings and progressing to the next stage of the research project. Also, if you are sharing lab space for testing participants you may find it helpful to create a shared calendar to help facilitate data collection in the group. To keep track of what happened in meetings, you could keep notes (see Box 2.2 for meeting notes template).

5. To ensure you will be able to generate creative ideas at any stage in the group activities relating to your research project, it is important for all team members to effectively research the topic and to create an atmosphere in meetings, whether face-to-face or virtual, where everyone feels they can freely contribute to the discussion. As a team, consider all ideas brought to the table, and then decide which idea to go with based on

BOX 2.2 Meeting Notes Template

Date: *2nd Nov*
Who was present: *Student 1 (S1), Student 2 (S2), Supervisor (SPV)*

	Question/item that was discussed	Actions needed and who by	Deadline
1	**Research design** A qualitative study is most appropriate for the research question. (see Research Diary for reasons and references). *S1* and *S2* think interviews would be the best way to collect data.	*S1* and *S2* to think about and draft questions.	15 Nov
2	**Ethics** Study will need to be approved by ethics committee.	*S1* and *S2* to find checklist and application form.	18 Nov
3			
4			

Date of next meeting:

available resources (e.g. equipment, software, time). Be sure to discuss these ideas with your supervisor during your next meeting. It may be useful to develop and circulate minutes or notes of your meetings (see Box 2.2 for a template) and incorporate any action points in your group action plan.

Remember, communication within the group is key to successful group work. You can also discuss any issues or concerns you may have about teamwork or any aspects of your project with your supervisor. For example, if you find that there are delays with certain aspects of the project it is often advisable to arrange a group meeting or even a one-to-one meeting with your supervisor to discuss such issues and to discuss a plan forward.

Handy Hint

Some dissertation projects require you to work with a partner. This can be seen as a negative for some, as it entails the relinquishment of total control over your project. However, two brains are often better than one! Be accommodating and collaborative with your partner. Try to be flexible in your ideas and have frequent discussions with your partner. This can help to generate new ideas and will allow your dissertation to evolve into a fantastic project.

Student, Durham University

Summary

In this chapter, we have covered key elements to get you started and to help you progress with and complete your research project. These involve:

- Project management skills, which include creating an effective, flexible action plan with deadlines, and prioritizing work depending on which stage of the project you are in.

Different research projects have different requirements, so it is important to develop a plan that is suitable for your project and that it works for you.

- Decide what you need to do for your research project, from the point where you have a topic up until project completion (i.e. submission of the research project report), then allocate time in your weekly timetable or time planner to work on tasks specified in your action plan.

- Try and engage with your project work throughout the timeline provided by your department. Often different elements of the research project overlap and often doing things in parallel can help with your progress.

- Some research projects may require students to work in pairs or small groups to complete certain tasks or aspects of the project. Good communication between group members and sticking to agreed deadlines can often help with this process.

 Go online to access further resources for the text:
www.oup.com/he/whitt1e.

References

Buehler, R., Griffin, D., & Ross, M. (1994). Exploring the 'planning fallacy': Why people underestimate their task completion times. *Journal of Personality and Social Psychology, 67*(3), 366–381. https://doi.org/10.1037/0022-3514.67.3.366

Cirillo, F. (2006). The pomodoro technique (the pomodoro). *Agile Processes in Software Engineering, 54*(2), 35.

3 Working With Your Supervisor

For most project work, students are allocated a supervisor. This person will guide you through the research that you will conduct, and it is important to establish a good working relationship with them. In this chapter, we will have a look at starting to work with a supervisor, communication, what a supervisor can help with, and how to ensure a good working relationship.

Most students are allocated a supervisor who they will work with for the research project's duration. This is likely to be an academic that you have seen before, but it could also be a researcher from your department, or a member of academic staff that you haven't encountered before. Whoever your supervisor is, please be reassured that they will have your best interests at heart and want you to enjoy the research project and for you to produce something that you are proud of. Your supervisor will be passionate about their subject area and will enjoy seeing your research ideas and understanding take shape and development.

To begin with, it's worth understanding that your supervisor will likely be a very busy person as academic staff hold a number of roles. They will teach face-to-face, assess work, prepare teaching sessions, have their own research projects ongoing, look after students in a pastoral role, and be on committees (which help the day-to-day and long-term running of the department). They will have administrative tasks to do in the department and around the institution, which is likely to include attending meetings. However, supervising research projects is something that academics do enjoy because they love research and will be interested to hear your ideas and generally see how you are getting on. The research project will involve you and your supervisor working collaboratively. An interesting qualitative study by Roberts and Seaman (2018) highlighted what can make a good supervisory experience. They found that a good experience comes from both the supervisor and the student. The supervisor provides support and advice, and students contribute through having an interest in the research and taking ownership of the research.

3.1 Preparing for the First Meeting

Sometimes, your first meeting with your supervisor might be with a group of other students. Your supervisor might be doing this so that you can all clarify expectations about the research project, but also share ideas with each other and, potentially, for students to find other students to work with. Working with other students on your project can be beneficial

---

BOX 3.1 Expectations to Clarify with your Supervisor

- Supervisor working days/hours/holidays.
- Your working days/hours/holidays.
- Communication preferences (including how long it will generally take for a response).
- Meeting preferences (e.g. are there office hours, booking system, email for appointment, drop in, and so on).
- How should you prepare for meetings (e.g. come with questions, write an agenda).
- Level of involvement of the supervisor.
- What your supervisor can help with (e.g. is it their topic area, who helps with technical issues?).
- What you think you might need help with (e.g. setting up an experiment, guidance on statistics).
- Create a timeline for the research project. Agree deadlines within this.

---

for a number of reasons (see Chapter 2). Clarifying expectations with your supervisor can help you to understand each other and have a positive start to your project (Shellito et al., 2001). This may include practical details such as when your supervisor is available. See Box 3.1 for ideas about what to talk to your supervisor about.

It is a good idea to do some preparation before the first meeting with your supervisor. Read over any project briefs or summaries they provided when you were making your choices and read any journal articles or textbooks they refer to. You could do your own literature search to help you to get a wide view of a topic (see Chapter 1 for more information); a review article or a meta-analysis can be a really useful place to start. Generally, these types of articles have evaluated a high number of studies investigating the same question and so give you an idea of the state of the research at the time the review was published. By doing some initial reading, you may be able to work out some gaps in the literature (i.e. questions that haven't yet been investigated) and you could talk to your supervisor about these. In Chapter 1 we provided a number of other suggestions of ways that you could prepare including:

- Narrowing down the general topic (potentially suggested by the supervisor) to something that you are interested in.
- Finding a research paper that you like and summarizing it.
- Thinking about what type of research to conduct.
- Identifying potential research questions or variables to investigate.

Doing one or more of these shows that you are interested in the topic area and even starting to take ownership of the research. Nothing is set at this point so don't worry if you change your mind later, but it is useful for everyone (you, other students, your supervisor) to have a starting point.

3.2 Communication with Your Supervisor

Good communication throughout the research project can make work much more pleasant and productive for both you and your supervisor. You may end up communicating with your supervisor in multiple ways if that is what you agreed (see previous section on 'Preparing for the First Meeting'). In this section, we will look at emails and meetings as it is likely most students will use these methods.

3.2.1 Email

It's always good to be polite and professional. The way emails are written can impact on how students are viewed, for example students who send emails that are polite are liked more by an instructor (Bolkan & Holmgren, 2012). Casual emails have the opposite effect and may even result in the student being seen as less credible and mean the instructor is less willing to agree to student requests (Stephens et al., 2009). To use these effects to your advantage, follow the five standards outlined by Sims (2015):

1. Make the email personal. This means writing a greeting, e.g. 'Dear Dr X' and signing off with your name. Make sure you are using the person's correct title (usually this is Dr or Professor rather than Miss, Mrs, or Mr, and so on).

2. Make the email precise. Keep the email short and have a clear topic. Include a subject in the subject line.

3. Prepare your email by checking in other places for the answer first. If you have checked and can't find what you need, then mention this.

4. Be polite. Make sure to use a formal tone and basic manners (i.e. use 'please', 'thank you').

5. Proofread your email. Check for any errors in spelling and grammar and check that the tone is appropriate.

As well as sending email, supervisors (and institutions) do expect students to read emails and manage them appropriately. This is important so you are up to date with everything that is going on and are aware of any changes that are made in the course of the term/ year. Use folders in your email inbox and sort your email according to categories (e.g. 'project', 'module x', 'module y'). Check settings on any automatic emails you are sent; for example, any that come from the institutional virtual learning environment (VLE; e.g. Moodle, Blackboard) forums. You may be able to change the settings to reduce the number of emails you get or set up a rule that puts all these emails in one folder. Although you should read and organize email, make sure that it doesn't become a distraction. You could set a particular 30 minutes each day to sort email, for example, rather than checking it continually.

3.2.2 Meetings

You are likely to have a number of meetings with your supervisor to discuss your research project work. These may be one-to-one or in a group and may be face-to-face or conducted over video call (e.g. Zoom, Microsoft Teams, Skype). One easy thing to do is to make sure that you are reliable and punctual. Turn up on time to all meetings. You and your supervisor are both busy people so make sure to stick to the meeting time you agreed. Sometimes, something may occur that means you cannot attend a planned meeting. If this happens, you should tell your supervisor as soon as you can.

Supervisors will likely take different approaches to meetings. Some will arrange a regular day and time to meet you (e.g. every second Thursday at 2pm) and other supervisors may expect you to arrange meetings. You may have already clarified this in your first meeting but if it's not clear which approach they take then do ask! If your supervisor expects you to take the lead in arranging meetings, then don't be put off and think they don't want to see you, they do, they are probably trying to help you to develop skills in self-management. If you would prefer regular, scheduled meetings, then talk to your supervisor about it. Some students may have restrictions on how much time they can have with their supervisor so make sure that you find out if this applies to you (check the module information) and ensure that any suggestions you make around a meeting schedule are within those boundaries. When arranging one-off meetings, it might be useful for your supervisor to know how long you are expecting to be there as it will help them to work out when they are free to meet you. Be aware that sometimes supervisors might need a bit of notice; you can't expect to email them on, for example, Monday afternoon for a meeting on Tuesday morning. A couple of days' notice is usually fine for most supervisors.

When you do have a meeting booked in with your supervisor, try to think beforehand what you want to get out of it. Creating an agenda (a list of discussion points) can be a really good way to structure a meeting and make sure that you cover everything that you want to. Your supervisor may give you a task or something to think about prior to the meeting so ensure you complete that and make some notes on it. For example, at the start of the research project you may need to think about a method to use to investigate your research question. What you could do in this case is to look at published studies and the methods they used, make notes on the types of tasks and any strengths or weaknesses (and how you might overcome those weaknesses). These notes could then form the basis of the discussion that you have with your supervisor.

You will not be able to remember everything discussed in a meeting and therefore taking notes is really important. Supervisors do expect students to take notes in meetings. Taking notes can help you to avoid asking your supervisor the same question multiple times. You could also use a research diary or log to keep track of all your work and meetings (see Chapter 2). This could be done in a paper or an electronic notebook. An advantage of using an electronic notebook is that you could share parts of it with your supervisor.

It is important to stay in touch with your supervisor. Even if you are getting on fine with your work, let your supervisor know what you are working on and how you are approaching tasks. Life events also occur during the time students are working on their projects. Let your supervisor know what you are dealing with so they can support you and signpost you to other professional support.

> **Handy Hint**
> Try to have regular meetings with your supervisor. This will ensure that you are on track and will ensure that both you and your supervisor know exactly where you are at in your project. This will also help you to avoid stumbling down the wrong path with your research.
> Student, Durham University

FUTURE FOCUS **Professionalism**

Think of your project as gaining experience in professionalism for future work. You may not do research in a university setting in the future, but the general setup of working with a supervisor mirrors a workplace situation quite well. For example, in a professional environment, you will be expected to attend scheduled meetings on time and well-prepared, complete tasks you have agreed to do, and take ownership of your work; these are all critical for a successful project. Building a good professional relationship with your supervisor will make it easy for them to provide you with an excellent reference if you need one. It may also encourage your supervisor to work with you themselves in the future if you are interested in applying for a postgraduate research degree with them.

3.2.3 **Question and Share Ideas**

Students may sometimes think that their supervisor knows everything about everything. This is not really the case. Supervisors will often have experience and knowledge of your area of research but will not know everything. Supervisors are there to guide your research and make sure you are conducting quality science. Question and challenge your supervisor. If something doesn't make sense or you've seen something you don't think your supervisor knows about then discuss it with them. Psychology supervisors are generally curious and open to ideas and will be thrilled to discuss the subject with you and will likely be impressed by you!

Handy Hint

It is important that you utilize your supervisor. Try not to treat them like a school teacher, responding "yes sir . . . no sir"; be inquisitive and pick their brain! After all, they are experts in their field, and it is crucial that you use their pool of knowledge to develop your own ideas. This will aid the development of your dissertation project and will result in a much more accomplished and up-to-date project idea.

Student, Durham University

3.3 **What Can a Supervisor Help With?**

As we've mentioned, a supervisor is primarily a source of support and advice (Roberts & Seaman, 2018). A supervisor's help can be key at particular points in the research project; for example, when you are working out the aim of your work and the methodology (Strebel et al., 2021). For a psychology research project, both of these come very early on in the process. At other times, you may need to recognize for yourself when you need help. This is a key aspect of self-directed study and project management. You may have already discussed the level of involvement your supervisor has in your research project, and this will vary depending on the project. In this section, we've thought about what a supervisor might do and not do when their aim is for students to develop skills in research and project management; here, this is in the context of a project in which students are running a study and collecting data.

3.3.1 At the Start of the Research Project

Background research

Your Supervisor Will . . .

- Often provide research articles as a starting point. You should make sure to read these and then search for other articles.
- Discuss articles with you, if needed. For example, if you don't understand an article, then meet your supervisor and explain as much as you can about the research paper and try to identify specific questions or issues to focus on. It is difficult for supervisors to help if you just say, "I've read this paper and don't understand it".
- Sometimes ask you questions about your background research to help you articulate your understanding of the topic.

Your Supervisor Will Not . . .

- Know all the literature. This is exciting because it means that you are the person finding the latest literature on your topic.
- Give you all the research papers that you need for your background research. Your supervisor will expect you to do literature searching on your own. There will likely be support you can get from your library if you need help.

Research questions and method

Your Supervisor Will . . .

- Expect you to draft your research questions and will discuss them with you.
- Discuss with you the method that you have chosen to use and talk through any issues. To help this you could outline to your supervisor any strengths and weaknesses and give an indication of your preference (and why).
- Check materials with you. If they offer suggestions for changes then think about how you would take those on board. Your supervisor doesn't want to make your life harder but wants you to have the best study possible.

Your Supervisor Will Not . . .

- Create your research questions for you.
- Create materials for you or solve problems for you. The research project is a brilliant opportunity to gain evidence for a variety of skills, problem-solving being a key one. Your supervisor wants you to have the experience of tackling problems and being able to say how you went about dealing with an issue and what the outcome was. There may be other staff, such as technicians, who can help with setting up studies.

3.3.2 In the Middle of the Research Project

Collecting and analysing data

Your Supervisor Will . . .

- Support you with guidance on working with participants (also see Chapter 6).
- Help with access to labs (if needed, and this might just be signposting to how to book labs).
- Signpost you to materials to support with analysing data (most likely if you have done the analysis before in research methods and/or statistics classes).

Your Supervisor Will Not . . .

- Recruit participants for you.
- Do your data analysis for you.
- Tell you what your results mean.

FUTURE FOCUS Being Proactive And Working Independently

My supervisor encouraged me to explore my questions I was interested in and provided some input into the analytics but for the most part gave me the freedom to try and find my own way. I was lucky to have someone who gave their time, honesty but also gave me scope for growth.

Student, King's College London

3.3.3 Towards the End of the Research Project

Assessment criteria

Your Supervisor Will . . .

- Help you understand the assessment criteria for the piece of work. Most departments will have criteria that they use to assess the research project report. It is a good idea to find this document in the research project module information and read it. It is unlikely that the criteria will be completely new to you as you are likely to have similar work such as laboratory reports in the first and second year of your degree. If there is something in the criteria that you don't understand, then highlight it and talk to your supervisor about what their expectations are. You should also check your module information to see if there are any other resources to support you with understanding the assessment, for example writing guides, example pieces of work, or even workshops that you can attend.

Your Supervisor Will Not . . .

- Tell you what specifically to put in any assessed work. For example, in the introduction and discussion, it is up to you to decide what to put in to support your argument. Sometimes this is assessed as a criterion, so it needs to be your work (not your supervisor's).

Feedback

Your Supervisor Will . . .

- Likely give you some feedback on a draft of the report. Different departments have different ideas about what supervisors do or don't comment on; however, if you are offered the chance to get feedback on draft writing then it is a good idea to take it. Once you get comments back, if you are able to talk to your supervisor about the comments then try to take that opportunity too, particularly if there are comments that you don't understand. Try to ensure you have enough time when revising your work to make use of your supervisor's comments as reading and applying comments can often take more time than you think.

Your Supervisor Will Not . . .

- Write or rewrite sections.
- Substantially edit or correct your writing.
- Give feedback on more than one draft.

3.3.4 **A Note on Feedback**

Your supervisor will be giving you feedback all the way through the research project, so it is important that you look out for it. Feedback is not restricted to written comments on work. When you ask questions and have a conversation with your supervisor you are getting feedback on your understanding and thinking. Really pay attention to what your supervisor says as sometimes they may give you hints in what they say.

3.4 Making the Relationship Work

There are challenges when doing the research project and being able to face these and work out solutions is a key part of project management. In this section, we provide some tips about how to foster a good working relationship with your supervisor. We also take a look at some questions students may have at times during the research project. These are common things students face in project work; but they are resolvable, and you will feel a great sense of accomplishment for making it through difficult times.

3.4.1 **Taking Ownership of the Research**

Remember that students can contribute to a successful research project by taking ownership (Roberts & Seaman, 2018). This can start by taking an interest in the topic. Most of the time, students have had a choice as to what topic they want to investigate for the project. Hopefully, you will be working on a research project of interest. However, it could be the case that you have been assigned a project that you had minimal or even no choice in. If you are in this position, it can be a little down hearting but the best thing to do is to begin reading some of the literature related to the topic and you will likely come across something that you find interesting. Have a chat with any other students who are doing the same or a similar topic (or your supervisor) about what the topic is about, why it is worth studying and what the possible impacts are of doing research in this area. This might ignite some excitement and energy for the task ahead. Psychology is so varied in topics and after a few weeks being involved in a research project, we find that students are generally really enthusiastic about their project topic. If you have chosen your topic, your supervisor will probably be aware of this and may expect you to be interested in the topic from the very start. Often, the topics an academic will supervise are related to their own research and so they will be delighted to see a student's interest in that topic. You may not find every aspect of your topic interesting but try and find something that enthuses you. Avoid telling your supervisor that you aren't interested in anything!

Taking ownership means being the one to drive the work forward and make progress. To help this, try to be prepared and contribute throughout your research project:

- Turn up to meetings with an agenda and take notes.
- Complete work you have agreed to do.
- Stick to a timeline you have drawn up.
- Make sure you know various deadlines throughout the year (check your research project module information).
- Read around the topic of your research.
- Put forward ideas.

Even if you are working in a group to complete your research project you can still take ownership as a group. Your supervisor will expect you to be able to work with other students and contribute equally to your project. One thing that supervisors sometimes have to deal with is group members complaining that other members are not putting any work in. Try to avoid this, if possible, by setting clear expectations and roles in the group (see Chapter 2). However, if you are having real difficulties and it is causing stress, then do approach your supervisor and they will try to help as much as they can. Whether working on your own or in a group, you will have a much better time working on the research project if you have a positive attitude and put effort in.

3.4.2 Using Time Effectively

On some research project modules, you may only have a certain number of hours contact with your supervisor. At first, it may seem like this allocation is not enough; however, your department will have decided this very carefully to ensure that all students receive adequate supervision time. So, it's up to you to be careful how you use that time. Here are some tips.

- Create an agenda for your meetings with your supervisor.
- Avoid asking long or complicated questions via email, book in a meeting instead.
- Try things yourself first (e.g. statistical analysis).

- Do some reading beforehand in order to understand the area and common methodologies.
- Talk to other students who you are working with or who are doing a similar research project to you.
- Reflect on what you might need most help with. Maybe this is setting up the experiment or maybe analysis. Make sure you don't use up all your time early on in the research project if you'll need help during the analysis stage.

Smart Solution—Reaching Out For Support

Upon falling behind on my dissertation I was very anxious about the consequences of this and my ability to produce a decent piece of work for my dissertation which did make me hesitant to reach out to my supervisor. However, I did realize that my supervisor was here to aid me in achieving my best piece of work. I advise any students who feel overwhelmed by the stress of working on their dissertation or those who feel as if they've fallen drastically behind to definitely reach out to their supervisors and avoid feeling as if it is too late to pick things up again and produce good standard of work because it most certainly is possible.

Student, University of Roehampton

3.4.3 **Difficult Times**

Research projects are often conducted across a whole academic year, which means they require perseverance and commitment. There will be low points, where you feel things are not progressing or you get stuck on a problem. These are the times when your supervisor could be really helpful and important. Let them know your worries or issues and they can help you work through them. Supervisors will have experienced and seen similar issues across the years and will likely tell you that these things are just part of the research process. Of course, if your problems relate to personal issues that you have no control over then you may be able to get support through your institution's relevant procedure for this (often called extenuating or mitigating circumstances). The most important thing whatever is happening is that you talk to someone about it.

There may be times when you are finding your supervisor difficult to work with. This could be for a variety of reasons. Here are some examples and solutions.

"My supervisor isn't replying to my emails"

How long ago was it that you sent your email? Supervisors are unlikely to read emails in the evenings and at weekends. Sometimes they might have a whole day of teaching and meetings or might be away at a conference. Sometimes they might be on holiday. Give them a few days then you could try sending a prompt or use their office hours (or any similar system in your institution). Academics receive so many emails each day that yours may just have been buried in their inbox or they may have seen it but then had something else come up, so sometimes a prompt will be appreciated by them. In this email you could suggest some days and times to meet or ask about the best way to contact them. Also think about what you are emailing about. Would it be something that would be better to talk through in person (e.g. statistics)? In which case, it might be better to book an appointment for a meeting.

"I can't ever find my supervisor in their office"

Check to see what the best way to meet your supervisor is. Have they said it is ok to drop into their office or not? Some supervisors might not have an office, or might share an office, in which case you will have to book a time to meet them. If you have agreed with your supervisor that you can drop in then you might just have missed them as they could be teaching or in a meeting or in a lab. In this case you could try to find them in their office a couple more times (maybe including the following day) but if you still have no luck, then send them an email requesting a meeting.

> ### Smart Solution—Making Progress While Your Supervisor Is Away
>
> One difficult situation that did arise was contacting my supervisor over the holiday periods. To work around this I wrote extensive notes on what I needed help with/what I was unsure about and as soon as was possible I scheduled a meeting and reported my specific problems. This allowed both me and my supervisor deserved time off but also meant after the break I could jump right back into my report with a comprehensive understanding.
>
> Student, Royal Holloway University of London

"They advised me to do one thing but now are telling me something else"

This is a common problem and probably comes down to the fact that supervisors are just human. The first time, they will have suggested what they thought was the best thing at the time, but the second time, maybe something else is better. This is also the nature of research, things may change during the initial decisions around methodology, for example. This is another reason why keeping your own notes can be useful.

"I find my supervisor quite scary"

Each supervisor approaches research projects and project supervision in different ways. Some people can be more direct than others and sometimes directness can be intimidating. If this describes your supervisor, then again remember they do want you to do well and bear in mind that they probably do not mean to criticize you personally (if this is what it feels like). If you can, try to separate out yourself from your work and associate the comments from your supervisor with the work rather than yourself. With a supervisor who is direct, they may appreciate you being direct too. This is where creating lists of questions in preparation for meetings may be helpful. There will also be a module convenor (or similar) who oversees the research project module. You can talk to this person when or if you need help from someone who is not your supervisor. You should also let your personal tutor or adviser know about any problems or issues.

> **FUTURE FOCUS Interpersonal Skills**
>
> While it may be tough at the time, having the experience of working with someone different from you is extremely valuable. In a workplace you will have to work with a whole variety of people and having examples and evidence to show a potential employer when you have done this in the past is useful. For example, you may be able to draw on your project experience to show your future employer that you are adaptable and can adjust to different styles of working.

"My supervisor cannot help me with the technique I am using"

There might be other people who can help. For example, is there a postgraduate student or a researcher who is using the specialist equipment or technique that you need to do? There may also be a technician who can support students with building and designing studies. This person could provide valuable help so do try to seek them out but be aware that they may also be assisting many other students too. Most universities also have librarians who might be able to help with literature and specialist techniques like systematic reviews. Before getting help from other people, make sure to ask permission from your supervisor.

"The equipment has broken/my program doesn't work, and I'm worried to tell my supervisor"

It is likely that at some point during your research project you will hit a problem while conducting your research. A very common problem is malfunctioning equipment or programming errors. Expect something like this to happen during your project then you will be much more prepared to deal with it. Supervisors know these are common occurrences and will appreciate you telling them as soon as possible if something breaks or goes wrong. You could tell a technician about the issues with broken equipment first, if you have one in your department. Supervisors might ask you to try and fix the issue first if they think you could solve it; but, if you must wait for a technician or your supervisor to help then be patient, it might actually take some time to fix equipment or work on a program. The timescale that you are given for a research project is designed to consider issues like this that you may come across.

"My supervisor hasn't given me enough feedback on my draft report"

Supervisors may give feedback on a draft version of your report. When giving feedback it might be that supervisors are following guidelines set out by the department or the institution in terms of what they can give feedback on. For example, they may not be able to comment on the arguments you have made in your writing and won't edit your work. This is to ensure that the work you hand in is your work, not your supervisor's work. Try to focus on comments or suggestions they have made. You could also have a look at the marking guidelines and assess your own work. You might then identify aspects of your report that you could work on.

Summary

In this chapter we have considered how to manage the relationship with your supervisor. Admittedly, this will take some effort on your part, and you may have some difficult points. The main idea to remember from this chapter is that your supervisor does want you to do well and to do well you need to take control and responsibility for your own work. You are the person who drives the research project. This can seem scary at first but the benefits you get from this are substantial.

 *Go online to access further resources for the text:* **www.oup.com/he/whitt1e**.

References

Bolkan, S., & Holmgren, J. L. (2012). "You are such a great teacher and I hate to bother you but . . . ": Instructors' perceptions of students and their use of email messages with varying politeness strategies. *Communication Education*, 61(3), 253–270. https://doi.org/10.1080/03634523.2012.667135

Roberts, L. D., & Seaman, K. (2018). Good undergraduate dissertation supervision: Perspectives of supervisors and dissertation coordinators. *International Journal for Academic Development*, 23(1), 28–40. https://doi.org/10.1080/1360144X.2017.1412971

Shellito, C. J., Shea, K., Weissmann, G., Mueller-Solger, A., & Davis, W. (2001). Successful mentoring of undergraduate researchers. *Journal of College Science Teaching*, 30(7), 460.

Sims, C. D. L. (2015). Competency and connection: Undergraduate students and effective email messages. *Communication Teacher*, 29(3), 129–134. https://doi.org/10.1080/17404622.2015.1028557

Stephens, K. K., Houser, M. L., & Cowan, R. L. (2009). R U able to meat me: The impact of students' overly casual email messages to instructors. *Communication Education*, 58(3), 303–326. https://doi.org/10.1080/03634520802582598

Strebel, F., Gürtler, S., Hulliger, B., & Lindeque, J. (2021). Laissez-faire or guidance? Effective supervision of bachelor theses. *Studies in Higher Education*, 46(4), 866–884. https://doi.org/10.1080/03075079.2019.1659762

4   Choosing Your Method

In this chapter we will cover some basic points about choosing and designing research methodology for a study. We assume that most people who are at the stage of conducting their independent research project have studied research methods deeply and so most things covered here will be familiar, and hopefully most of this is a brief reminder (see Box 4.1 for glossary of terms). When you come across points that are relevant to your study, note them down and if you need more information look back at your course materials or a research methods textbook. We divide the chapter into two sections, focusing on quantitative and qualitative methods, respectively.

> **FUTURE FOCUS Research Skills and Data Analysis**
>
> Students who aren't intending to pursue research after they graduate can sometimes fail to appreciate the value of the research skills and data analysis developed during their project. In actual fact, these are a real selling point and something which you can use to set yourself, as a psychology graduate, apart from other applicants. While it may not be immediately apparent, the ability to design, conduct, and interpret research with human participants is fundamental to many professional settings. This could involve evaluating the impact of: a new reading programme for school children; changes to recruitment processes to promote inclusivity; a marketing strategy to attract funding; or a team-building event to boost productivity—your ability to understand and explain patterns in human behaviour can give you the edge in a professional workplace.

4.1 Quantitative Methods

In this section, we will look at quantitative methods. These are methods in which you gain numerical data by measuring behaviour. You will be measuring and/or manipulating variables. Working out what the variables are in your own study is one of the first things you will do and it is a good idea to write them down and keep reminding yourself of them as they are core to your research. Your department may ask you to submit details of your study before you begin data collection to ensure that you have a good design and plan for your study. This might be done at the same time as an application for ethical approval. Writing and submitting a research proposal is a bit like the process of preregistration (see Box 4.2).

BOX 4.1 Glossary of Terms Used in this Chapter

Causation—when one variable (X) brings about a change in another (Y). For example, eating biscuits makes you feel less hungry.

Correlation—when two variables show an association. For example, when there are many biscuits in the common room there are many psychologists there too. However, we cannot say that the biscuits cause the psychologists to be there or, the opposite, that the psychologists cause the biscuits to be there.

Validity—whether your experiment or survey measures what it is supposed to measure.

Reliability—whether your measure/experiment/survey will produce the same results time after time.

Independent measures (or between subjects or between groups)—separate groups of people participate in the different conditions.

Repeated measures (or within subjects or within groups)—the same group of people complete all the conditions.

Predictor—a variable that is assumed to impact on another variable (also called an independent variable)

Outcome—a variable that is impacted by a predictor variable (also called a dependent variable).

Replicating—re-running a study in the same way as someone else has reported it to see if the same results are found.

The APA dictionary is a great source for other terms: https://dictionary.apa.org/

BOX 4.2 Preregistration

There is a movement in psychology to try to address some issues with creating good quality designs and methods for experiments as well as publication bias. A type of journal article is available for researchers called registered reports. Authors first submit their introduction, methods, and analysis plans. These are then reviewed, and authors receive feedback on their suggested study. Authors then collect the data in accordance with methods outlined in the first part of their registered report. They then publish the entire report containing their original introduction and methods and new sections of results and discussion.

This way of publishing is more transparent as the researchers announce what they are going to do before they do it. It should help researchers to manage and avoid issues such as low power and floor and ceiling effects as these have to be addressed in the first report before any data collection. It also means that researchers cannot engage in HARKing (hypothesizing after results are known).

This practice is filtering into psychology journals and it might be that you as students are required to submit your report in a similar two-stage way or that your lecturers are thinking about how to incorporate these practices into undergraduate project modules.

For further information, Chris Chambers' book *The 7 Deadly Sins of Psychology* is a clear overview of current practices and the preregistration movement.

4.1.1 Experiments

Experiments are likely to be a method of research that you have come across again and again when reading research papers and in previous research methods classes. Research conducted using experiments is often considered highly but this means it is subject to much scrutiny too.

4.1.1.1 Aim

Experiments are important in psychology, and other areas of science, because they can be used to establish causality. This means that if you conduct an experiment in which you manipulate a variable and you observe a change in a behaviour that you are measuring then you would be able to say that your manipulation had an effect, or it caused the change in behaviour. For example, imagine you are investigating the effects of learning techniques on memory. You want to see if highlighting or quizzing results in better memory. In your experiment, you get participants to study a set of information on two topics and for one they use highlighting and another they use quizzing. You give everyone the same final test and analyse the results. You find that participants remembered more information from the topic that they studied via quizzing than the one they studied via highlighting (see e.g. Dunlosky et al., 2013). If your experiment were well controlled, you would be able to say that studying using quizzing results in better memory than studying using highlighting. You can say this because you have directly manipulated the learning technique and by using statistics you can be sure of what those results show.

So, if in your own research you want to be able to make a causal claim about a variable affecting behaviour, then you have to use an experiment. If you want to measure lots of variables and aren't concerned about causality then you may be better off using a survey (see later in this chapter). For you to be able to conclude causality from your experiment you need to ensure that it is tightly controlled and you have considered various threats to internal validity.

4.1.1.2 Principles

Variables

Variables are core to experiments. In an experiment, the researcher is manipulating one or more variables (the independent variable; IV) and measuring one or more other variables (the dependent variable; DV). One well-used way is to remember this is that the dependent variable "depends on" the independent variable. The DV is measured by the experimenter and so will always be a variable that is continuous, that is, it will always be numbers. So that could be, for example a time, a rating, an accuracy score, a weight, or a volume. In simple experiments, you might only choose to measure one DV, or perhaps there is only one DV that could be measured. In other experiments, you might measure two DVs. For example, in studies looking at reaction time, it is common to also record errors that are made by the participants. Think carefully about how many DVs you want to measure and why this is needed for your research question. When you have taken the trouble to gather the data, it is generally expected that some analysis of it will appear in the research project report. The IV is what you are changing in the experiment. An IV will have two or more levels. For example, imagine you were investigating participant's reactions to emotional stimuli, here your IV is the emotional nature of the stimuli and you have three levels, for example: positive, negative, and neutral.

Identifying IVs and DVs in experiments, whether this is in reading a research paper or in making your own experiment, is vital. Try to get some practice in identifying IVs and DVs by actively seeking them out in any research article that you are reading. For example, you should be able to identify IVs and DVs from an abstract. Try to find the IV and DV in this extract of an abstract:

Participants ($N = 22$) judged the heaviness of identically weighted cylinders across three conditions: (1) objects appeared different sizes but were physically the same size, (2) objects were physically different sizes but appeared to be the same size, or (3) objects which looked and felt different sizes from one another. Consistent with prior work, haptic size cues induced a larger SWI [size-weight illusion] than that induced by visual size differences. In contrast to prior work, however, congruent vision and haptic size cues yielded a larger still SWI. These findings not only add to our understanding of how different modalities combine to influence our hedonic perception but also showcase how virtual reality can develop novel cue-conflict paradigms. (Buckingham, 2019)

The IV is the heaviness of the cylinders: this is what the researcher has altered. In this abstract, the different levels (or conditions) are helpfully numbered: '(1) objects appeared different sizes but were physically the same size, (2) objects were physically different sizes but appeared to be the same size, or (3) objects which looked and felt different sizes from one another.' The DV is mentioned in the same sentence: it is the judgement of the heaviness of the cylinder. The variables you choose for your own experiment should come from your research question (see Chapter 1 about research questions).

Design

Once you know what your variables are then you can think about how the participants are going to experience these: so do you want to use an independent measures design in which different groups experience different levels of the IV or do you want to use a repeated measures design in which participants experience all levels of the IV? Which you choose may depend on a few considerations. There is a general consensus that repeated measures designs are best to use if at all possible. This is because the participants act as their own control and so any differences between groups are eliminated (because there are no separate groups). However, there are challenges with all types of design and these are listed along with possible solutions. See if you can come up with a solution to the challenge before reading our suggestions.

Challenge: confounds. Confounds are other variables that could be contributing to the manipulation.

Solution: control all variables other than those assigned as IVs. Each condition or group should have the exact same experience apart from the condition to which they are assigned.

Challenge: observer bias. You as a researcher may know something about the condition participants are assigned to, which may influence your perception of their behaviour.

Solution: ensure that observers are unaware of the condition the participant is in. This could be challenging as you are unlikely to have a team of assistants you can employ but you might be working in a team and you could assign some of the team to being observers, while others assign the participants to conditions. Interrater reliability checks (e.g. Cohen's kappa) will also be important if you have two people observing.

Challenge: manipulation checks. Sometimes it is important to make sure that the IV has manipulated what it was supposed to.

Solution: you could use questions to establish participants' knowledge or thoughts related to the IV. For example, if you used a mood induction to make participants feel happy then you should think about measuring their mood before and after the induction. This allows you to check to see if the induction was successful.

Challenge: regression to the mean. At the outset of the research, scores on a pretest might be very low or high (possibly due to biases in sampling) which will lead to performance in the experiment becoming better or worse.

Solution: you need to make sure that any differences seen at test are not due merely to a group with low scores (for example) moving back towards the mean. To help with this issue, make sure to have a comparison or control group and to randomly assign participants to groups after the pretest.

Challenge: demand characteristics. Participants have some awareness of the purpose of the experiment, what condition they are in, and change their behaviour.

Solution: avoid giving away details about your predictions in the introduction to your experiment. Consider if you need to use a between-subjects design.

Challenge for within-subjects designs: order effects. Completing every condition (level of an IV) can be time consuming and tiring. This might lead to participants getting bored. Participants may also get better at whatever task they are doing (practice effects) and participation in one condition may carry over to the next.

Solution: it is fairly easy to deal with order effects by counterbalancing conditions. This means that you make sure that half of the participants complete, e.g. level 1 first and then level 2 and the other half of participants complete level 2 first then level 1. When there are many levels that need to be counterbalanced, then a Latin Square could be used to define the orders (see Figure 4.1). Try to avoid very long experiments to stop your participants getting tired. If lots of trials are necessary, then make sure to add in breaks.

Challenge for between-subject designs: selection effects. When using two or more groups of participants, you need to be sure your results are due to the manipulation and not because people have ended up in a non-random group.

Solution: for a number of IVs you should be able to randomly assign participants to a particular group. For other IVs this is not possible (e.g. gender, race, degree course) and so if you have an IV like this you now have a quasi-experiment and should note that your ability to draw causal inferences is reduced.

Quasi experiments

The definition of an experiment is quite specific and random allocation to group or condition is important. This means that if you have an experiment in which you are observing a variable that already exists (called a quasi-variable), such as gender or degree subject, then you cannot really establish causality in your study. Of course, you cannot change these attributes,

Order Participant	1	2	3	4
1	A	B	C	D
2	D	A	B	C
3	C	D	A	B
4	B	C	D	A

Figure 4.1 Latin Square for Counterbalancing Orders of Conditions in Within-Subject Designs

so you just need to be careful about how you write about your findings and acknowledge that there is a limitation in your study.

4.1.1.3 Practical Thoughts about Setting Up Experiments

Now that you have considered aspects to ensure that you have controlled your experiment as much as possible you should think about practical aspects to conducting your experiment. We have provided a list of possible questions and solutions. Again, try to come up with a solution before reading ours.

"Can I copy someone else's experiment?"

Replicating a study can involve using a method that has been used in a published study. Replications are important as they can add support to the original finding or show a different finding. Replications might use different samples and so extend our knowledge about behaviours in different populations. If you note a limitation in a published study, then see if you can address it in your own experiment to make it a better experiment.

"Should I use specialist software or equipment?"

Think about what you want to measure. Are you doing a cognitive task in which you need to measure reaction times? To do this you will need to use some specialist experimental software. You will probably have used such software in your laboratory or practical classes. An example of open-source software that is used in many departments is PsychoPy, available at https://www.psychopy.org/PsychoPy which is free for anyone to download. If your institution has a licence and funds, then you may be able to run experiments online via Pavlovia. PsychoPy is user-friendly and most experiments can be constructed using the Builder (Figure 4.2). This means you can make experiments with a limited (and sometimes no) knowledge of programming code.

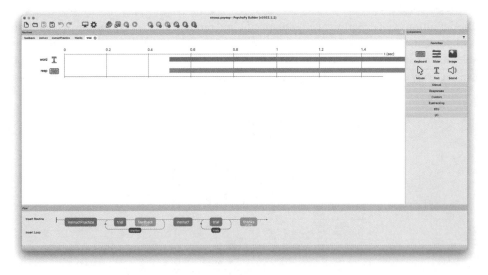

Figure 4.2 Screenshot from PsychoPy of the Builder View of a Stroop Task

Are you doing other tasks which do not require you to measure reaction time? If so, then perhaps you don't need to use PsychoPy but you can use other software (e.g. survey software) or even paper and pencil. However, using software has other advantages too, such as control over the presentation of the stimuli (e.g. you can set how long a participant views a stimulus for) and data are collected digitally, which could save time later and minimize errors. There is often support available if you are using experimental software like PsychoPy; for example, there is a book called *Building Experiments in PsychoPy* (Peirce, Hirst, & MacAskill, 2022), which will talk you through making an experiment in PsychoPy. There are also videos on YouTube and an active community on the PsychoPy forum. Your department may also have psychology technicians who could help.

Depending on the resources available in your department you may be talking to your supervisor about using equipment to measure brain activity, for example electroencephalography (EEG) or functional magnetic resonance imaging (fMRI). You may also be measuring other physiological activity such as heart rate or galvanic skin response. Students who use these measures usually work as part of an established lab team and such equipment is not available to everyone due to cost and training.

FUTURE FOCUS Proficiency With Psychological Tools

An important skill expected of psychology graduates is the ability to use a range of psychological tools; this might include specialist software, equipment, or psychometric measures (QAA, 2019)—all of which you may have the chance to work with during your project. If you are interested in going into research or pursuing a professional psychology career pathway in the future, then the particular experience you develop here may be directly applicable. Even if this isn't the case, graduate employers will be keen to know that you can develop proficiency in novel tasks quickly and are often on the lookout for applicants with a 'can-do' attitude.

"What task should I use?"

It depends on what you are measuring, but there are some measures and tasks in psychology research that are well-known, and you can use them in your own research. Here are some standard tasks. You will need to evaluate these to see if they are suitable for use in your own research.

- Corsi block-tapping task: working memory
- Stroop task: inhibition
- Flanker task: attention
- Visual search: attention
- False memory paradigm: memory
- Raven's matrices: intelligence
- Working memory span tasks: working memory (Conway et al., 2005)

Pavlovia has a great feature in which you can adopt PsychoPy experiments that have been built by someone else and adapt them to your own research (obviously you will need to check to make sure the task is one you want).

"How long should my experiment be? How many stages, trials, and so on?"

It is important to consider the balance between making sure you have included all the conditions in your design and are collecting enough data and making sure the overall experience for participants is not too long. In experiments that take longer than 20 minutes to complete you should consider how you are going to keep the participants comfortable and motivated. You also need to make sure that aspects of the stimulus presentation are controlled; for example, that stimuli are presented equally often on the left and right side of a stimulus display. When you start looking at this it could be that you have lots of things that need counterbalancing. This can increase the time duration of the experiment. If the amount of counterbalancing that you would need to do is not practical then you could consider randomization instead.

Smart Solution—Know Your Limits

For our study we required sentences of text to move across the screen at a set rate. This turned out to be very difficult and we had to compromise on the length of the sentences compared to the other conditions. To avoid any technical troubles or difficulties with designing experiments/surveys it is a good idea to reflect on your abilities and if your research requires anything beyond your abilities, ask for help.

Student, Royal Holloway University of London

"Where should I conduct my experiment?"

If you're not collecting data online, you should see what facilities are available in your department. There might be lab rooms or testing cubicles you can book out.

"Where do I get equipment from?"

Sometimes you might need equipment like a response box or headphones. Check with your supervisor or department as you may be able to borrow these sorts of items.

4.1.1.4 Summary

You should consider using an experiment when you are investigating causality. If your research questions do not investigate causality, then you should consider another type of research that we cover in the next section: 'Surveys'.

4.1.2 Surveys

In this section, we have a look at another common methodology used in psychology research, surveys. Surveys are used as a measurement tool to collect information on people's opinions and behaviours. In a survey, you are not manipulating any variables and so some of the challenges around control are reduced. That doesn't mean that surveys don't have their own challenges, however.

4.1.2.1 Aim

Using a survey will not allow you to make any claims about causality, but it is still an important research tool. Lots of researchers are interested in finding out people's views and real-life behaviour and surveys are used to collect that sort of information. Before using a survey, you should have a clear research question that you will be able to answer from your research (Kelley et al., 2003).

4.1.2.2 **Principles**

Surveys are all about asking people to report on their own behaviour or beliefs. Lots of surveys comprise a written questionnaire that the participant fills out themselves. The questionnaire is the list of questions that the participants will answer. As a researcher, you are trying to gather opinions or measures of behaviour from participants, so you need to make sure that your questions are measuring what you think they are measuring. It is most likely that you would use published tests or scales to measure a characteristic about a participant, such as individual differences, rather than making one yourself. You should of course critically evaluate these tools before using them (see Handy Hint). You can see some examples of these measures in Table 4.1. Of course, this table does not cover all tests that you might use. To find other tests that you might need, you could look in published research papers (see section 'Tips to Find Measures from Papers') or on websites that have catalogues (see Table 4.1).

You might also include individual questions to gather further data and for those, you still need to consider what those questions are and how to get good quality data from them.

Handy Hint

Make sure that you know the flaws in the key research before you even begin to design your own project. For example, it is crucial to know whether the instruments you plan to use, such as a questionnaire, are valid and reliable measures of the construct you are attempting to measure. Knowing the issues in the key research will help you to avoid the same pitfalls and will generate discussion of the limitations of your own design.

Student, Durham University

Tips to find measures from papers

1. Search some key words on a search engine like Web of Science, e.g. 'measure stress psychology.'

2. Browse results and look at titles. Click on titles that look relevant. For example, a title like 'the psychology student stress questionnaire' indicates that the study is likely to present a questionnaire that measures stress in psychology students. Check if the paper reports reliability and validity measures. If it does not, see if you can find other papers that do.

3. Look at papers that have cited one of the papers chosen in step 2. This will show you research where the measure may have been used. This may also help you to find shortened versions of the questionnaire.

4. Questionnaires are often put in appendices or as supplementary material on the journal webpage.

Table 4.1 Examples of Commonly Used Tests and Measures

Behaviour/ Characteristic	Suggested source
Anxiety	Grös, D. F., Antony, M. M., Simms, L. J., & McCabe, R. E. (2007). Psychometric properties of the state-trait inventory for cognitive and somatic anxiety (STICSA): Comparison to the state-trait anxiety inventory (STAI). *Psychological Assessment*, *19*(4), 369–381. https://doi.org/10.1037/1040-3590.19.4.369
	Spitzer, R. L., Kroenke, K., Williams, J. B., & Löwe, B. (2006). A brief measure for assessing generalized anxiety disorder: The GAD-7. *Archives of Internal Medicine*, *166*(10), 1092–1097. https://doi.org/10.1001/archinte.166.10.1092
Autism	Baron-Cohen, S., Wheelwright, S., Skinner, R., Martin, J., & Clubley, E. (2001). The autism-spectrum quotient (AQ): Evidence from Asperger syndrome/high-functioning autism, males and females, scientists and mathematicians. *Journal of Autism and Developmental Disorders*, *31*(1), 5–17. https://doi.org/10.1023/A:1005653411471
Depression	Kroenke, K., Spitzer, R. L., & Williams, J. B. (2001). The PHQ-9: Validity of a brief depression severity measure. *Journal of General Internal Medicine*, *16*(9), 606–613. https://doi.org/10.1046/j.1525-1497.2001.016009606.x
Handedness	Nicholls, M. E., Thomas, N. A., Loetscher, T., & Grimshaw, G. M. (2013). The Flinders Handedness survey (FLANDERS): A brief measure of skilled hand preference. *Cortex*, *49*(10), 2914–2926. https://doi.org/10.1016/j.cortex.2013.02.002
Impulsiveness (Barratt)	Patton, J. H., Stanford, M. S., & Barratt, E. S. (1995). Factor structure of the Barratt impulsiveness scale. *Journal of Clinical Psychology*, *51*(6), 768–774. https://doi.org/10.1002/1097-4679(199511)51:6%3C768::AID-JCLP2270510607%3E3.0.CO;2-1
Motivation (BIS/BAS)	Carver, C. S. & White, T. L. (1994). Behavioral inhibition, behavioral activation, and affective responses to impending reward and punishment: The BIS/BAS scales. *Journal of Personality and Social Psychology*, *67*(2), 319–333. https://doi.org/10.1037//0022-3514.67.2.319
Personality	Feher, A. & Vernon, P. A. (2021). Looking beyond the Big Five: A selective review of alternatives to the Big Five model of personality. *Personality and Individual Differences*, *169*, Article 110002. https://doi.org/10.1016/j.paid.2020.110002
Schizotypy	Mason, O., Linney, Y., & Claridge, G. (2005). Short scales for measuring schizotypy. *Schizophrenia Research*, *78*(2-3), 293–296. https://doi.org/10.1016/j.schres.2005.06.020
Catalogues	The Society of Behavior Change (based in the USA) has a catalogue of measures available here: https://measures.scienceofbehaviorchange.org/
	PsyToolkit contains a library of measures: https://www.psytoolkit.org/
	Journals that specialize in publishing about methods and assessments: • Psychological Assessment • Methods in Psychology • Assessment • Applied Psychological Measurement

4.1.2.3 Types of Question

In a questionnaire, you have two options of question: open-ended and forced choice. In open-ended questions, participants can write (or speak) whatever they like when answering the question. In forced-choice (or fixed-alternative) questions, the researcher provides alternative answers, or a rating scale, and the participants pick an answer or give a rating on the scale. Sometimes, which question you use will be obvious. For example, if you want to know what country participants live in, you might provide a list for participants to choose from.

Forced-choice questions are used frequently by researchers within the context of quantitative research because the data they produce are clear and reasonably straightforward to analyse. Text comments from open questions will require some kind of coding and interpretation and so are subject to further challenges around how to do this. However, open-ended questions may give you richer insights into the behaviour or viewpoint you are investigating and so should not be completely disregarded.

4.1.2.4 Practical Thoughts about Setting up Surveys

If you are using a questionnaire that you are designing yourself, make sure to think about ways to eliminate bias and potential problems with your questionnaire. Here are some of the challenges and possible solutions to think about when writing a questionnaire.

Challenge: fair questions. The questions must be written in such a way that they are easily understandable by participants and should not be leading and push participants to answer in a particular way.
Consider the following question:

"How good was the last series of The Masked Singer?"

Very good, good, neither good nor bad, bad, very bad

This is a leading question: it is already framed in a positive way and participants may feel they have to answer in a positive way and so their answer may not actually reflect their true opinion.

Solution: rewrite the question and consider asking participants to rate their point of view. You could use Likert scales for this. For example:

Please indicate your response to the statement: "I thought the last series of The Masked Singer was . . ."

Very good, good, neither good nor bad, bad, very bad

This takes the judgement out of the question and lets the participant respond with their true opinion. Check a draft of the questions with people to see how they interpret them and if they are clear.

Challenge: scale points. How many points should be used on a Likert scale?

Solution: how many points you use on a scale may depend on who your participants are going to be. Weijters et al. (2010) suggest using five or seven points with a student sample and five points with a sample drawn from the general population. Whoever is in your sample, the points on the scale should all be labelled.

Challenge: number of questions. Do more questions in a questionnaire mean more drop out?

Solution: there is a little evidence we can look at to inform guidance on this. Regarding questionnaires printed on paper, Robb et al. (2017) found no difference in response rates to a mailed survey that was short (four pages) compared to long (seven pages). In a study looking at drop-out in online studies, Hoerger (2010) reports that 10% of participants will drop out early on in the questionnaire. After this, drop-out may relate to the number of items, and you should allow for a further 2% of participants dropping out per 100 questions. Thinking about these findings, it is worth allowing for some rate of drop-out depending on how many items you have. From an ethical point of view too you should think about how long it will take participants to fill out your questionnaire and not make it too long.

Challenge: reliability and validity.

Solution: where possible, try to use a questionnaire or measure that has already been used and has good reliability and validity. Be aware that if you adapt surveys, for example by changing question wording or removing questions, then this could impact on their reliability and validity. Constructing a scale where you use multiple questions to measure the same thing (e.g. attitudes to recycling) is a lot of work and you will likely need to refer to a research methods textbook for more specific information about this.

- Check construct validity (does the questionnaire measure what you think it does?). This includes:
    ○ content validity: does your measure include all aspects of the topic you are looking at? (It should.)
    ○ convergent validity: does your measure compare well to other measures of the same thing? (It should.)
    ○ discriminant validity: does your measure correlate to things unrelated to your chosen topic? (It should not.)
- Check that the questionnaire is consistent and measuring the same thing throughout (internal reliability) by using Cronbach's Alpha.
- Check test-retest reliability to make sure that participants respond similarly across time.

Challenge: survey presentation. How you present a survey can influence participants' responses. For example, Galesic and Tourangeau (2007) altered the title and sponsor of a survey for two groups of participants and found that people responded differently depending on the frame. Participants responded in a way that was in line with the title of the survey.

Solution: ensure that the information you provide at the start of the study is an accurate representation of what you are investigating and is clear to participants. As part of piloting, you should check that participants understand the instructions.

Provide all participants with the same instructions, as far as possible.

Challenge: delivery method. How should the questionnaire be delivered: on paper or online?

Solution: online methods do allow you to gather lots of responses in a short space of time and the data are usually output in a spreadsheet, which saves you lots of time and avoids mistakes compared to inputting data from a paper questionnaire. You should check with your supervisor or department as there may be particular software that you need to use, for example some departments might pay for certain software as it has good security and useful features. Paper questionnaires might be useful if you are conducting your study in person and you do not have access to a computer or device at the time you are with the participant. Make sure to check with your supervisor about the costs of printing.

Challenge: getting responses. How can you encourage participants to complete your questionnaire whilst maintaining the participants' right to withdraw? This may be a particular challenge if you are using online surveys.

Solution: you may be able to offer small incentives to participants who take part in your survey. A prize draw is a very common technique used, especially on a limited budget. However, be aware that this may not help response rates (Robb et al., 2017). You may also be able to make use of recruitment platforms like Prolific (https://www.prolific.co/) but you should always check with your supervisor about using these platforms.

4.1.2.5 Summary

Surveys allow you to collect lots of data from participants but need to be carefully constructed to make sure that data is of good quality. Ensure that your questionnaire is fair and doesn't lead participants to respond in a particular way. Survey software can really aid you with questionnaire construction.

4.1.3 Sampling Methods

In quantitative research a key priority in determining your recruitment strategy is about ensuring that your research is generalizable (i.e. your results are applicable to the wider population) ideally by random sampling (drawing your participants at random from a fully specified population). In practice, a fully random sample is not necessarily achievable and typical alternatives include convenience sampling (recruiting from participants you know) and snowballing (asking your participants to identify potential participants that they know). For some research you may need to use more targeted methods such as stratified sampling (recruiting subpopulations based on attributes such as age to ensure proportions that align with the general population).

4.1.4 Power

As well as carefully choosing your method and designing your study you need to make sure that you collect enough data to have a good chance of finding an effect if it exists in the population. This means you need to make sure your study is sufficiently powered. Unfortunately, many published studies in psychology are not sufficiently powered and this is a problem because it means that we cannot say for sure if such findings are true and studies that are published have exaggerated effect sizes. Before you conduct your study, you need to work out what is the minimum number of participants you need to detect an effect if one exists. This will depend on your design and what statistical test you will perform on the data, so you need to plan the tests you are using before you start collecting data (see Handy Hint). See Figure 4.4 if you need help working out which statistical test to do.

> **Handy Hint**
> Plan what statistics to use in your analysis at the start of your project. It is a frequent occurrence that students run their experiments and later find themselves unable to analyse their data in the manner they had initially planned. So plan out what statistics you plan to use before you even start testing!
> Student, Durham University

There are calculators freely available to help you calculate power. One such is called G*Power and is available at https://www.psychologie.hhu.de/arbeitsgruppen/allgemeine-psychologie-und-arbeitspsychologie/gpower

The G*Power website also contains instructions for how to use it with examples. Here is an example of how to compute power for a between-subjects t-test. We have chosen a medium effect size ($d = 0.4$) with a power of 80% as reasonable values. If you want to use a larger effect size, you will need to justify why. In G*Power enter the following:

Test family: t tests

Statistical test: Means: Difference between two independent means (matched pairs)

Type of power analysis: A priori: Compute required sample size

Input: Tail(s) = Two, Effect size d = 0.4, α err prob = 0.05, Power (1-β err prob) = 0.80, Allocation ratio N2/N1 = 1.

Once you have input the parameters, click 'calculate' and you are shown the output (copied here and Figure 4.3). We can see that the suggested sample size is 100 participants per group, meaning a total of 200. Using the same values for a within-subject t-test, G*Power suggests 52 participants.

Output: noncentrality parameter $\delta = 2.8284271$

Critical t = 1.9720175

Df = 198

Sample size group 1 = 100

Sample size group 2 = 100

Total sample size = 200

Actual power = 0.8036475

Note that the number you enter into the effect size box will be different depending on the test you have chosen. So, for t-tests it is labelled as 'd' and for f tests it is 'f', so you need to make sure you are entering the correct number. For example, a medium effect size d is 0.4 but a medium effect size f is 0.25 (see the G*Power manual).

It is worth bearing these sample sizes for simple tests in mind when computing sample sizes for more complex designs. Brysbaert (2019) has an interesting paper that reports minimum numbers for common designs with an effect size of $d = .4$ and power of 80%. Keeping designs as simple as possible can help with power (Brysbaert, 2019). As you can see from Table 4.2, more participants are needed the more complex the design and generally most analyses require at least 100 participants.

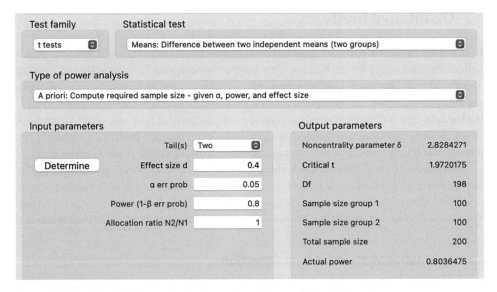

Figure 4.3 Screenshot of G*Power App for Computing a Between-Subjects *t*-test

Table 4.2 Sample Sizes Needed for Common Statistical Tests for the Alternative Hypothesis. From Brysbaert (*2019*)

Design	Number of participants needed for frequentist statistics (p < .05)	Number of participants needed for Bayesian statistics (BF > 10)
1 between-groups variable, 2 levels (e.g. *t*-test)	200 (100 per group)	380 (x2 190)
1 within-subjects variable, 2 levels (e.g. *t*-test)	52	100
1 between-groups variable, 3 levels (e.g. One-way ANOVA)	1740 (x3 groups of 580)	2850 (x3 groups of 950)
1 within-subjects variable, 3 levels (e.g. repeated-measures ANOVA)	300	540
Two-way repeated measures ANOVA		52 210
main effect	27	
interaction	110	
Two-way mixed ANOVA		
Main effect (repeated measures variable)	55 (x2 groups of 27)	100 (x2 groups of 50)
Main effect (between-subject variable)	190 (x2 groups of 95)	360 (x2 groups of 180)
Interaction	200 (x2 groups of 100)	390 (x2 groups of 195)
Correlation	195	370
Multiple regression		
One predictor	200	
Two predictors	300	

4.2 Qualitative Methods

In this section, we will focus on qualitative methods of data collection and analysis. When conducting qualitative research, there are a number of decisions that you will need to make about your study, depending on your research question. For example, you will need to think about the epistemological standpoint you will take in conducting your research and analysing the data. This will form the basis of your research, in terms of what questions you can ask about the data and what conclusions you can draw. More detailed information about epistemological standpoints in qualitative research can be found in Braun and Clarke (2013).

Additionally, you will have to think about the method of data collection you will employ in your study. This will likely be influenced by a number of factors, such as the nature of your research question, and what resources you may have available. Refer back to Chapter 1 (Starting Your Research Project) for further information on research questions in qualitative research.

4.2.1 Qualitative Methods of Data Collection

The approach to data collection methods and analysis is largely determined by your research question and the aims of your study. In qualitative research, you can use methodologies, such as interpretative phenomenological analysis (IPA), grounded theory, and discourse analysis. These are examples of theoretical frameworks which offer guidelines on methods of data collection, analysis of data, and what conclusions can be drawn about the data. A detailed narrative of different methodologies is beyond the scope of this chapter so for a more in-depth description we recommend having a look at introductory textbooks to qualitative research (e.g. Braun & Clarke, 2013; Bourne et al., 2021). This chapter will instead focus on qualitative methods of data collection, specifically interviews, and focus groups, and thematic analysis as a method of data analysis (Braun & Clarke, 2006; Braun & Clarke, 2012). These are independent of epistemological positions and a broader theoretical framework.

Methods of data collection within qualitative research can include gathering data from primary sources, such as interviews, focus groups, diary studies, and questionnaires with open-ended questions. This is where the researcher will recruit participants and collect the data first hand. Alternatively, the researcher can use secondary data. Examples may include newspaper articles, discussions in online forums or discussion groups, or information seen on social media. Each of these methods may be associated with different ethical risks and considerations, so you will need to ensure that you consider and address these, for example within an application for ethical approval, as specified by your department.

The choice of method will depend on your research question, the aims of your study, and what resources you have available to conduct your research. For example, it may be the case that a questionnaire with open-ended questions would suit your research question and have the added benefit of being less time consuming in terms of collecting data as well as preparing the data for analysis. This is because you can distribute the questionnaire to large numbers of individuals, and avoid the need to transcribe recorded speech, as you would have to for an interview or focus group. However, a potential drawback to qualitative surveys may be variability in the depth of participants' responses, and hence, the richness in the data that you may obtain from qualitative surveys may be lacking. Reviewing research papers that take a similar approach to your own will give a good idea about the types of methods that are most typically used.

In this chapter we will focus on two common methods of data collection that you may be likely to use as part of your research project—interviews and focus groups. We will outline the aims of each method, the basic characteristics and principles, the advantages, and potential challenges associated with each method and provide some tips on how to overcome these. We will focus specifically on how to conduct interviews and focus groups, constructing an effective interview and focus group schedule of questions, and how to structure and phrase your questions.

4.2.2 **Methods of Data Collection**

Interviews

In research, an interview is a professional conversation between a researcher and a participant, which involves asking the participants questions to capture their perspectives or experiences on a specific topic. Interviews offer an opportunity for participants to talk about their experiences on a particular issue and for researchers to capture the language participants use when talking about those experiences (Braun & Clarke, 2013). Interviews are useful when you want to explore individuals' views, experiences, and perceptions on a specific topic or research question, particularly for individuals who are personally affected by an issue or who may have a personal stake in the subject matter (Braun & Clarke, 2013). As with any approach, interviews have their advantages and disadvantages (see Table 4.3 for some examples), and this is something you will need to consider when designing your research project.

Interviews can take on a number of different forms. These include a structured interview, where all participants are asked the same questions in the same order, and responses are typically confined to a range of pre-determined options, similar to administering a questionnaire with closed-ended questions verbally. This approach is typically employed within a quantitative study. On the other end, you may have a purely unstructured interview schedule, where the research begins with a very broad question, and the process and the nature of subsequent questions depend on participants' responses. This may be useful if you are investigating a previously unexplored topic, for example. The most common method employed by qualitative researchers is the semi-structured interview, and this will be the focus of this chapter.

Semi-structured interviews

In semi-structured interviews, the researcher develops an interview schedule with a list of questions that address the objectives of their study and their research question. In addition to the main research questions, the researcher will also develop some probes to encourage further conversation with the participant. What is important within the context of an interview is to adopt a flexible approach, offering scope for participants to discuss issues that are important to them. Issues may fit in with the research question but may also explore unplanned topics if they are relevant to your research. There is also flexibility in terms of how questions are phrased as well as the order in which questions are asked, depending on the conversation with the participant.

Table 4.3 Advantages and Disadvantages of Using Interviews in Qualitative Research (Adapted from Braun and Clarke, *2013*)

Advantages	Disadvantages
Interviews have the potential of offering rich and detailed data about individuals' lived experiences and perspectives on a given topic (see 'Designing Effective Questions for Interviews').	Interviews can be time consuming to schedule and run. For example, depending on your research question and the number of questions you want to ask participants, an interview could take between 20–90 minutes.
Interviews can offer a flexible approach to data collection; the use of probes and the flexibility of asking additional, unplanned questions, can offer deeper insights into people's experiences. See 'Designing Effective Questions for Interviews' for some tips.	Careful consideration should be taken when developing your interview schedule to be able to build rapport with participants that will allow participants to feel comfortable to share their experiences with you. See 'Designing Effective Questions for Interviews' for some tips.
Depending on your research question and the nature of your research project, qualitative studies using the interview method of data collection typically tend to recruit a smaller number of participants in comparison to other methods (e.g. surveys). The number of participants that you need for your study will depend on your research question and the aims and objectives of your study. The quality of the data you obtain, in terms of richness and depth, can also affect the number of participants that you need to recruit. This is something to consider and factor in when designing your study.	Verbal data from interviews will need to be transformed into a written account of the conversation for analysis. Transcribing data can be time consuming and this needs to be factored in your research project timeline.
Interviews may be a good method of data collection if you are seeking perspectives or experiences on sensitive issues, as opposed to a group setting (e.g. focus group).	
Interviews can be more accessible to participants, in comparison to other methods of data collection, and can thus be used to collect data from vulnerable populations.	

For example, you may be conducting a study about people's experiences with a particular health issue. You would typically have a list of questions relating to the different topics you want to cover in the interview. You may ask your first question, and responses from a participant dive into a topic that you originally planned to cover later on in the interview. Depending on the flow of discussion, you may wish to focus on that particular topic at that point in the interview, given that the participant has already raised it, and then follow on with your remaining questions. Allowing this level of flexibility, provided that the conversation is still directly relevant to your research question, will enable you to obtain rich, detailed data from your participants and allow the conversation within the interview to flow well. Similarly, if a topic comes up in the conversation, which is interesting and relevant to your research question, this may provide the opportunity to follow it up with some targeted, unplanned questions to help you gain additional insights or perspectives into the topic you are investigating. It is important that the conversation remains on topic and relevant to your research question. With this in mind, you may want to plan some phrases in your interview schedule that would help you to bring the conversation back to the aims and objectives of the interview. Here are some important points relating to designing your interview questions, some challenges which you may come across, and some possible solutions:

Challenge: designing open questions. In qualitative research we aim to obtain rich and detailed data from participants. In-depth responses can provide key insights into perspectives, beliefs, experiences. A key consideration is, therefore, to develop open questions for your interview schedule.

Consider the following question: *"Would you say you have been affected by the Covid-19 pandemic?"* This question will likely lead participants to answer with a yes or a no, or to restrict their responses in a particular way.

Possible solution: although this type of question could be followed up with additional questions, you may want to consider phrasing it in more open terms. For example, *"Were any aspects of your life affected by the Covid-19 pandemic in any way? Please provide some examples".*

The phrasing in this question would enable more varied responses that can be followed by probes for more in-depth exploration of the impact of the Covid-19 pandemic on individuals.

Challenge: neutral questions. Similar to survey questions, questions written for an interview should not lead participants to respond in a particular way.

Consider the following example: *"In what ways has your experience with online assessments impacted you negatively?"*

This is a leading question: it is framed to focus on the negative impact of a given situation and probes participants to respond in a specific way or to focus on the negative aspects, rather than potentially gaining a true reflection of their experiences.

Possible solution: your initial question on this topic could be phrased in more neutral terms to gauge individuals' experiences and based on their responses, follow up with more targeted questioning (probes). For example, an initial question may be:

"Could you tell me about your experience with online assessments?"

This could be followed by additional questions to ask about different aspects of their experience, and impact (depending on what you want to ask participants, relating to your research question). For example:

"What has been the effect of online assessments on your learning experience, either positive or negative?"

The aforementioned examples are likely to provide participants with the opportunity to reflect on their experience with a particular topic or issue and offer their insights on different aspects, as relevant to them. This may be preferable rather than trying to preempt or assuming a-priori that a person's experience with *online learning* would be a negative one.

The use of probes can also help with following up on participants' responses, but also ensuring that important aspects of a topic are covered in the interview. With careful probing you also increase the chances that you will get richer data, with a more detailed narrative of participants' experiences, as opposed to having a single question on a specific aspect of the topic you are investigating with no follow-up points or questions. Some examples may include 'Could you tell me a little bit more about this?' or 'Could you give an example of that?'.

Challenge: clear questions that avoid asking multiple things. You want to be including questions that are clear and use non-ambiguous language. You should avoid asking participants multiple things in a single question as this can be confusing, and participants may not give equal attention to all elements of your question.

Consider the following question: *"What effect does consuming chocolate and coffee have on your health, lifestyle, and overall sleeping pattern?"*

There are too many elements in this question. You are asking participants to talk about the effects of two separate things (chocolate and caffeine) on a number of different aspects of their lives (health, lifestyle, sleeping pattern).

Possible solution: you could perhaps break up this question into a number of questions, each focusing on a single element. For example, you may want to ask participants.

"What effect does consuming caffeinated drinks have on your sleeping pattern?"

"What effect does consuming caffeinated drinks have on your health?"

This could then be followed by additional probing, depending on participants' responses (e.g. participants may say they are not impacted at all, in which case it may not make sense to probe further in this case). Some example probes may include asking for experiences or perspectives in relation to different aspects of sleeping or health.

Challenge: order of questions. The order of the questions in your interview schedule is important to build rapport with your participants.

Possible solution: *opening* and *closing questions* are really important in any interview schedule. You may want to consider starting with some general, open questions, that participants would feel that they could easily respond to. This can help with building rapport with participants and enable them to feel more comfortable having a conversation with you. This may lead them to open up about more sensitive or personal issues (depending on the nature of your research question) later on in the interview.

You will want to think about your closing question as well. This would be a good chance to give your participants the opportunity to add any further information they feel is important to them but did not have the opportunity to do so through the questions covered in the interview thus far. For example, you could ask participants if there is anything else they would like to mention in relation to the topic covered in the interview.

Challenge: making sure the conversation in the interview flows. It is important that you are responsive to the person you are interviewing, and you are listening actively to what they are saying and following up key points with additional questions or asking participants to expand on their response. It is also important to consider the nature of the topic you are investigating, that questions are phrased appropriately and don't offend or challenge participants in any way.

Possible solution: once you have developed your interview schedule, it would be beneficial to pilot it on a few of your peers or family members before you run the interview with your first participant. You can also ask your friends and family for feedback on the questions. This will give you an indication of how questions are being perceived by people and how well they work in relation to the objectives of your research project. By piloting your interview schedule, you are also likely to gain more experience and confidence in asking the questions before you start collecting data.

> **Handy Hint**
> When delivering the interview questions, what you want to be aiming for is to have a conversation with your participants around the topic you are investigating. You don't want the questioning to come across as very formal and staccato. Once you have developed your interview schedule you may want to practise with friend or family members and get some feedback on your questions and delivery style.

Focus groups

A focus group involves a number of individuals having a discussion that is focused on a particular topic. Participants may be recruited based on shared experiences or characteristics. For example, you may want to investigate the effect of technology use on learning in higher education. You would then want to recruit participants who are students in higher education and, depending on your research question, these may be students from a particular discipline (e.g. psychology or history). Careful consideration of who you want to recruit will help to yield some rich, meaningful data in relation to your research question. As such, recruiting individuals who may have a stake in a particular topic (e.g. recruiting students in higher education for the discussion about technology use) may help to generate greater, more in-depth discussion, compared to individuals who may not be invested in a particular topic or where the topic may not be personally relevant to them (e.g. individuals in retail as opposed to education).

Focus groups are different to an interview. The aim here is not to ask each person taking part in the focus group the same questions in turn, but rather to facilitate or moderate a discussion between a group of individuals. You will still need to develop a series of questions (called the focus group schedule) and some probes for each of your questions, where relevant, to ensure that you cover all aspects relevant to your research question. Like an interview, typically there would be flexibility within the focus group schedule to focus discussion on particular points raised by participants and to change the order that the questions or topics are covered in the focus group, depending on the discussion. In a focus group, in addition to a group discussion on a topic, the researcher may also wish to get participants' responses to stimuli or to include group activities and get some input from participants (Colucci, 2007).

Facilitating focus groups effectively is a skill acquired through experience. As with interviews, you may want to consider having a run-through the questions with friends or family members to practise before running your focus group with participants. Table 4.4 presents some advantages and disadvantages of using this method of data collection in a research project.

As with interviews, focus groups may also pose some challenges to the researcher. Here are some potential challenges to think about that are associated with focus groups and some possible solutions.

Challenge: managing the focus group discussions. One potential challenge when moderating a focus group discussion is to ensure that the conversation stays on topic. In a group, the conversation may easily get off-topic and this can be challenging for the researcher to manage.

Table 4.4 Some Advantages and Disadvantages of Focus Groups

Advantages	Disadvantages
The focus group discussion resembles an everyday conversation about topics. This can facilitate contribution and discussion by group members.	A focus group requires a group of individuals to all attend at the same time and same location (focus groups might take place virtually, depending on your study and resources available). Thus, it can be quite time consuming to schedule and you may also need to deal with cancellations from participants (see below for possible solutions to some challenges associated with focus groups).
Given the context of how a focus group would typically run, this can facilitate personal disclosure from participants.	Transcribing the focus group discussion can be very time consuming. Assuming that you would be transcribing the data verbatim (where the transcript is an accurate representation of what was being said in the discussion and by whom), then this would require repeated listening to the recording and checking for accuracy afterwards.
Interaction between participants is a key feature of a focus group. Rich data can potentially be obtained as points raised by some participants may trigger further discussion and additional viewpoints and experiences shared by other participants.	There are some additional ethical considerations associated with focus groups. Everyone in the group will be aware of who said what. Information around privacy and confidentiality (i.e. for participants to avoid discussing what was being said in the focus group outside of that setting) would need to be included in the information sheet and/or the consent form.

Similarly, you may find that one individual may be dominating the conversation, meaning that other participants may not have the opportunity to contribute their thoughts to the discussion.

Possible solution: when developing your focus group schedule, you may want to include some phrases that you could easily refer to in the focus group to try and steer the conversation back on topic.

Some examples may include, 'Thank you for that point. Perhaps we could take the conversation back to X', or 'Thinking about X [reminding participant of the question you are referring to] are there any further thoughts on this?'. You want to ensure that you are not dismissing participants' comments, even if unrelated to your research question/point of discussion at the time or making them feel uncomfortable in the situation. Thus, thinking beforehand of some strategies on how to bring the conversation back to the main topic of discussion may help within the context of the focus group.

When one individual may be dominating the conversation, again, planning ahead on different ways in which you could address this in the focus group, and discussing your strategies with your supervisor, could prove to be helpful. For example, you may wish to thank the individual for their contributions and ask other participants more generally if they had any thoughts on the topic at hand.

Setting some ground rules at the start of the session may also be a useful strategy to adopt. For example, when explaining the aim of the focus group and how the session will run, you may also want to comment that it is important for everyone to have an equal opportunity to talk about their experiences or perspectives.

Another point to consider is the number of participants you may want to have in each focus group. Many people in a single focus group may pose a challenge in terms of managing the conversation and providing the opportunity for all participants to contribute to the discussion. On the other hand, having too few participants may not provide grounds for detailed discussions and a range of perspectives on the particular topic you are investigating. Typically having six to eight participants in a focus group may help to moderate the discussions and address some of the challenges we have listed.

Having a second researcher in the focus group to take notes can be a useful consideration. This could be another student working on the research project. This may be particularly useful if you are asking participants to comment on certain things that you bring to the focus group (e.g. materials) or if you are asking participants to take part in an activity within the focus group. These are instances where the recording may not capture participants' actions or responses to the stimuli or activities. This is something that you can discuss with your supervisor, in terms of the practicalities of having a second person present in the focus group to support the process and what their role will be in the session.

4.3 Handling Data

Whatever type of method you use to gather your data you will end up with lots of it, in the form of numbers or text. It is important that you keep your data secure by storing it appropriately. Your department may have guidance on how you are expected to store data so do follow that, where available. If in the UK, guidance will likely come from the general data protection regulation (GDPR) which cover rules around gathering and using personal data. If in the UK, you must follow GDPR rules when collecting personal data. You may pseudonymize your data. This is where you give the person's data a code (e.g. rather than using their name) so that the data cannot be linked back to a person, but you could find the name that the code was linked to in another source. Similarly, when conducting interviews and focus groups you will need to anonymize your interview or focus group transcripts, such that you remove all potentially identifying information and replace these with a neutral word that serves as a description of the information provided (e.g. if a participant mentions the street they live in, you could replace this information with [location]). Personal and pseudonymized data are subject to GDPR. Data that are anonymous (i.e. cannot be tracked back to an individual) is not covered by GDPR; however, it is good practice to apply the principles set out by GDPR, for example, thinking about which data you need to collect and keeping data secure. For more information about GDPR see these guidelines from UK Research and Innovation: https://www.ukri.org/about-us/policies-standards-and-data/gdpr-and-research-an-overview-for-researchers/

4.3.1 Storage of Data

Always follow any guidelines from your department or supervisor about storing data. General good principles are to store:

- In a location accessible to your supervisor.
- In a location that is protected by security provided by your institution (e.g. One Drive).
- Not on a personal device.

4.3.2 Sharing Data

Supervisors will likely want you to share the data you have collected, and you might decide together to make the data available to other researchers. Sharing data helps others to replicate your analysis, and perhaps even to replicate and extend your study. You might look at websites like the Open Science Framework (OSF; https://osf.io/) to do this (see Soderberg, 2018 for instructions about sharing data via OSF). Here, we provide a checklist about how to format your data in a clear way based on information from OSF. This is good to follow even if you are only sharing data with your supervisor.

Checklist for formatting data for sharing:

- Have a raw data file that contains data but no analysis. OSF suggests making this a read-only file or a pdf.
- Have a file that contains the data after any collation (e.g. averaging across trials, converting units).
- Have a file for data summaries (e.g. descriptive statistics of the data).
- Keep a file of any code that was used for analysis (e.g. if you used R or SPSS syntax).
- Create a README file so that other people can understand your data. A README file is a document that contains information about that file. For a data file, this includes information like:
  - an abstract (a brief description of the data and study);
  - a list of data files and information about how they relate to each other;
  - methods of how the data were collected;
  - a data dictionary. This can be used to give details of the variables in the data set, for example, what they are called, what the unit of measurement was, what possible values were;
  - any abbreviations used in the data set.

4.3.3 Analysing Data

You likely already have an idea about how you are going to analyse your data based on your design and, if so, make sure to follow any analysis plan you had created and avoid questionable research practices (see Box 4.3). Alternatively, you might be doing exploratory research and perform a variety of analyses. Whatever type of research you are doing, when analysing your data it will help to keep notes on what you did so that you have accurate records that will help when writing the research project report. Notes may also help when talking to your supervisor about analyses. Theory and practice relating to individual tests for quantitative data is out of scope of this book but there are many statistics textbooks and websites you can refer to for that sort of detail (see Box 4.4 for a selection).

Qualitative data analysis

Your research question and the theoretical framework within which your research is situated will inform the analysis of your data. One common method is thematic analysis, a

BOX 4.3 Questionable Research Practices

There is lots of momentum to move psychology forward as a discipline by removing questionable research practices. These are practices that involve the researcher not being completely transparent in what they have done or manipulating analysis or reporting of analyses so it looks as though significant effects have been found. It is worth being aware of these to avoid doing them.

Students show low levels of engaging in these practices (Krishna & Peter, 2018), which is great and establishing good habits and practices will help if you are interested in a career in research. The following list of questionable research practices is taken directly from John et al. (2012).

- In a paper, failing to report all of a study's dependent measures.
- Deciding whether to collect more data after looking to see whether the results were significant.
- In a paper, failing to report all of a study's conditions.
- Stopping collecting data earlier than planned because one found the result that one had been looking for.
- In a paper, 'rounding off' a p value (e.g. reporting that a p value of .054 is less than .05).
- In a paper, selectively reporting studies that 'worked'.
- Deciding whether to exclude data after looking at the impact of doing so on the results.
- In a paper, reporting an unexpected finding as having been predicted from the start.
- In a paper, claiming that results are unaffected by demographic variables (e.g. gender) when one is actually unsure (or knows that they do).
- Falsifying data.

BOX 4.4 Statistics Resources

Your department

Don't forget to use any materials or resources from statistics modules that you have already completed. Check reading lists from your department too.

Books

- Bourne, V. (2017). *Starting out in Methods and Statistics for Psychology.* Oxford University Press.
- Bourne, V., James, A. I., & Wilson-Smith, K. (2021). *Understanding Quantitative and Qualitative Research in Psychology: A Practical Guide to Methods, Statistics, and Analysis.* Oxford University Press.

Websites

- StatHand. For help choosing a test: https://stathand.net/
- Discovering statistics. For lots of types of statistical tools. https://www.discoveringstatistics.com/statistics-hell-p/
- Laerd statistics covers many statistical tests with clear examples. A subscription is required. https://statistics.laerd.com/

foundational approach in qualitative research. Thematic analysis is considered a flexible approach to data analysis as it is not directly linked to a specific theoretical framework and can be applied within the context of different epistemological approaches and for a range of data collection methods. It is important to discuss your analytic approach with your supervisor, as they may have suggestions for what would be the most appropriate way to analyse your data depending on the nature of your research project, the aims of your study, and importantly, your research question.

Braun and Clarke (2006) outline six key steps in undertaking a thematic analysis, whether you are adopting an inductive or a deductive approach to your analysis: (1) familiarizing yourself with your data by repeatedly reading through your entire dataset, (2) conducting initial coding, (3) collating and refining your codes, (4) grouping your collated codes into candidate themes, (5) reviewing your themes in relation to the codes and data extracts and the entire dataset, and (6) naming your themes to reflect the nature and content of each theme and its relationship to other themes in your thematic map. An in-depth discussion of the basis of thematic analysis is beyond the scope of this chapter, and we would recommend engaging with relevant literature to become familiar with this approach (e.g. Braun & Clarke, 2006, 2012, 2013). Some key points to keep in mind when conducting thematic analysis include being thorough and systematic in the approach that you take and to clearly outline all the steps you have taken when presenting your analysis in your research project report.

Disseminating

Once you've analysed your data and have your results, it is very common to tell other people about your research (dissemination). You might be asked to write a report (see Chapter 7) and to prepare and give a poster or oral presentation (see Chapter 8). Doing either (or both) of these is a fantastic opportunity to make sure that you are knowledgeable about the research you have conducted and understand what you have found and how it relates to the wider research area. You could talk to your supervisor about the possibility of submitting your work to a peer-reviewed journal. This will generally depend on the rigour of the study (e.g. was it well-designed, was data collected appropriately, how much data was collected?).

Summary

Which type of research methodology you choose will depend on your research question. Within the context of quantitative research, experiments need to be used when you have a question about causality and surveys can be used when you have questions about frequency and want to measure people's current thoughts and behaviours. Both methods require careful implementation to ensure that you collect data of good quality. When undertaking qualitative research, your research question, the aims of your study and the epistemological standpoint that you take will help to inform the design of your study and your analytic method.

Summary of Tips for Quantitative Research

Experiments

- Keep the design simple and know what your variables are.
- Think about how to control your experiment so that you can ascribe the results to the manipulation and not to other factors.
- Use materials that have already been used in research.

Surveys

- Use a reliable and valid measure. It is a good idea to use measures that have been published.
- If creating your own questions, make sure the questions are fair and if creating a measure from multiple questions, check the reliability and validity.

Summary of Tips for Qualitative Research

- Your approach to data collection methods and analysis will largely be determined by your research question and the aims of your study.
- Interviews can be useful when you want to explore perspectives or experiences on a specific topic, particularly with individuals who may have a personal investment in the topic under investigation.
- When designing your interview schedule it is important to carefully develop your questions. Some points to keep in mind include designing open questions, avoid leading questions; the use of prompts can help to obtain rich responses from participants.
- When delivering the interview, a flexible approach is desirable that is responsive to participants' responses.
- Focus groups are different to interviews. The aim is to facilitate a group discussion between participants.
- In managing focus group discussion, consider the size of your group, participants' characteristics, and setting some ground rules.

Data

- Calculate the sample size needed to detect an effect.
- Comply with data protection regulations.
- Format your data to facilitate sharing.

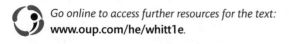

Go online to access further resources for the text:
www.oup.com/he/whitt1e.

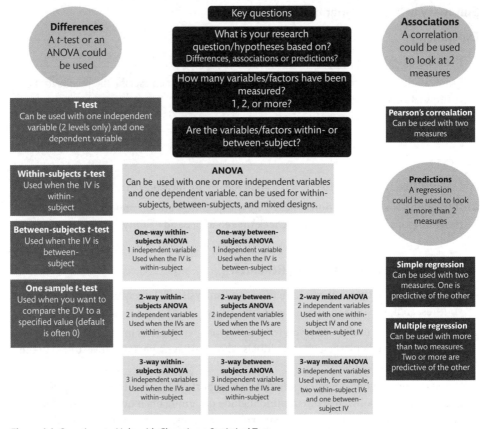

Figure 4.4 Questions to Help with Choosing a Statistical Test

References

Bourne, V., James, A. I., & Wilson-Smith, K. (2021). *Understanding Quantitative and Qualitative Research in Psychology: A Practical Guide to Methods, Statistics, and Analysis*. Oxford University Press.

Braun, V., & Clarke, V. (2006). Using thematic analysis in psychology. *Qualitative Research in Psychology, 3*, 77–101. https://doi.org/10.1191/1478088706qp063oa

Braun, V., & Clarke, V. (2012). Thematic analysis. In H. Cooper, P. M. Camic, D. L. Long, A. T. Panter, D. Rindskopf, & K. J. Sher (eds.), *APA Handbook of Research Methods in Psychology, Vol. 2. Research Designs: Quantitative, Qualitative, Neuropsychological, and Biological* (pp. 57–71).

American Psychological Association. https://doi.org/10.1037/13620-004

Braun, V., & Clarke, V. (2013). *Successful Qualitative Research: A Practical Guide for Beginners*. Sage.

Brysbaert, M. (2019). How many participants do we have to include in properly powered experiments? A tutorial of power analysis with reference tables. *Journal of Cognition, 2*(1), 16. https://doi.org/10.5334/joc.72

Buckingham, G. (2019). Examining the size-weight illusion with visuo-haptic conflict in immersive virtual reality. *Quarterly Journal of Experimental Psychology (2006), 72*(9), 2168–2175. https://doi.org/10.1177/1747021819835808

Chambers. (2019). *Seven Deadly Sins of Psychology: A Manifesto for Reforming the Culture of Scientific Practice*. Princeton University Press.

Colucci, E. (2007). "Focus groups can be fun": The use of activity-oriented questions in focus group discussions. *Qualitative Health Research*, *17*(10), 1422–1433.

Conway, A. R. A., Kane, M. J., Bunting, M. F., Hambrick, D. Z., Wilhelm, O., & Engle, R. W. (2005). Working memory span tasks: A methodological review and user's guide. *Psychonomic Bulletin & Review*, *12*(5), 769–786. https://doi.org/10.3758/BF03196772

Dunlosky, J. A, Rawson, K. A. A, Marsh, E. J. B, Nathan, M. J. C, & Willingham, D. T. D. (2013). Improving students' learning with effective learning techniques: Promising directions from cognitive and educational psychology. *Psychological Science in the Public Interest*, *14*(1), 4–58. https://doi.org/10.1177/1529100612453266

Galesic, M., & Tourangeau, R. (2007). What is sexual harassment? It depends on who asks! Framing effects on survey responses. *Applied Cognitive Psychology*, *21*, 189–202. https://doi.org/10.1002/acp.1336

Hoerger, M. (2010). Participant dropout as a function of survey length. *Cyberpsychology, Behavior, and Social Networking*, *13*(6), 697–701. https://doi.org/10.1089/cyber.2009.0445

John, L. K., Loewenstein, G., & Prelec, D. (2012). Measuring the prevalence of questionable research practices with incentives for truth telling. *Psychological Science*, *23*(5), 524–532. https://doi.org/10.1177%2F0956797611430953

Kelley, K., Clark, B., Brown, V., & Sitzia, J. (2003). Good practice in the conduct and reporting of survey research. *International Journal for Quality in Health Care*, *15*(3), 261–266. https://doi.org/10.1093/intqhc/mzg031

Krishna, A. & Peter, S. M. (2018). Questionable research practices in student final theses– Prevalence, attitudes, and the role of the supervisor's perceived attitudes. *PloS one*, *13*(8), e0203470. https://doi.org/10.1371/journal.pone.0203470

Peirce, J., Hirst, R., & MacAskill, M. (2022). *Building Experiments in PsychoPy*. Sage.

QAA (2019). *Subject Benchmark Statement for Psychology*. Quality Assurance Agency.

Robb, K. A., Gatting, L., & Wardle, J. (2017). What impact do questionnaire length and monetary incentives have on mailed health psychology survey response? *British Journal of Health Psychology*, *22*(4), 671–685. https://doi.org/10.1111/bjhp.12239

Soderberg, C. K. (2018). Using OSF to share data: A step-by-step guide. *Advances in Methods and Practices in Psychological Science*, *1*(1), 115–120. https://doi.org/10.1177%2F2515245918757689

Weijters, B., Cabooter, E., & Schillewaert, N. (2010). The effect of rating scale format on response styles: The number of response categories and response category labels. *International Journal of Research in Marketing*, *27*(3), 236–247. https://doi.org/10.1016/j.ijresmar.2010.02.004

5 Conducting Your Research Ethically

A key principle guiding all research in psychology is that studies or experiments are conducted in an ethical manner, whereby the rights and safety of participants are respected in the research process. Psychological research with human participants, in the UK, is currently guided by the British Psychological Society (BPS) *Code of Ethics and Conduct* (2021) and the BPS *Code of Human Research Ethics* (2021). The BPS has further published guidelines for psychologists working with animals and these can be found on their website as well. Similar guidelines for researchers also exist in other countries; for example, in the US researchers are guided by the American Psychological Association (APA) ethical guidelines. This chapter is designed to map to and reflect the ethical guidelines set out by the BPS *Code of Ethics and Conduct* and the BPS *Code of Human Research Ethics* and how these apply to undergraduate research projects. It is also important, before undertaking a piece of research, to familiarize yourself with the procedures set out in your department, and that you discuss these along with a plan of action with your supervisor. We recommend that you start thinking about the ethical requirements and potential ethical risks associated with your study right at the start of your research project.

Once you have designed your study, and before you start collecting data, it is important that you obtain approval from your relevant research ethics committee (or equivalent). Depending on the research project you are conducting, this is likely to be run by your department. Gaining approval from a research ethics committee or relevant team ensures that potential ethical risks have been assessed (see section on 'Risk' for further information) and that necessary procedures are in place by the researchers to address such risks. It also ensures that both participants' and researchers' interests are protected in the research process.

In this chapter we present key principles and some key points to consider when designing your study or experiment and preparing your paperwork for ethical review. We also outline what the relevant documentation may entail. It is important to ensure that you are also following the guidelines and procedures set out by your department.

5.1 Why Do I Need to Obtain Ethical Approval for My Research Project?

Ethics forms a key part of psychological research, which aims to protect participants as well as researchers. The BPS Code of Ethics and Conduct (2021) outlines four main ethical principles that members of the Society should follow. These are respect, competence, responsibility, and integrity. More information on these principles can be found in the relevant documentation on the Society's website (www.bps.org.uk). The BPS also provides a set of principles on conducting research with human participants through their *Code of Human Research Ethics* (2021). This document can also be found on the society's website. This chapter will focus on these guidelines and how they are relevant to conducting your undergraduate research project. If you are conducting your research in an online context you should also ensure that your research is conducted in line with the BPS *Ethics Guidelines for Internet-mediated Research* (2021).

Clinical studies may need to go through a different route and may have additional requirements. If you are conducting research with a clinical population or research that involves collecting data in a healthcare setting (e.g. in the National Health Service (NHS)) then you are likely to go through the ethical approval procedures outlined by the NHS. You will need to consult the relevant website (NHS Research Ethics Service) to obtain information on this. The procedures involved in such routes are beyond the scope of this chapter.

FUTURE FOCUS Behaving Ethically

Ethical Awareness is the ability to recognize what ethical issues are created by a particular course of action; if you can do this, then it is much more likely that you will go on to act in an ethical way. This is important, not only in a professional context, but more broadly across all aspects of your life.

5.2 Key Principles Underlying Psychological Research

Research in psychology can employ a range of different methodologies, methods of data collection, and different populations, some of which are vulnerable or may not be able to provide informed consent. Some key principles to think about when designing your research study include risk, informed consent, confidentiality, deception, and debriefing. These are outlined in the BPS *Code of Human Research Ethics*, a summary of which is presented in what follows (www.bps.org.uk).

5.3 Risk

The BPS defines risk as 'the potential physical or psychological harm, discomfort or stress to human participants that a research project may generate' (BPS, *Code of Human Research Ethics*, 2021, p. 10). When designing your study you will need to consider potential risks to participants and to develop procedures to manage those risks.

The BPS outlines examples of research that are considered to involve more than minimal risk. See Box 5.1 for some of these examples, which may be relevant to undergraduate research projects. If your study involves any of these instances, then these will have to be acknowledged in your application for ethical approval, with relevant details of how you will address those risks. For example, your study may involve showing participants emotional

> **BOX 5.1 Examples of Research which Would Normally be Considered to Involve More Than Minimal Risk. Taken from the BPS *Code of Human Research Ethics* (2021, p. 10).**
>
> - *Research involving vulnerable groups (such as children aged under 16; those lacking capacity; or individuals in a dependent or unequal relationship, or who have prior experience of psychological or physical harm or adversity in its broadest sense);*
> - *Research involving potentially sensitive topics (such as participants' sexual behaviour; their legal or political behaviour; their experience of violence; their gender or ethnic status);*
> - *Research involving a significant and necessary element of deception;*
> - *Research involving access to records of personal or confidential information (including genetic or other biological information);*
> - *Research that might open access to potentially sensitive data through third parties;*
> - *Research that could induce psychological stress, anxiety or humiliation or cause more than minimal pain (e.g. repetitive or prolonged testing);*
> - *Research involving invasive interventions (such as the administration of drugs or other substances, vigorous physical exercise or techniques such as hypnosis) that would not usually be encountered during everyday life;*
> - *Research that may have an adverse impact on employment or social standing (e.g. discussion of an employer, discussion of commercially sensitive information);*
> - *Research that may lead to 'labelling' either by the researcher (e.g. categorization) or by the participant (e.g. 'I am stupid', 'I am not normal');*
> - *Research that involves the collection of human tissue, blood or other biological samples.*

images which can be quite negative in nature, or you may include a questionnaire which contains items measuring participants' levels of anxiety (e.g. State-Trait Inventory for Cognitive and Somatic Anxiety, STICSA; Ree, French, MacLeod, & Locke, 2008). Although these studies may not pose any physical harm to participants, they do carry an element of risk in terms of psychological harm. In the first example, participants may be adversely affected by viewing negative emotional images; and in the second example, some of the questions may be deemed sensitive in nature, and may trigger recall of personal negative memories, or even the possibility that participants may feel that this instrument is diagnostic. Therefore, such risks need to be acknowledged in the study's ethical application, and necessary procedures need to be put in place by the researcher or research team to address these risks. If we take the earlier example of a questionnaire measuring levels of anxiety, a potential procedure could, for example, entail informing participants of the nature of the questionnaire at the start of the study, and further stating that it is not intended as a diagnostic tool. A further procedure could also involve the researcher ensuring that participants' mood does not change in a negative manner as a result of participation in a study; an evidence-based mood enhancement technique may help to address this aspect of your study. Further information and support contact details can also be presented in the debrief section of your study for participants to refer to (see section on 'Debriefing'). Such procedures need to be discussed with your supervisor to ensure that they are appropriate for your study design and included in your application for ethical approval.

It is important to be aware that not all supervisors will be willing or able to supervise 'high-risk' projects. Equally important is considering whether you are happy with the level of risk involved in research you might undertake. If you are proposing a research project idea of your own that is high-risk, you may need to make sure that any potential supervisors are comfortable with this and feel equipped to oversee the work you are suggesting.

5.4 **Informed Consent**

When deciding whether or not to take part in a research study, participants need to be fully informed of the nature of the study, what they will be expected to do, and how their data will be used (see also Chapter 4). They also need to provide their consent for taking part. Therefore, informed consent involves two key processes: (1) the researcher needs to provide appropriate information to participants about the study; and (2) obtain their consent for participation. It is important to note that informed consent is an ongoing process in the research process (see section on 'Right to Withdraw').

It is common practice for researchers to provide an information sheet to participants prior to the start of the study, and this needs to precede a consent form. Box 5.2 presents some key information to include on the participant information sheet, which could be provided to participants as a hard copy or presented online depending on the nature of your study (see also bps.org.uk). Critically, to meet the ethical standards required by psychology research, it is important that any participant materials you use are clear and easily understandable by the target audience (i.e. your specific participant sample); without this, it is not possible for a participant to provide informed consent. This means that you need to think carefully about the language you use, and make sure to avoid overly technical terms and unnecessary jargon.

FUTURE FOCUS Communicating With Different Audiences

An important skill which you will likely have plenty of opportunity to practise during your project is the ability to tailor your communication style to suit a variety of audiences. When composing your participant-facing materials (e.g. your Information Sheet and Debrief), you will need to give careful consideration to who will be reading them and what they need to understand from them. Getting the right balance between scientific depth and straightforward language is not always easy, but if you can do this, then you probably have a very good grasp of the research you are carrying out.

It is important that participants are adequately informed about the nature of the study they are agreeing to take part in (see also 'Withholding Information and Deception'), and that they have the opportunity to raise any concerns or ask any questions they may have about the study. When conducting a study in a laboratory, for example, it can be straightforward for participants to ask the researcher any questions they may have. When conducting a study

---

BOX 5.2 Participant Information Resource

Participant Information Sheet

The following information is typically presented to participants prior to obtaining their consent for participation in your study.

- Who the **researchers and project supervisors** are and their contact details.

- The **title of your study**.

- An **ethical approval reference number** (or equivalent) to indicate that your study has been approved by a research ethics committee (or equivalent).

- **Key details** about the study. These include the **aims of the study**, **procedures** (i.e. what participants are expected to do as part of this study), **duration of the study**, and some information on how participants' **data** will be used and stored (e.g. compliance with the Data Protection Act (2018); privacy notice and compliance with General Data Protection Regulation (GDPR), where relevant—see Chapter 4 for further information on this). If applicable to your study, you can also include details of an inconvenience allowance given for participation.

- Information on **anonymity** and **confidentiality** (see also section on 'Confidentiality').

- Participants should also be informed of the voluntary nature of the study, and that they are **free to withdraw** their consent and means to do this (see further information on this in text).

- If the data collected in your project is going to be shared openly (e.g. through being deposited in a publicly available repository)—which is quite likely if you hope to publish your project findings in a peer-reviewed journal—you should include details of this here.

- Participants may also be provided with **relevant contact details**, independent of the research team, should they wish to raise any concerns or complaints about the study.

- **Signposting participants**. Where relevant, details of appropriate support organizations and websites can be provided should participants wish to obtain further information about the topic of the study or if they would like to discuss their personal circumstances with a relevant professional. Common examples of useful support services might include: The Samaritans, Shout Crisis Text Line, your University Nightline (for students), a local General Practitioner (GP) Service or Health Centre, Beat Eating Disorders Helpline.

---

online or remotely, you will need to consider how you can provide participants with such opportunities. For example, you may wish to inform participants that they can contact the researcher(s) via email should they have any questions about the study.

Also, within the context of online studies, there may be further risks you will need to consider and inform participants of. For example, online questionnaire data might be stored on the server of a third-party software provider which reduces the amount of control that you might have in protecting confidentiality. Stating how data will be stored and managed on the information sheet can ensure that participants are aware of such risks prior to participation. For more information refer to the BPS *Ethics Guidelines for Internet-mediated Research* (2021).

Where your research project involves collecting data on potentially sensitive topics (e.g. sexual behaviour, gender), you must be particularly mindful of your consent procedures. This is especially the case when you collect data in a way that is personally identifying (e.g. video- or audio-recorded focus groups or interviews, or data collected through diary studies). If your project topic involves a potentially sensitive area, then you should be prepared to include extra informed consent procedures in your research. For example, it is not uncommon to ask participants to provide general consent and then, separately, consent for any additional sensitive data that may be collected. Similarly, it might be necessary to obtain separate informed consent for your data collection in addition to any planned dissemination of findings from your research project.

5.4.1 "How Much Information Should I Give Participants about the Nature of My Study?"

Participants should be adequately informed of what it is you will be asking them to do as part of your study, and overall what your study involves. However, in some cases, providing explicit information as to the aims of your study may affect people's responses or behaviour in the study. Imagine that you wanted to investigate whether people recall more words if these are presented randomly on a computer screen or in an organized hierarchy. Consider the following statement: *The aim of the experiment is to investigate whether people remember more words depending on how these words are presented, either randomly or in an organized hierarchy.* Providing information about the explicit aims of your experiment in this way may influence participants' responses to your stimuli. Alternatively, consider the following statement: *The aim of the experiment is to investigate whether people remember more words depending on how these words are presented.* This second statement provides an accurate reflection of the purpose of the study, however, the way that this information is presented is less likely to influence participants' responses in a specific direction, in comparison to the first statement.

Similarly, if you wanted to investigate the effects of different techniques on memory, explicitly informing participants, such as *in this study you will be provided with a list of words; we will ask you to try and remember these words, and for half of the words we will ask you to use a specific technique A and for the remaining words we will ask you to remember these using technique B. We expect participants to remember more words using technique B in comparison to technique A,* may again influence participants' responses to the task. Instead, you can inform participants of the general, rather than explicit aims of the study, and provide adequate information about the procedures. You can then discuss what your specific aims and hypotheses are when you debrief your participants. Note that withholding some information about the explicit aims or anticipated findings of your study is not the same as your study involving an element of deception (see section on 'Deception').

Handy Hint

Students often feel apprehensive or uncertain about the style and level of detail to include in important documentation such as a Participant Information Sheet or Debrief. It is not unusual for initial drafts to be overly formal or casual in their language or for the information provided to be too scant or extremely lengthy! Making sure you are familiar with the guidelines of your institution is essential but having the chance to see a few authentic examples can also be really handy. Lots of Psychology departments offer the chance for students to be involved in research projects as participants themselves—you may have the chance to participate in other undergraduate research projects earlier in your degree programme, or you might participate in a project being run by a postgraduate student or a member of staff. Doing this is a great way to get some experience of what it is like to be a research participant, and to get a feel for the type of information provided to participants and how this is best presented.

BOX 5.3 **Anonymity and Confidentiality**	
Anonymity	**Confidentiality**
• You do not collect any personally identifying information that would allow a link to be made between the data and a particular individual.	• You separate personally identifying information from the data you collect (e.g. using ID numbers or pseudonyms).
• No one, including you, as the researcher— can identify participants in the study.	• You, as the researcher, know the identities of your participants, but you do not disclose this outside of your research project team.

5.5 Confidentiality

The principle of confidentiality relates to respecting someone's privacy. It is linked to, but distinct from, another important principle: that of anonymity. The differences between the two, in the context of carrying out a research project, are outlined in Box 5.3.

Data provided by participants should be treated with confidentiality and any reports that may be produced from your research (e.g. research project report, presentations) should not identify any individual participants, unless you have their consent for doing so (depending on the nature of your study). If confidentiality and anonymity of participants cannot be maintained, this needs to be made explicit to participants prior to them agreeing to take part in the study. You and your supervisor will have discussed any anticipated risks and potential scenarios which may warrant that confidentiality cannot be guaranteed, and you may need to disclose information to relevant individuals to ensure the wellbeing of participants: it would be important that participants understand this before consenting. It is important to think of such instances when designing your study and your application for ethical approval. Further details on the issue of confidentiality can be found in the BPS *Code of Ethics and Conduct*.

5.6 Right to Withdraw

The point at which participants can withdraw their consent is typically specified by the researcher on the information sheet provided prior to the start of the study. As a minimum, participants can withdraw before or during the study; participants may also be able to withdraw after the study. Depending on the nature of the study, it may only be possible for participants to withdraw their consent up until the point of data analysis or publication of results. When conducting anonymous online surveys, for instance, and depending on the nature of the survey, participants may only be able to withdraw prior to or during the study, as the researcher may not be able to identify an individual participant's responses and remove these from their dataset.

It may, however, be possible to have processes in place where anonymous data can be retrieved, such as using anonymous identifiers in your study that participants can easily remember. This will then enable the researcher to remove any individual's responses should they wish to withdraw their data. Withdrawal is particularly important for online studies because it might not be immediately obvious when a participant has withdrawn. For example, if participants work through several frames of an online questionnaire what happens to the data in previous frames if the participant shuts down the questionnaire part of the way through? Having appropriate processes in place to address participants' ability to withdraw their data is, therefore, important. The researcher would need to explicitly state on the information sheet given to participants how they can withdraw consent at different stages of the study.

5.7 The Consent Form

Once participants have received information about what they are going to be asked to do and have been provided with opportunities to ask any questions they may have, then the researcher will need to obtain their consent for participation. The consent form, which can either be presented as a hard copy or an online document to participants depending on the nature of your study, would typically include key information, as presented in Box 5.4. You will also need to consult relevant guidelines set out by your department on the content of the participant consent form and means of seeking consent. The BPS *Code of Human Research Ethics* provides some further details and examples of consent procedures relevant to different types of research topics and study design (see bps.org.uk). It is important to retain a copy of completed consent forms for your records. In order to ensure that the identity of individual participants is not linked to their responses, it would be advisable to store signed consent

---

BOX 5.4 Typical Contents of a Participant Consent Form

The following information is typically included in the consent form. Participants are generally asked to confirm that:

- They have read and understood the information they have been provided with about the study.
- They have had the opportunity to ask questions about the study, they have been provided with the means to do so, and that their questions have been answered.
- They understand that they are free to withdraw consent from the study without giving a reason for doing so; the means and timeline for this are made explicit to participants.
- If you are collecting data in a way that is personally identifiable (e.g. video- or audio-recorded focus groups or interviews) you will need to state this so that participants can provide explicit consent for this.
- If the data collected in your project is going to be shared openly (e.g. through being deposited in a publicly available repository) you should include details in your information sheet, together with how participants' anonymity will be maintained, and seek participants' consent for this.

Participants are then asked to declare that they agree to take part in the study.

forms separately from your dataset. It is important to have a discussion with your supervisor about study documentation, such as consent forms, to agree how and where these will be stored following completion of your research project.

The aforementioned information is intended to serve as general guidelines on the content of relevant study documents. Please follow the guidelines provided by your institution, which may include standard information and consent forms that need to be used in research studies.

5.8 Observational Studies

In the case of observational studies, informed consent should be sought from participants when such studies are carried out in non-naturalistic settings such as the laboratory. When observational studies are conducted in natural settings, it is important that participants' privacy and wellbeing are respected. Observational research where informed consent is not obtained from participants can only take place in public where individuals would expect their behaviour to be viewed by others. An example of an observational study in a natural setting would be exploring individuals' behaviour and interactions in a restaurant, where participants may anticipate that their general behaviour would be observed by strangers. On the other hand, listening in to people's private conversations and using these for your research without obtaining consent from these individuals would not be acceptable! A similar expectation applies for online research. For example, collecting data from a 'members-only' discussion group is not dissimilar to listening in on a private conversation and would require informed consent.

5.9 Vulnerable Populations and Informed Consent

When working with vulnerable populations, such as children, individuals with learning difficulties, or individuals who have experienced physical or psychological harm or adversity, additional ethical procedures and safeguards should be in place with regard to obtaining informed consent. For example, when conducting research with children in schools, you are likely to need the consent of the head teacher. Depending on the nature of your study, you may also need to inform children's parents or carers of your study and obtain their informed consent for their child's participation. It is also good practice to seek assent from the child. To accommodate this, be aware that you will need separate information sheets and consent forms for caregivers, gatekeepers, and for the participants themselves. Additional safeguarding procedures will need to be in place during and after the study. For example, in the event that a child becomes upset you will need to identify a key contact in their school that the child can talk to. It is important that any information provided to children in relation to the study is clear and presented in a way that is appropriate, so that the child is able to understand what they are agreeing to take part in and that they understand that they can withdraw from the study at any time without any consequences. Ensure that you consult your department's guidelines on research involving children when developing and running your study.

5.10 Your Role as a Researcher

As previously mentioned, as researchers we are bound by key principles such as respect, competence, responsibility, and integrity. When undertaking a research project it is important to consider your role as a researcher, what that entails, and what the boundaries are. Think of the following example. You may be conducting a study investigating the effects of workload on psychological wellbeing. What is your role as a researcher in this study?

5.10.1 Giving Advice

Your role as a researcher working on your undergraduate project is to collect data from participants for research purposes only. As a researcher you are not in a position to be giving advice to participants. This is something that you can make explicit in the information you give to participants. For instance, you can state both verbally (if applicable to your research project) and in your information sheet or debrief form that the data that you are collecting are merely used for the purpose of research, that any measures (e.g. questionnaires) that you are using are not intended to be diagnostic, and that you are not able to provide personal advice to or on behalf of participants. Even if you are presenting health-related information as part of your study, you can inform participants that this information is used for the purposes of this study and should not be taken as individual medical advice.

If participants require further information or would like to discuss their personal circumstances with someone, provide relevant contact details and resources for further information. You might detail how they can find additional information related to the topic covered in your research project (e.g. websites of relevant trusted organizations) and relevant contact details should they wish to speak to someone about their personal circumstances. This information can be presented in the debrief form given to participants at the end of the study. Remember that any contact information or other information that you provide should be appropriate and accessible to every participant in your study. Participants can direct any questions about the study to the research team, but for general information or advice in relation to the topic covered in your study you can signpost them appropriately.

5.10.2 What to do if You Identify Issues?

Where an issue may be detected as a result of participants taking part in your study, which can be either psychological or physical and may affect the future wellbeing of participants, then relevant procedures should be in place prior to the start of the research on how to address these instances. For example, you may be conducting a study using a magnetic resonance imaging (MRI) scanner. You, or a suitably qualified individual in the research team, may notice something in the scan which may appear abnormal, based on the training that you may have had, and you may need to refer this for further investigation. Your study design, which you will develop together with your supervisor, should detail what procedures you need to follow, and participants will need to be informed of these when they are provided with information about your study. Guidelines relevant to studies using specialized software or procedures should already be available in your department and you will need to consult these.

If you are in doubt about any aspect of your research project, have a discussion with your supervisor, and consult your department's guidelines and guidelines set out by the BPS.

5.11 Deception

As mentioned earlier in this chapter, providing participants with explicit details of the purpose of the study and the study's hypothesis may drive participants to change or adapt their behaviour in line with those hypotheses, so it may be necessary to withhold certain information. However, there is a difference between withholding details of the specific aims and hypotheses, and deliberately providing information to participants contrary to what the aims of the research are or withholding information for no good reason. Some examples of the use of deception in research may include: informing participants that they are taking part in a study measuring response times to a computer-based task when in fact you may be investigating a more sensitive topic such as attitudes towards minority groups, or not informing participants that they are being filmed during the study. You should aim to disclose as much information as possible about your study prior to participation. If an element of deception is employed in your study, then a full debrief should be provided to participants explaining the nature of the study and the purpose of the deception. Relevant procedures should be in place to ensure that the autonomy and dignity of participants are protected. This aspect of your study should be fully disclosed in your application for ethical approval.

Before embarking on a research project that entails a degree of deception, you should consider carefully whether it is necessary and whether the potential value of the research findings justify the use of deception. The BPS position on it is that 'Deception or covert collection of data should only take place where it is essential to achieve the research results required, where there are no alternatives, where the research objective has strong scientific merit and where there is an appropriate risk management and harm alleviation strategy' (BPS *Code of Human Research Ethics* 2021 , p. 23). Ultimately, the decision on whether to go ahead with a study involving deception comes down to you and your supervisor and is a matter of judgement. This is something that your research ethics committee will consider seriously if your application for ethical approval details the use of deception.

Your own decision on using deception will probably be influenced by how you expect it might affect your participants. If participants are likely to get upset or angry after they have been informed of the deception, then the BPS *Code of Human Research Ethics* states that deception is not appropriate in this case. To decide how likely this is, ask yourself how you might feel if you were a participant in your research study. What about one of your friends or a family member? If your research intends to involve vulnerable participants, consider if this may make them more likely to be distressed by the deception. Assuming your supervisor has conducted similar research before, then they may have a good idea of how participants typically react and be able to offer guidance on appropriate ways to manage the risk of participant distress. Consulting previous research using similar methods is another useful way to find strategies to alleviate potential harm, and to assess how extensively your planned approach has been used in the past. It is important that both you and your supervisor are comfortable with any suggested use of deception in your project, and be aware that a supervisor may decline to supervise a research project if this is not the case.

BOX 5.5 Typical Contents of a Participant Debrief Form

Debrief form

- Title of study and contact details of researchers and project supervisor, should participants wish to discuss the study further.
- The nature of the study, aims, and hypotheses.
- The measures used in the study.
- How the findings may inform literature and practice.
- What participants need to do should they wish to withdraw their data (e.g. contact the research team by a specific date).
- Depending on the nature of your study, it may be relevant to ask participants to reiterate their consent for the use of their data.
- Signposting participants. Where relevant, details of appropriate support organizations and websites can be provided should participants wish to obtain further information about the topic of the study or if they would like to discuss their personal circumstances with a relevant professional. Common examples of useful support services might include:
  - The Samaritans
  - Shout Crisis Text Line
  - Your University Nightline (for students)
  - A local GP Service or Health Centre
  - Beat Eating Disorders Helpline

5.12 Debriefing

As outlined in the previous section, where studies include deception or withholding of information, researchers need to ensure that participants are appropriately debriefed afterwards. It is also good practice to debrief participants even if your study does not involve such instances. A further purpose of the debrief procedure is to ensure that participants leave your study in a positive mood, and that they have not been adversely affected by any of the information or stimuli that they have been exposed to as part of your study. For example, if you have asked participants to recall potentially unpleasant memories, then you may wish to include a mood enhancer, where participants are given the opportunity at the end of the study to think about a positive memory or write down something they look forward to doing in the near future. You might produce a form to summarize debriefing information for participants (see Box 5.5).

5.13 Some Tips on Filling in Your Ethical Approval Documentation

Obtaining ethical approval can be a lengthy process. Depending on where you are carrying out your research there may be other organizations that you need to approach for permission or ethical clearance. If you are at all uncertain, seek your supervisor's advice. Relevant policies and procedures associated with obtaining ethical approval for studies can differ between institutions, so it is worth spending a bit of time at the very start of your research project familiarizing yourself with those for your department. A few things you might look out for are:

- Are there different research ethics committees that you could apply to? Do these have different timeframes?

- Are there some types of research project which can be signed off by your supervisor rather than requiring an application to a research ethics committee?

- Is there an expedited process for low-risk research, or research projects which are a variant on a study which already has ethical approval?

- Are there any topics which are not permitted?

It may be the case that your supervisor already has approval for the research project that you are running, or you may be required to obtain full ethical approval for your project. Some departments offer an expedited ethical approval process for research that poses only minimal risk. Your supervisor will be able to provide some guidance on where to find relevant information in relation to ethics, such as consent forms, participant information documents, and the ethical approval procedures in your department. Some departments will offer additional forms of support to guide you through the ethical approval process, such as related teaching sessions, e-modules, or further guidance within your module documentation. If you are applying for ethical approval for your project, we recommend that you engage with this process early on as it does take some time to fill in the relevant paperwork, and it may take several weeks for this to be processed and approved by the ethics committee or another relevant team. It is highly likely that reviewers on these committees respond with some comments and may even request revisions to the paperwork which you have submitted before they review it again. Make sure you leave time in your planning to make changes based on the reviewers' feedback and to submit your paperwork for a second ethical review where needed.

> ## Smart Solution—My Ethics Application Has Been Rejected
>
> Apply for your ethics proposal early. It is common for ethics proposals to be rejected and this can delay starting the whole project. Therefore, it is important to plan for the worst and get your ethics application in early!
>
> Student, Durham University

We have provided some tips to consider when filling in the paperwork to ensure that your application meets the requirements of the research ethics committee (or equivalent team). It is important to also check what the requirements are for your department's research ethics committee.

- Be transparent: include as much detail as is relevant and necessary to explain to the reviewers what your study involves, that you have thought about all potential ethical risks associated with the study, and that these risks have been addressed with appropriate safeguarding procedures in place. Keep in mind that research ethics committees will usually want to see quite a high degree of detail in your application, and it is easy to underestimate what is needed. For example, it will typically be expected that you outline details of all stimuli (with examples where appropriate), full questionnaires (or relevant links/citations for standard measures), and each step of the process involved for a participant in your study.

- Go through the ethical risks checklist and others listed in your department's guidelines, to ensure that you have covered everything that is needed for your study in your application.

- Ensure that all relevant forms are completed, such as the information sheet, consent form, debrief, and any resources used to advertise your study, if applicable. You should follow your department's guidelines on advertising research studies to participants, as these may specify what information you will need to include in resources such as posters or recruitment emails. Typical information incorporated in recruitment material includes study details, researcher contact details, details about ethical approval of the study, how participants can express an interest in taking part.

And remember, if you are unsure about any aspect of your study, consult the relevant procedures in your department and have a discussion with your supervisor.

FUTURE FOCUS Resilience

If your ethics application comes back with revisions from the committee, then this can feel disheartening and unnerving, especially if amendments to your research design are required. Try not to worry if you don't get things perfect first time! It is extremely common to experience setbacks in a professional environment, and gaining experience in 'bouncing back' during your project can stand you in good stead for the future. Employers are often keen to know that applicants have demonstrated resilience, so when you feel you have done this well, note it down to draw on later.

Summary

Ethics forms a key part of research in psychology. When designing your study it is important that you consider the ethical requirements and potential ethical risks associated with your study right at the start of your research project. Be sure to consult relevant guidelines and to familiarize yourself with the relevant ethical procedures in your department and to discuss these along with a plan of action with your supervisor. Obtaining ethical approval can often be a lengthy process so planning your application for ethical approval early can help with project management.

 Go online to access further resources for the text:
www.oup.com/he/whittle.

References

The British Psychological Society (2021). *Code of Ethics and Conduct*. https://www.bps.org.uk/guidelines-and-policies; https://www.bps.org.uk/node/1714

The British Psychological Society (2021). *Code of Human Research Ethics*. https://www.bps.org.uk/guideline/bps-code-human-research-ethics-0

British Psychological Society. (2021). *Ethics Guidelines for Internet Mediated Research*. https://www.bps.org.uk/guideline/ethics-guidelines-internet-mediated-research

Ree, M. J., French, D., MacLeod, C., & Locke, V. (2008). Distinguishing cognitive and somatic dimensions of state and trait anxiety: Development and validation of the State-Trait Inventory for Cognitive and Somatic Anxiety (STICSA). *Behavioural and Cognitive Psychotherapy, 36*(3), 313–332.

6 Working With Participants

It is quite easy to underestimate how valuable the experience that you gain simply by recruiting participants and running research studies is but there is a real need for a great deal of planning and coordination involved in the running of your research and a lot of skills to be gained in this process. When you are conducting your research, you will become a representative for your institution and will need to demonstrate a good level of professionalism. This next chapter is intended to help you to understand where the pitfalls might be and to plan and run your research study in such a way that you aim to avoid them. We will provide pointers on recruiting participants and then running your research with adults and children.

6.1 Recruitment

Planning an effective recruitment strategy often starts at the design stage, particularly where you are needing to seek ethical approval (see Chapter 5), and you should therefore expect to be able to be specific about who you will recruit and the means that you will employ to recruit them as a part of your research proposal and/or application for ethical approval. You will need to take into consideration the number of participants that are required for your study which will be determined in conversation with your supervisor taking into account your proposed method and will include consideration of issues such as power (for quantitative studies), your research and analysis methods, and the quality and quantity of data that you collect from your participants (see Chapter 4 for further details of how to determine your sample size).

Effective recruitment is essentially a networking process. It starts with identifying the networks and channels that are available to you and then identifying the most appropriate means of contacting members of that network, and the most convenient means of enabling your participants to complete the study that you have devised. It also requires a degree of sensitivity to the needs and expectations of the groups and organizations that you are seeking to work within. Different institutions/organizations will all have their own processes and expectations in place and what works for one population might not be so effective for another population. For example, where student populations might actively prefer to complete an online survey or task that has been shared over social media, other groups of participants might prefer to express interest over the telephone or in person and complete a pen and paper task. Similarly, organizations, charities, and other social interest groups, particularly networks for a protected characteristic or health condition, will require close liaison with any relevant gatekeepers prior to conducting any data collection to ensure that you are compliant with any safeguarding measures which are operated by the network. It is therefore important that you have a clear plan in place well before you start conducting any research. Therefore, plan to speak to your supervisor and any other contacts that might be helpful (for example PhD students or other contacts who have conducted research with similar populations) about what works with the population you are planning to recruit.

Whatever network you seek to approach it is important not to assume that you will be able to achieve a 100% participation rate. In fact, for some means of recruitment (social media being a good example) you might be needing to reach over ten times your planned sample size to find enough participants to complete your study. People find it much easier to ignore an email or social media post than they do a human with a clipboard and a clearly articulated explanation as to how they can help and what impact their participation could have. So, when it comes to recruitment, it is a good idea to be willing to consider all options, sample size permitting. It is also worthwhile making sure that you are aware from the beginning what steps you need to take in case you need to change any element of your recruitment strategy. Having a clear idea about who needs to be informed and what changes they need to be informed about is important in making sure that you are compliant with the ethical approval processes associated with your institution and any other organization that you work in.

FUTURE FOCUS NETWORKING

Networking is a very useful employability skill which will be helpful both with respect to gaining relevant employment but also as a skill in the workplace itself. Effective networking requires strong communication skills and a clear sense of professionalism and is important in maintaining good working relationships between colleagues, clients, and other key stakeholders.

6.1.1 Recruiting Student Populations

If your study is based on a student population then you may well find that there is infrastructure in place at your institution to support the recruitment of student participants. For example, your department may have a points-based research participation scheme you can use, and you may be able to arrange reciprocal arrangements with other students in your department, in other words "you do my study and I do yours". It goes without saying, but if you are open to supporting each other's research participation (and if you encourage students in earlier years to understand how valuable this support is) then the recruitment process becomes much more seamless for everyone concerned. The experience of being a participant is as valuable a part of your training as the experience of running research studies after all.

Smart Solution—Getting Enough Participants

The main challenge for recruiting participants is mainly getting enough and ensuring you stick to any requirements of your study. The best way to get a large cohort is to use your university's platforms. Any group chats you're in too. Exchanges work as well by offering to do other experiments/surveys in return for them doing yours. As well as this don't feel bad for asking, a lot of students are more than happy to help others and are often very helpful participants.

Student, Royal Holloway University of London

You are also likely to find that the wider student population at your institution may well be primed to expect that, as part of a community of learning, they may be asked to volunteer to participate in other student research and you may be able to cast your net a little wider using posters and adverts that you can share in designated areas across your campus. An example poster has been provided as part of the additional online resources. As a responsible researcher it is always important to identify the relevant gatekeepers for the physical and virtual spaces you are using and seek their permission. You should not post flyers if there is any doubt as to whether you have the permission to do so. It is also important to keep in mind that some research ethics committees will expect to see all recruitment materials (e.g. adverts/flyers) and approve where the materials will be posted/shared.

In promoting their research some students have been known to get creative. For example, by handing out the details of their research project on keyrings or wrapped around sweets. These small gestures can work well in garnering interest. Larger gestures may be harder to refuse, so do be aware of the professional boundaries and avoid anything that could be interpreted as peer pressure or coercion (for example do not be tempted to target people after a few drinks in the university bar). If you are in any doubt what may or may not be appropriate, then check with your supervisor. Also do not underestimate the power of a human, face to face conversation. Sometimes, if you are polite and open to refusal then just taking the time to explain to people what you are doing and how they can help can be very persuasive.

6.1.2 Recruiting Non-Student Populations

Although student populations are often convenient, they might not always be suitable for the research that you wish to conduct. Student samples are often of higher socioeconomic status than the general population, and typically younger in age. Psychological research has been criticized for the overrepresentation of Western, educated, industrialized, rich, and democratic (WEIRD) societies and this can have implications for the generalizability of psychological research to non-student populations (see e.g. Henrich et. al., 2010). For these reasons it might be that you and your supervisor choose to work with a non-student population. In this case then you will most likely need to think differently about how to go about the recruitment process.

If you intend to work with non-student populations then it is going to be particularly important to the success of your research project that you plan your recruitment strategy well. Have a look for social media sites, or community groups, particularly if your participants have a specialist interest: for example, they might have formed part of a support or community network who may be able to support you with gaining access. Ask around and seek recommendations from other researchers (those could be staff, PhD students, or your peers) who have worked with similar populations before and find out what the most effective approaches might be. If you have any contacts who are part of the population to which you are seeking access, then speak to them: what networks are they part of, who coordinates those networks and would be able to support you in gaining access (i.e. who are the gatekeepers) and how might you contact them. Think very clearly about the number of people within the networks that you identify and the number of participants that you will need to test. If you have a group of 30 people that you intend to approach to participate, then you cannot assume that all 30 will be willing to take part. In fact, you are more likely to find that less than half this number will be willing to complete your study.

Before you plan to recruit from a specific network or community then you should always plan to contact the gatekeepers of your population (for example these might be moderators on social media sites, or community group leaders) and make sure that they are on board with your research project and have offered their recorded approval. Always make sure that you have their consent and permission to recruit within the population and seek their advice about what approach is appropriate and works most effectively. This is good practice in all cases, but it is particularly important if a group is vulnerable, and where the gatekeepers may feel they have some responsibility in protecting that population. In this case, if you do not gain upfront permission then you may later find that you are refused access to the population entirely.

6.1.3 Recruiting Vulnerable Populations

According to the British Psychological Society (BPS) definition of Human Research Ethics (2021a) vulnerable populations include children, persons lacking capacity, those in a dependent or unequal relationship, people with learning or communication difficulties, people in care, people in custody or on probation, people who have suffered physical or psychological trauma, and people engaged in illegal activities, such as drug abuse. You should only plan to recruit vulnerable populations with the express agreement of your supervisor and with full compliance of any institutional requirements for working with such populations. You may well find that, due to the complexities of gaining ethical approval and safeguarding you and your participants, you are advised that research with vulnerable populations is not within the scope of your final year research project. This may particularly be the case if, for example, you are studying your degree programme at distance, and your supervisor does not have close links with the associations through which you may be seeking access. For information on the ethical considerations of working with vulnerable populations then please refer to Chapter 5.

When recruiting vulnerable populations, you will need to be particularly sensitive to the risk of unintentional coercion. You should carefully consider the power dynamic between you and the participant. If you are in a position of responsibility (for example perhaps you are conducting your research with care recipients in your place of work) then they are likely to feel a pressure to participate in your research which should be mitigated or avoided. If you are working with children or other populations that may lack the awareness or confidence to refuse consent, then you should make sure that you are aware that you monitor for any signs that your participant is not giving their assent. Signs of withdrawal, or a lack of attention and engagement are an important cue that the participant no longer wishes to participate in your research, even if consent has been provided.

6.1.4 **Recruiting in Organizations**

Some student research may take place in organizations such as businesses and workplaces, or charities. Schools are treated separately in the next section. Before you recruit participants in organizations it is important to make sure that you have permission from the relevant gatekeeper such as a manager, executive, or human resources (HR) representative with overarching responsibility for the whole population that you wish to test. If in any doubt about who has appropriate authority, then ask. When you do seek permission, do keep in mind that you must receive that permission in writing. Verbal permission is not sufficient. You should also be prepared to provide a copy of the permission that you receive as part of your application for ethical approval. Organizational permission is required over and above ethical approval from your institution, but you do also need to make sure that you are aware of, and compliant with, any ethical procedures that are in place within that organization. It is not advisable to conduct your research in organizations that require additional layers of ethical approval (in the UK context this would include organizations such as Her Majesty's Prison and Probation Service (HMPPS) and the National Health Service (NHS)) since going through these processes can add substantial time to your ethical approval process. For more information about applying for ethical approval from your own institution and other external parties please refer to Chapter 5.

Once you have permission to access the organization you may still need to consider appropriate channels to advertise your study. Large organizations are unlikely to be happy to allow you to send an 'all-staff email' and you may need to look to advertise through newsletters, noticeboards, and so on. Also, if you already have any responsibility within the organization where you are conducting your research, then you need to make sure that any communications that you share about your research are very clearly delineated from other communications that you might routinely send to make the distinction between your role as a researcher and your role within the organization. This is particularly important if, as part of your role within that organization, you have direct responsibility (e.g. line management responsibility) for the participants you are hoping to recruit. It is very important to be sensitive to any power relationships that may exist because of your role within the organization that you are recruiting within. For example, if you are recruiting staff who you have a line management or a supervisory responsibility for then they may not feel comfortable to refuse to participate. It is therefore important that you are transparent with your research project supervisor where there is any risk of unintended coercion and that you have discussed the implications for your research strategy.

6.1.5 **Recruiting in Schools**

Gaining access to young populations in schools can be a challenge and there are often several layers of approval and consent that you may need to work through before you begin testing. The process for obtaining permission to conduct your research in schools can vary widely by context. For example, in some areas it is also necessary to gain permission for research from your local education authority but in other areas permission from the headteacher may be sufficient. Therefore, make sure that you are familiar with the permissions required in your context. As with testing in organizations you will need to gain written consent from the relevant gatekeeper (usually the headteacher). An example organizational letter is provided in the additional online resources. It is worth bearing in mind that headteachers are often exceptionally busy and may receive many requests from different parties who wish to conduct their research with young people. You are therefore likely to have the most success in gaining their agreement if you have pre-existing relationships with the school (for example you might have connections with one or more of the teachers). You are also most likely to gain approval if you can demonstrate that your activities are going to have minimal impact on the day-to-day activities of the school. You may also want to consider offering something back to the school, for example you could run an after-school psychology club.

Whilst having contacts can be helpful in gaining access to students, if you work for the school then you need to make sure that you clearly differentiate your role as researcher in any communication that you have with parents and children. This is so that your participants understand that their engagement in your research project is voluntary. It should be clear in your information sheet and recruitment strategy that your research is secondary to your participants' schoolwork, and that your research will have no negative implications for any aspect of their participation at school. According to the BPS *Code of Human Research Ethics* (2021a) it is important that the child is given an age appropriate opportunity to offer consent and ask questions (for example by indicating how they feel about taking part in your research activity by pointing to a smiley/sad face), but during the research activity itself you should also plan to monitor for assent (active agreement) from the participant and any signs of withdrawal or disengagement should be taken as a signal of a withdrawal of consent.

If your participants are below 16 then you will at least be expected to inform parents and other legal guardians about the research and offer them the opportunity to withdraw their child from it, but you may need to seek parental consent to opt your participants into the study. This depends on the nature of the task you employ. The BPS Code (2021a) stipulates that if the head is satisfied that the activities fall within the range of usual curriculum or other institutional activities, and no significant risks have been identified, then parental consent may not be required. However, this is not a decision that you should take on your own and you should consult with your supervisor regarding any specific institutional or contextual requirements.

Communicating information to parents is fraught with challenges and you must take steps to make sure that you can be confident that your parents have received your communication and it has not just found its way to the bottom of a child's school bag. Schools often have their own processes for making sure that communications have been received by parents and you should find out what these are and make sure that you adhere to them.

6.1.6 **Recruiting Online**

In some research scenarios using online data collection methods you may never physically meet your participants to recruit them to your study. Importantly, according to the BPS Guidelines for Internet Mediated Research (2021b) whatever your method of data collection it is still important that participants are offered the opportunity to provide valid consent. This means that your participants may need to be actively recruited to the study you wish to carry out. This depends on the nature of the data to be used. Where you are asking your participants to respond to tasks and/or questions that are set by you there is a clear need to recruit your participants and, in doing so, gain their consent. However in other cases the need to seek consent can be a little less clear. If you are working with data (such as forum or blog posts) which has not been specifically generated for the purposes of research then it is important to consider whether or not you will need to gain consent from your population prior to analysing data.

According to the BPS *Code of Human Research Ethics* (2021a) consent is required in all circumstances except in public spaces where participants might reasonably expect their behaviour to be observed. The challenge in conducting research in online settings is that it is not always clear cut what is seen as public and what is seen as private. For example, if participants post information to a locked social media account which later becomes publicly archived then there is a clear argument that the data could be considered private because the participant may not have been aware that their data would be publicly shared. For the purposes of informed consent, it is a good principle to make sure that, if there is any doubt about whether the data is public or private, then consent to use the data should be sought from the contributors and gatekeepers (e.g. moderators, blog/website owners) of the data source that you are analysing.

Recruitment for online studies can take place by several different means including both paid services and unpaid survey swapping websites (see Box 6.1 for a list of sites you may wish to use). You might also want to advertise your study through social media groups, particularly where you are seeking a specific population or studying a research question that may be of special interest (for example Support Groups). If you are using survey swapping sites, it is a good idea to spend some time getting to know the website that you are working with and how it prioritizes the studies that are advertised. This will help you to optimize your own data collection on the site (particularly when you release your study for participants). Sites often reward members for being active participants in other studies and will use activity data to prioritize studies in the site listings. It can be possible to get your data collection done very quickly if you make optimal use of the website. If you are wanting to advertise by special interest groups, then it is important that you make sure that you are familiar with any rules in place for the special interest group and seek the permission

---

BOX 6.1 Recruitment Resources

Your department

Don't forget to check out the information from your department with respect to ethical compliance and research recruitment. Also find out whether your department offers any platforms for recruiting participants which you could employ in your research.

Websites

Here are a number of websites that can be used to recruit participants:

Survey swap is a free resource where you can participate in other research projects in return for participants for your own experiment: https://surveyswap.io/

There are also some research sharing groups on Facebook, for example.

The Research Survey Exchange Group: https://www.facebook.com/groups/1376853029260212

The Student Survey Exchange Group: https://www.facebook.com/groups/225472898392397

Prolific is a paid platform for recruiting research participants. If you consider using this platform you should discuss the financial implications with your supervisor. https://www.prolific.co/

of the gatekeeper before you share any adverts. Failure to gain the correct permissions and comply with the rules of the group could mean that you are barred from gaining access to the population at all.

When networking online, it is tempting to snowball, i.e. one webpage might lead to another, or whilst you are sharing your research a contact from one network might suggest an additional network that may be of relevance to your research. If, in the process of collecting your data, you do find additional networks that may be of relevance to target then be cautious about making changes to your recruitment strategy without approval and, where necessary, seek advice about how to update your application for ethical approval to reflect any amendments that you are making.

6.1.7 Offering Incentives for Participation

To encourage participation, you may wish to incentivize your study for example by offering a small inconvenience payment (if your supervisor has some available funds to support this). Younger participants enjoy small trinkets like chocolate and stickers and older participants may appreciate travel and/or refreshment vouchers if they are going out of their way to attend the study location. Student populations may be interested in a reciprocal arrangement or vouchers to support their studies (e.g. for books). Any incentives that you offer should be ethical and appropriate to the population and should not in any way make your participants feel obliged to participate. If using payment then you should not offer amounts that a participant is likely to be unable to refuse. This may be a particular consideration if working with vulnerable participants, particularly if they might be experiencing any financial hardship. Remember as well that it is important to attract a diverse sample and aim to be culturally aware. For example, as ingenious as it might feel to offer a voucher for the university bar, it is important to bear in mind that campuses are very diverse places and alcohol is not always culturally appropriate and may deter some prospective participants from taking part.

You should also make sure that if the provision of any incentive requires that your participant provides their personal data then this should be collected and stored separately from any research data that you collect. For example, let us say that you are providing your participants with an electronic voucher for their participation that requires collecting your participants' contact details. If you are using an online form then you should make sure that you provide a link to a separate form to collect this information at the end of the study so that your research data is stored separately from any personal information that might identify your participant. If you are using a paper form then this should not be linked to any of the data collection methods in the study or to your participant's consent form.

To briefly conclude this section then, with respect to recruitment and incentivization aim to adhere to the following key principles/checklist.

- ✓ Different recruitment approaches work for different populations. Speak to other researchers or contacts that you have from within the population to find out what networks you should seek to include and who the gatekeepers for those networks are.
- ✓ Make sure that you are familiar with institutional requirements for approval of your recruitment strategy, your supervisor is aware how you will be recruiting participants

and you have made sure that your approach is aligned with anything described in your application for ethical approval.

✓ Network, network, network. It is unusual to achieve a 100% participation rate so be sure to cast your net wide.

✓ Get the right approval. Know who your gatekeepers are and make sure that you are aware of any additional ethical approval or permission processes that apply for your specific context, organization, or jurisdiction.

✓ If you are recruiting student populations then be sure to help each other out!

✓ Do not underestimate the power of the personal touch. Try to speak to people about your research if you can.

✓ Incentivize but do not coerce. Carefully consider any imbalances of power that you have and design your strategy around these. Remember coercion can be intentional or unintentional.

6.2 Conducting Your Research

When you carry out your research keep in mind that effectively you are taking a position of responsibility and assume a professional approach with your participants. If you are working in lab space or using equipment that is shared with other students, then you may need to be organized in gaining access through a rota system, for example. If this is the case, it is critical that you do not leave your data collection to the last minute. It is invariably the case that demand for lab space increases as you get towards the submission deadline and those students who are proactive and get things up and running quickly may find they have a lot more access than those who leave it late.

6.2.1 Managing Appointments

When you conduct research under the name of your university, you become a representative of that institution. The experience that you give your participants will impact their willingness to engage in institutional research activity in the future and the behaviour of peers in your cohort will influence other students' willingness to participate in your research. It is therefore important that you treat your role as you would any other professional activity. Remember that your participants are taking time out from their day-to-day activities to participate in your study and be appreciative of this and respectful of their time and commitment. Make sure that you have carefully timed your research study or experiment so that you do not leave other participants waiting and leave a buffer in between appointments in case another participant arrives late or finishes slowly. Have a clear timetabling system so that you do not miss appointments and only arrange appointments with participants if you are confident that you are available at that time. If you do need to cancel an appointment, then aim to give plenty of notice and provide a timely apology and mitigate any shortfall on the part of the participant (for example if you have committed to providing points then you should still offer at least a proportion of those points if you cannot rearrange the appointment).

> **Handy Hint**
> Working with participants can be nerve-racking, particularly when you're constantly meeting new people. However, it is important that you make a good impression. Maintaining a positive and upbeat manner with your participants will make them more comfortable and result in better engagement in your experiment. It is also important not to 'write off' participants that have cancelled; try and re-arrange a time, as finding willing participants can be difficult!
>
> Student, Durham University

6.2.2 Managing the Physical Test Environment

Take time to set up your testing space so that it is organized and everything that you need for your study is readily available and well stocked. It can help to have physical materials (e.g. paper consent forms, questionnaires, and so on) organized chronologically according to when you need them in your research study or experiment. This enables you to work through everything in a set order and means that you do not neglect to provide any information to your participants. You should also make sure that you are familiar with any emergency procedures for the test space that you are working in, particularly where the closest emergency evacuation routes are and where to go/who to contact if you require a first aider. Although emergency situations are very rare in research, it does help to be prepared.

6.2.3 Managing the Online Test Environment

If you are running your test online then you will have less opportunity to clarify any task instructions and it is therefore particularly important to ensure that your study is presented in a logical sequence and that instructions that you provide are given step by step and are easily understood.

6.2.4 Preparing to Run the Study for the First Time

Before you run your study for the first time it is a good idea to complete a pilot test, perhaps with a friend or lab partner. You could even offer to do a reciprocal arrangement and complete their study. Make sure that you are familiar with the procedures that have been approved during the ethical approval process and trial how they will work in practice. When you have completed the trial ask your friend for feedback.

- How did it feel, were there any aspects of the study that were unclear and needed further clarification?
- Were they comfortable and able to remain focused on the tasks?
- Were there sufficient rest breaks built in?

Record the timings and make a note of any points of confusion or difficulty. If you need to change any aspect of your procedure then be sure to update your ethical approval submission and seek reapproval if required.

You will be providing your participants with written information about the task in your participant information and consent form, but you will want to make sure that you also provide information to the participants verbally to ensure that they understand the task. You should aim to make these instructions as consistent as possible. Use the feedback that you have gathered from your pilot testers to prepare a script around your task instructions. Rehearse them so that every participant is provided the same explanation of the task and they are confident what to do at the point of completing it.

Here are some pointers that you may wish to explain in your verbal instructions:

If you are conducting an interview then you may wish to explain the nature of the questions, how you would like your participants to respond and how you will be interacting with your participant during the interview session. For example, are your questions open-ended, will you be working through them in a fixed order or are you using a more semi-structured approach? Will you be prompting your participants for expansion and how? How will you be making a record of the interview? Will you be taking notes or recording the session?

If you are conducting an experimental task that may be unfamiliar to the participant, then plan to have some practice activities that enable them to familiarize themselves with the task before they start the task itself. Before participants start the task then explain how to carry out the task and consider demonstrating how responses are made. To ensure total clarity, you will also wish to accommodate some of the design elements described for the online tasks in the next paragraph. Once participants have completed the practice items then check verbally that they have understood before proceeding.

If you are conducting an online experimental task or interview, then you cannot provide verbal instructions, but you will still want to make sure that the instructions that you are using are in a clear format that is easy to understand. Aim not to have too much written information per page and break down your instructions into clear steps. You should plan to have some practice activities if there is a need to familiarize your participant with the task and consider building in some feedback to ensure that participants are aware whether they have been responding appropriately. Remember to reiterate the task instructions prior to starting the main activity. You could consider offering participants the opportunity to repeat the practice items if they choose. You may also wish to consider including questions to provide an attention check to make sure that your participants are actively engaged in your study. However, do be aware that excluding participants who fail an engagement check may have implications for the external validity of your study (see for example Berinsky et al., 2016).

6.2.5 Running the Study

The process of running your study is very similar regardless of the type of research you are conducting. Here is a straightforward checklist to make sure that you start your study on the right foot and can be confident that your participants are fully prepared to take part in the research.

✓ Greet your participants warmly and make sure that they are comfortable and prepared to take part in the study.

✓ Take participants through the relevant paperwork, including participant information and informed consent forms. Make sure that participants are not rushed at this stage and are able to make an informed decision.

✓ Confirm that your participants understand exactly what will happen during the research study. Make sure that participants have time at the beginning of the research study to ask questions (both for reasons of informed consent, but also to ensure data integrity).

✓ In all cases make sure that your participants are participating in a comfortable environment that is free from distractions. Keep in mind that unexpected circumstances can happen and keep a logbook to record anything that may impact the integrity of the data you collect.

✓ Allow sufficient time at the end of the research study to debrief your participant and confirm their consent for the study.

Smart Solution—When Testing Goes Wrong

When I was collecting data as part of my PhD I did a lot of my work using eye-tracking. Prior to one of my test sessions the equipment crashed, and I couldn't figure out how to get it working in time for my participant to arrive. I was still frantically testing bits of the equipment when I was due to go and collect my participant to start the study.

Knowing that it was unclear how long it was going to take me to get the equipment up and running again I made my apologies to the participant and rearranged the study for an alternative convenient time. By being honest with the participant and being considerate with their time I was able to avoid any frustration that may have impacted on the test findings. People generally do understand that unplanned things do happen and will be patient with you as long as you are up front with them.

6.2.6 Storing Your Data

Remember that any data that you collect from your participants needs to be stored securely and confidentially so make sure that you have space to keep this data. It is a requirement under European Union (EU) Law that any research is fully compliant with the Data Protection Act (2018) which is designed to protect personal data and makes certain requirements about how personal data is used, stored, and shared. Prior to collecting any data you should make sure that you are familiar with the data protection principles that are in place at your institution and ensure that your data storage methods are compliant with them. If you are storing your data digitally then you should take steps to ensure that your data is stored securely, for example by using cloud software that has been approved by your institution. If you need to remove the data from the lab space in which you are testing, make sure that you move it directly to a secure place and never leave confidential data unattended in a public space. Create good habits from the outset and stick to them to avoid complacency. This is when mistakes happen.

6.3 Additional Things to Consider when Working with Children and Young People

From a methodological perspective, children can be great fun to work with, but they can also be somewhat unpredictable and need to be given the space, time, and information to complete the task at hand effectively. You may find that your department has special ethical approval processes in place for working with children and other vulnerable populations due to the ethical considerations involved. There are several considerations that you should make when planning to conduct research with children. Some of these are around duty of care, and others are around effective study design to ensure valid results.

6.3.1 Safeguarding

Safeguarding is any action that is taken to promote welfare of individuals, particularly children under the age of 18 or other vulnerable adults, and offer protection from harm. As a researcher you have a duty of care to offer this protection and it is therefore important to make sure that you do not put yourself in any position where you may be vulnerable to allegations of abuse or where you inadvertently put a child or vulnerable person at risk. These considerations are important in determining the setting that you conduct your research in and the activities that you carry out. For these reasons you should plan your research to be conducted in a public place (for example, in classroom) and not in a private location (for example, a bedroom) and you should plan your design so that it limits the risk of your young participant disclosing anything that could be considered a safeguarding issue. You should also be careful with respect to the information that you provide to your young participants about your role. It is particularly important (despite the commitment that we make to protecting a participant's anonymity) that you do not commit to secrecy and that any sensitive information that might suggest that a child is at risk of harm is shared with someone (for example a guardian or teacher) who is legally responsible for that young person. Plan to find out the relevant legal framework for your jurisdiction and make sure that your design is fully compliant with any safeguarding expectations. Discuss the steps that you are taking to ensure appropriate safeguarding of your participants with your supervisor before you carry out any research and as part of gaining ethical approval.

6.3.2 Consent and Assent

Connected with the issue of safeguarding is the need to gain relevant informed consent. Competent minors who understand the process of consent should be given this opportunity, even if you have consent from another responsible adult. With younger children who are not capable of providing informed consent themselves it is still important that the child does not participate in any activities that cause them distress or that they actively do not wish to be part of even if you have informed consent from a parent/teacher. It is therefore important to have a process of assent (or active agreement) to protect the child from doing anything that makes them feel uncomfortable and to confirm that the child is motivated to complete the task that you have set. As well as this you should make sure that you are fully informed of the requirements of your local research ethics committee as well as the legal requirements of your jurisdiction and that your strategy for gaining assent/consent from your participant is consistent with these requirements.

> ### Smart Solution—Expect The Unexpected—Be Prepared!
>
> When I was collecting data for my undergraduate project, I wanted to collect some spellings of non-words with primary school aged children. By using a network of my own connections, I was lucky to gain the consent of a few local schools to come into the classroom and conduct the research during class time. To help my participants understand the task I devised a game—the premise being that children were helping a group of alien beings translate words from their language to write an English dictionary by sounding out the words. At the start of the activity, and to gain the assent of the class, I asked the children whether the task sounded like fun. One child gave a frank "no" from the back of the classroom which could have indicated he was declining assent.
>
> Classroom settings are managed by the classroom teacher, and it is ultimately their decision what activities the class participate in. It is important to make sure that you have a conversation with the classroom teacher prior to starting the task about how to deal with children who may not wish to participate in the activity. It may be that the teacher still wants the students to engage with the activity, but you discard the data from the child. Alternatively, it may be that the classroom teacher will set a different activity for the child. Either way this should be the teacher's decision.

6.3.3 Experimental Design for Children

When you design an experiment to be run with children it's worth trying to look at the activities that you set through a young person's eyes. Do not assume that tasks that have been prepared for adults will be appropriate for children and, where you can, try to identify relevant tasks in the literature that have already been prepared for young people.

If you are needing to devise a task yourself then consider what your young participants are going to understand about the study. What do they think their role is? Will they enjoy it? Bear in mind that children do not have the same attention and memory span as adults and there is also a power differential between you and the child. All these factors this will have an influence on how they understand the intention behind your study. For example, children are quite used to adults asking them questions that they know the answer to and might be inclined to try and offer the answer they "think" that the experimenter wants rather than the answer they know to be correct. In addition, children are more sensitive to prior knowledge than you might first anticipate. They are quite often in a position where adults seek to teach, ask questions, or direct and for this reason they may not respond appropriately to a question or task which they see as nonsense. To help children understand the purpose of the task and keep motivated you could seek to frame it as a game, for example by involving a toy or puppet or building in feedback or rewards to bolster motivation. You should also make sure that you provide regular opportunities to take a break during the task to ensure that your participants remain engaged.

When you introduce your task to children, make time to explain the task properly and provide children with plenty of opportunity to practise and ask questions. Plan the instructions that you provide so that they are simple and clear. To ensure that they are consistent for each participant then plan to practise them first, ideally with young people if possible. You might find that having a recorded video is helpful to ensure clarity and consistency.

6.3.4 Designing Surveys and Questionnaires for Children

When using closed questions that can be analysed quantitatively (e.g. Likert scaled data) it is worth keeping in mind that children may not have the same understanding of numeric scales as adults and considering this in your survey design. For this reason, using linguistic scales or even pictorial scales such as faces (sad and smiley) which you can convert to a numeric scale for analysis might make the task clearer for children to understand and engage with.

6.3.5 Interviewing Children

If you would like to use a more open-ended research design with children then you need to consider the child's ability to understand the questions that you are asking, but also matters around safeguarding. Remember that you cannot commit to absolute secrecy on behalf of the child and make sure that the questions that you ask are unlikely to put you in a position where the child is likely to disclose safeguarding issues. In planning your interview schedule think about how you will make sure that the child feels comfortable addressing your questions. Use simple language, particularly at the start, and consider having a few warm-up questions that will help you to establish rapport and ensure that the young person feels comfortable in the interview setting. Build in breaks and rest if you are interviewing children over a long period of time. There are alternatives to a sit-down interview that you may wish to consider: for example photovoice (see for example, Abma & Schrijver, 2020) where participants use photographs to document and reflect on their emotions and experiences. When you conclude the interview, be sure to end positively even if you have been disappointed with the data provided.

Summary

This section has covered working with participants during recruitment and data collection.

For recruitment, the key things to keep in mind are to get to know and make the most of your available networks, offer appropriate non-coercive incentives and to make sure that you get the right approval.

In terms of data collection, a summary of top tips from this section is as follows:

1. Be proactive in arranging access to lab space and testing equipment.
2. Remember you are representative of your institution and take a professional approach.
3. Take active steps to make sure that your participant understands the expectations of the task, both for reasons of consent and to ensure the integrity of your data.
4. Have a managed system for storing your data securely from the outset of the study.

When working with children you should additionally:

1. Ensure that you gain active assent from the child.

2. Make sure that you provide clear instructions and establish rapport.

3. Pay close attention to your task design so the child will understand what is expected.

4. Plan your task with safeguarding in mind.

Overall, since you are working directly with parties that are external to your institution or department then you should plan to demonstrate professionalism throughout your recruitment and data collection. By working with participants, you will be able to demonstrate your ability to be organized and communicate clearly. There is undoubtedly lots to learn and lots to enjoy during this stage of your project life cycle.

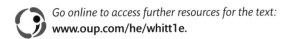

Go online to access further resources for the text:
www.oup.com/he/whitt1e.

References

Abma, T. A., & Schrijver, J. (2020). Are we famous or something? Participatory health research with children using photovoice. *Educational Action Research*, 28(3), 405–426. https://doi.org/10.1080/09650792.2019.1627229

Berinsky, A. J., Margolis, M.F., & Sances, M.W. (2016). "Can we turn shirkers into workers?". *Journal of Experimental Social Psychology*, 66, 20–28. https://doi.org/10.1016/j.jesp.2015.09.010

British Psychological Society. (2021a). *BPS Code of Human Research Ethics*. https://www.bps.org.uk/guideline/bps-code-human-research-ethics-0

British Psychological Society. (2021b). *Ethics Guidelines for Internet Mediated Research*. https://www.bps.org.uk/guideline/ethics-guidelines-internet-mediated-research

Henrich, J., Heine, S. J., & Norenzayan, A. (2010). The weirdest people in the world? *Behavioral and Brain Sciences*, 33(2–3), 61–135. https://doi.org/10.1017/S0140525X0999152X

7   The Report

The report is the main part of the research project where you can showcase what you have done, what you think about it, and reflect on the contribution of your work to the psychology community. It is your opportunity to bring together everything you have been reading and researching and it is really satisfying to see the end result once it is complete. Lots of students mark the occasion by taking photos with their final piece of work! It is worth being aware of the weighting that your department has put on the research project. Sometimes reports, and research project modules generally, can make a big contribution to your mark for the final year so it really is worth making the most of that and putting your best efforts into the report. Writing a report about a piece of research is likely something you have done before (especially if your course is British Psychological Society (BPS) accredited) and so you should be able to apply your learning from previous reports to the report for the research project module.

In this chapter, we are going to provide some main pointers about how to write up a study you have conducted. Your own department may have set guidelines about writing the report and you should make sure to look for those and follow them if they exist. We will be following guidance from the American Psychological Association (APA) Journal Article Reporting Standards (JARS; https://apastyle.apa.org/jars/index) since this is the most comprehensive at the current time and is commonly followed in many institutions. APA JARS are designed to help researchers report in a clear and transparent way, with the aim of increasing the reproducibility of the work. Essentially, the written report of your project should reflect the same style that researchers would use to report their own research for publication in a journal. Many journals have their own style guides which interpret the APA conventions for a specific audience and your supervisor may advise you to follow a specific style guide in the write-up of your report. This chapter will be a particularly useful point of reference if you are not working to a particular style guide or to support any gaps in information.

In an APA guide on reporting research, Cooper (2011) compares a journal article to a recipe. In both these types of writing the reader is being instructed how to do something and if the ingredients and descriptions are not accurate, the reader will not be able to replicate what you have done. We like this analogy as it makes writing a report seem manageable! Being able to replicate a study from its description is really important so that other researchers could redo your experiment or study if they wanted to and then compare results. Having findings replicated means that we can have more confidence that they are 'true' or at least not due to error or poor practice.

7.1 Structure

You are probably reasonably familiar with the overall structure of a report by now as you are likely to have written reports across the other years of your degree. However, it is a good idea to review what should go into a report to ensure that you are reporting your study as fully as possible. Most departments will give a recommended or maximum word count and it is worth being aware of this before you begin any planning about the report. Word counts differ across institutions so we won't be giving suggested word counts per section (these can differ quite a lot depending on your research study anyway). Table 7.3 shows a summary of the sections of a report. You may be asked to submit different sections of the report at different times to reflect preregistration practices (see Chapter 4). This would likely mean you would submit the title, introduction, method (including analysis plan) before collecting any data or analysing results. Make sure to check what your assessments are in your module handbook.

7.1.1 Title

Writing the title is something that students may spend lots of time on (see following 'Smart Solution') but there are certain pieces of information that should be included in your title, which should help. The title should be an accurate reflection of what you are investigating. For quantitative studies, the title should include the variable(s) that you measured and manipulated and the relationship between them. For qualitative studies, the title should contain details about the topic or issues you are looking at. Overall, aim for a title that is focused and succinct. Avoid phrases such as 'a study of' and don't use abbreviations.

> ### Smart Solution—Perfecting Your Title
>
> One of the most frustrating aspects of writing a dissertation is finding the perfect title. Hours can be spent deliberating over the nitty gritty details of your title when setting out on your project. However, the title should evolve with your project and by the time you have completed your dissertation, your end title will likely be unrecognizable from the start! So don't panic too much over the title and focus on the main ideas of your dissertation.
>
> Student, Durham University

Examples of titles
Quantitative: Bauer et al. (1996)

> Visual search for colour targets that are or are not linearly separable from distractors.

Qualitative: Clark et al. (2018)

> Housemate desirability and understanding the social dynamics of shared living.

The quantitative title is a good title because it tells you about what is measured (the dependent variable; visual search) and what was manipulated (the independent variable; the linear separability of the target from the distractors). The qualitative title is good because it tells you about the topic under investigation (shared living) and what was analysed (housemate desirability).

7.1.2 **Abstract**

The abstract is a summary of your research. The main objective for the abstract is to outline the problem you are investigating and to describe what you did and what you found. To construct an abstract, a common piece of advice is to summarize each section of the report in one or two sentences:

- Describe the topic of the research, including past findings. Describe the problem including your hypotheses or aims;

- Make sure to include details around the method you used (including design, sample size, materials, the dependent variable);

- Give a brief summary of your findings (in words, don't include statistics) and your conclusions; and

- Include any implications or applications of your results.

Example abstract—Weber et al. (2020)

Some research suggests that compared with younger adults, older adults have more homogeneous, less diverse daily life experiences because everyday situations and activities become increasingly stable and routine. However, strong empirical tests of this assumption are scarce. In two complementary studies, we examined whether older age is associated with less diversity in daily life experiences (e.g. regarding social interaction partners, activities, and places across and within days) and, if so, to what extent health limitations account for these age differences. In Study 1, we used daily diaries to investigate diversity across days among younger (N = 246; M_{age} 21.8 years, SD = 2.5) and older adults (N = 119; M_{age} 67.7 years, SD = 5.3). In Study 2, we investigated diversity within days employing experience sampling methods over three weeks in an adult life span sample (N = 365; range 14–88 years). Results showed that across and within days, the daily lives of older adults were less diverse regarding their social interaction partners. Yet, older adults reported more diversity in activities within days and across days in the afternoons, whereas younger adults reported less diverse activities partly due to working or studying more often. Age differences remained statistically significant when controlling for health limitations. We conclude that age differences in the diversity of daily life are nuanced, depending on the domain and the level of analysis.

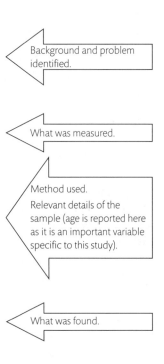

Background and problem identified.

What was measured.

Method used.
Relevant details of the sample (age is reported here as it is an important variable specific to this study).

What was found.

It can be very tempting to include a lot of information in the abstract, so the challenge is to keep it short. The APA notes that abstracts are generally no longer than 250 words. Abstracts tend to be written in one paragraph but may sometimes be structured. A structured abstract contains labels for the various sections (e.g. objective, method, results, conclusion). Check any guidelines from your department as they might specify what type of abstract you need to do. You might find it easier to write the abstract after writing the other sections of the report as then you have a clearer idea about the key points from those sections.

7.1.3 Introduction

The introduction should tell the reader why it was important to conduct your study. What was your research question and how did you come to it? What are the aims or predictions of your study? You may have already heard about the 'funnel' approach to an introduction. This metaphor is useful as it describes how the introduction often takes a broad view of the topic of investigation at the start and narrows and finishes with description of the current study.

You should begin the introduction with a statement about the area that you have identified and why it is important; this could include any practical or theoretical implications of researching this topic.

For example, this is the first paragraph in a study about humour at work:

> Humor, defined as expressions that are appraised by others as funny or cause others to experience amusement (Cooper, 2005, 2008; McGraw & Warren, 2010), is considered a universal behavior that exists in nearly all cultures (Apte, 1985). The benefits of using humor include reduced stress (Bizi, Keinan, & Beit-Hallahmi, 1988; Martin & Dobbin, 1989; Nezu, Nezu, & Blissett, 1988), improved social interactions (Martin, Puhlik-Doris, Larsen, Gray, & Weir, 2003), and increased positive affect and motivation (Kuiper, McKenzie, & Belanger, 1995). At work, the benefits of leader humor include increased employee creativity (Csikszentmihalyi, 1996; O'Quin & Derks, 1997), subordinate job satisfaction and commitment (Decker, 1987), and individual and unit-level performance (Avolio, Howell, & Sosik, 1999). In summary, humor appears to have positive consequences, in both work and nonwork contexts.
>
> (Evans et al., 2019)

You can then move on to the literature review aspect of the introduction. Here it is important that you only include literature that is relevant to your research. It is likely that you have read lots of articles that are vaguely linked and while it is tempting to put in everything it will not make for a high-quality introduction. Make sure that you make explicit links between the sources cited and your study and try to stay on track. Importantly you should aim to do this throughout your introduction, not just in the final paragraphs (see Handy Hint).

Handy Hint

When you're writing a dissertation it's so easy to get side-tracked, and without realizing you can end up on some weird and not-so-wonderful tangents. Going off topic costs time and words (something which we don't have many of in Psychology!), so as you're writing *keep reminding yourself of your title and your specific aims*. I do this by going back to my title after every paragraph, and having a good think about whether it's relevant and whether it fits with the flow of my work. It sounds brutal, but even though a piece of research might be super interesting, it shouldn't be in the dissertation if it's out of place/isn't closely relevant to your question!

Student, Bangor University

As we advised you in Chapter 1, it is likely that you will use other studies as the basis for your own design. You should include these studies in your introduction, pointing out any differences between them and your current study. This middle part of the introduction is all building up to the study you are doing so try and structure it into an argument. Listing descriptions of studies is not going to get you top marks, you need to weave an argument through. Comment on the studies in terms of what they tell us, what they don't tell us and link studies together so that you are using a body of evidence to support your ideas. Paragraph structure can really help here so do take note of the section on 'notes on writing paragraphs'. Following your review of relevant literature, you should then summarize what your study is, along with stating the aim, and what your hypotheses are.

For example, in a study investigating moderating effects of maths achievement, the authors stated:

> Here we explore the association between mathematics achievement and procedural skill, conceptual understanding and working memory in children who are at the early stages of learning mathematics. We predict that mathematics achievement will not only be associated with the main effects of procedural skills, conceptual understanding and working memory, but also with the interaction between them. Specifically, we predict that conceptual understanding and working memory will moderate the relationship between procedural skill and mathematics achievement.
>
> (Gilmore et al., 2017)

Even without reading the rest of the paper, you can understand what variables the researchers are measuring. Don't worry about writing a perfect introduction on your first draft. Everyone has to edit their writing at least once. Sometimes it can be difficult to see the big picture of the topic you are investigating and work out the best way to present the different research papers you have found. The next 'Smart Solution' can help with this as it shows that writing is not necessarily linear and looking at topics or paragraphs in context with the rest of the introduction can help to identify links or where the argument is not as strong.

Smart Solution—Creative Approaches To Writing

When writing my introduction I often hit points where I was like "how can I make this paragraph flow?", or "this piece of research just won't fit!". In situations like this it's easy to get frustrated and deflated, but there are things you can do in this situation. For example, I find it super useful to step away from the computer and write key topics/papers on individual pieces of paper/post-its. I then put the pieces of paper on the floor and rearrange them until they're in an order which flows. Sometimes I might have to add extra pieces of paper, or take bits of paper away. Although it might feel silly, I find that this allows me to see things more clearly, discover gaps in my work, and also realize if a piece of research isn't relevant and shouldn't be in the piece at all! Give it a go, trust me!

Student, Bangor University

7.1.4 Method

The method section is probably the section that you will write early on. Lots of students write the method section at the same time as collecting data while they are still familiar with how the study is run (see Chapter 2 for some tips on managing your project). There is a lot of information to report in the method section to ensure that a reader will be able to replicate your study. Information is generally reported under the sub headers we have used here (participants, measures/materials/stimuli, design, procedure) but see the section on 'Qualitative Studies' for differences. These headers should allow all the information you need to be reported. The aim you should have in mind when writing the method section is

BOX 7.1 *P-hacking*

Be transparent about the data you collected and how it was analysed. The term '*p*-hacking' can cover a number of behaviours relating to data collection and analysis, from removing conditions from analyses, and collecting more data after initial analysis. It seems to result from the pressure to publish significant findings and is problematic because it leads to lots of false positives being reported, which may then wrongly inform policy and future research (Simmons et al., 2011). Nuzzo (2014) provides a clear and interesting discussion about the *p* value.

As a researcher, you can make it clear to your readers that you have not engaged in behaviours related to *p*-hacking by including the following sentence in your methods section:

We report how we determined our sample size, all data exclusions (if any), all manipulations, and all measures in the study.

(Simmons et al., 2012)

to be transparent (see Box 7.1) so that a reader is able to reproduce your study based on the information you have provided.

Participants

Generally, the first section of the method is about who participated in your study. There are a number of things to include here (note, you do not have to use these headings):

- Inclusion and exclusion criteria

  This means that you explain if participants had to have or not have particular characteristics in order to participate. An example might be a study in which only right-hand dominant people could take part or a study that only required female participants. You might also detail who was invited to participate. For example, in research that uses surveys, those surveys are sent out to many more people than actually take part and return the survey.

- Participant characteristics

  Here you should report relevant characteristics of your sample, which may include age, gender, and ethnicity. If recruiting students, you might name the country or the area of the country where their education institution is located, or even the name of the institution. Depending on your study, you may also have other characteristics to report here, for example, IQ.

- Sampling procedures

  Describe how you selected participants. With student research projects this is often convenience sampling, and you may have used a participant pool set up by your department. For example, lots of departments require first-year students to participate in research for course credit. You should mention how many people dropped out of your study (i.e. how many you recruited but did not complete the study). Mention any payments or incentives made to participants. Mention which research ethics committee you received ethical approval from.

- Sample size

  You should report your final sample size and mention what your intended sample size was. In the context of quantitative research, it is quite important that you ensured that your study had enough power in order to detect an effect if there was one to detect (i.e. to avoid Type II errors). Sample size is an important part of this so you may have conducted a power analysis to determine how many participants you needed for your study (see Chapter 4). For more detail about significance, errors, and power, the YouTube channel Crash Course Statistics have a video about this topic, as well as others about statistics.

This all seems like a lot of information, but it is possible to write this succinctly. Here is an example participants section from a study about processing of faces.

> One hundred ninety-four undergraduates at the University of Texas at Dallas (M_{age} = 21.30, SD = 2.90) with normal or corrected-to-normal vision participated in Experiment 1 for course credit.[1] Sixty-seven percent of the sample self-identified as female, and 80% self-identified as Caucasian (most of the remainder identified as Hispanic or Asian). They were randomly assigned to one of eight conditions created by the factorial manipulation of test instructions (exclusion and inclusion) and stimulus type (upright, inverted, misaligned, and misaligned-inverted) with twenty-three to twenty-six participants in each condition. All gave informed consent, and the institutional review board approved the study.
>
> (Meltzer & Bartlett, 2019)

The footnote linked to the superscript 1 in this quote refers to a power analysis that was conducted. In your report, you can include it in the main text—it doesn't have to be a footnote. Here is an example where authors include the detail of the power analysis in the participants section. Notice that the authors justify the effect size they used.

> Appropriate sample sizes for adult samples were estimated a priori via a power analyses in G*power 3.1 (Faul, Erdfelder, Lang, & Buchner, 2007) using a Cohens effect size of 0.5. This was assumed based upon well-documented unimodal Stroop effects in young adults, and greater unimodal Stroop effects in children and older adults (Comalli et al., 1962; MacLeod, 1991) while considering the limited cross-modal Stroop effects literature. We calculated the sample size required to detect a Within × Between interaction with three groups and four measurements. Thus, the sample size was large enough to detect a difference between unimodal and cross-modal stimulus and response-interference between age groups (i.e. a 2 [sensory condition: unimodal vs. cross-modal] × 2 [interference type: stimulus vs. response-interference] × 3 [age group] mixed analysis of variance [ANOVA]). The exact parameters used within the power analysis were, therefore; a 'Repeated measures within-between interaction', α = .05, power = .95, number of groups = 3, number of measures = 4, nonsphericity correction = 1. This analysis indicated a need for a minimum of 29 participants per age group (87 in total), a criterion that was met by all three samples.
>
> (Hirst et al., 2019)

Measures/materials/stimuli

In this section, you should report the measures you included in your study. For quantitative studies, this section is often labelled as 'materials' or 'stimuli'. You should be able to choose whichever is most appropriate for your report.

You should report anything that you measured in your study, whether you later report it in your results or not. It is fairly common for students to work together measuring or manipulating a number of variables but then to only focus on a small number in the overall report. When reporting measures, you should mention the method used to collect data (e.g. questionnaire, observation, interview, and so on).

Describe any procedures used to ensure quality of measurements. For example, were the people collecting data trained or were multiple observers used? You will likely know about the importance of reliability from previous studies about research methods. The reliability and validity of measures used needs to be established so that a researcher can be confident in the data they will collect or have collected. One in particular that you may have to consider, and report, is interrater reliability. In observational studies there might be two or more researchers measuring or scoring data. You need to check how much they agree in their scores. This can be done using a correlation (*r*) or, if the variables are categorical, kappa. Another you should report, if applicable, is a check of the internal consistency of a measure using Cronbach's alpha.

Here is an example of reporting of observational measures:

> First, one primary coder was trained on the Actions or Distractions component of the Actions, Distractions, and Chaos (ABC's) of Family Mealtimes system (Fiese, Winter, & Botti, 2011) and another primary coder was trained on the Feeding Behavior Interaction Scale (Hughes et al., 2007). Training occurred using previously collected videos of family mealtimes (*n* = 7) from a different study. After primary coders attained adequate interrater reliability with the previous coders on the training videos (intraclass correlation coefficients [ICCs] >= .70 for distractions, ICC = .90 for observed responsive feeding), each primary coder trained two undergraduate coders using the same videos. Once adequate interrater reliability between all coders was established, the undergraduate research assistants each coded about half (*n* = 55) of the mealtime videos, while the primary coder coded 20% of these, overlapping equally with each research assistant, to guard against rater drift. Coding was completed using Mangold's INTERACT (Mangold International, 2016).
>
> (Saltzman et al., 2019)

You may have used a well-known or standardized measure or a measure used previously in which case you should provide some details on the measure.

Here is an example of how to report a measure:

> **Working Memory Capacity.** WMC was measured with the Composite Complex Span (CCS; Gonthier, Thomassin, & Roulin, 2016), a French-speaking battery of three classic complex span tasks: the reading span, symmetry span, and operation span (see Redick et al., 2012; Unsworth, Heitz, Schrock, & Engle, 2005). In each trial of a complex span, participants have to alternate between solving simple problems (deciding whether sentences are correct, whether spatial displays are symmetrical, and whether mathematical operations are correct, respectively) and memorizing unrelated stimuli (digits, locations in a 4×4 grid, and consonants, respectively). At the end of a trial, all to-be-memorized stimuli have to be recalled in the correct order.
>
> The CCS includes a total of 22 trials, with set sizes ranging from 3 to 8. Performance in each complex span is computed as the total number of stimuli recalled in the correct position (partial-credit load scoring: see Conway et al., 2005). A domain-general WMC estimate is then computed as the performance over the three complex spans, averaged after standardization. The CCS has demonstrated both internal consistency (ω_t = .86) and convergent validity with the APM (Gonthier et al., 2016), and has been used with over 1,500 participants.
>
> (Gonthier & Roulin, 2019)

In this section, you may be required to report equipment that you used, such as a computer, monitor, and if you used more specialist equipment like an eye tracker, an electroencephalogram (EEG) system, and so on.

Here is an example of reporting stimuli that were presented in experimental software:

The experiment was programmed and run using PsychoPy3 (Peirce, 2007). The search stimuli were presented on a 21-in. monitor with a gray background. Viewing distance was set to about 57 cm. Participants were required to fixate on a small white dot ($0.1° \times 0.1°$ of visual angle) presented at the center of the screen throughout the experiment. The target of the search task was a green T rotated clockwise or counter-clockwise by 90°, while distractors were 90°-rotated red Ts (RGB: 255, 0, 0) and green Os (RGB: 0, 255,0). The search items, each of which subtended 0.6°, were presented on an imaginary circle with the radius of 5°. The search display had five or nine stimuli. The target rotation direction and the target position were balanced across trials and distractor rotation directions were balanced within displays.

(Lee et al., 2021)

Design

In the method section, you need to report the design of your research. This means whether you used an experiment (manipulated the conditions) or a non-experimental design (e.g. an observational study). This does not need to be a separate section, some researchers sometimes combine it with the participants or procedure section, but it needs to be clear what type of design you used.

Here is an example from a study that used an experimental design:

We examined our hypotheses with a 2 (Music Complexity: simple, complex) ×2 (Volume: low, high) + 1 (Control: no music) between-subjects experimental design. Participants in the control condition were not exposed to the music complexity and volume manipulations, given that music was not played for these individuals.

(Gonzalez & Aiello, 2019)

Procedure

Although not specifically identified as a section by the APA as details are covered in other points, you may be expected to have a section that details the procedure of your study, particularly if you conducted an experiment. This is often a description of what the participant experienced while interacting with the researcher. This section could also be used to highlight similarities or differences to procedures of similar research (for example if you are conducting a replication study).

If you have conducted an experiment, then you need to provide detail about the manipulations, including:

- Context: description of how the manipulation was delivered, for example did you use any equipment or instructions? Where did the experiment take place? Who conducted the manipulation, for example, was it one researcher or two?
- Timing: how long the manipulation took and how many sessions and trials occurred.

Here is the beginning of a procedure section from a study conducted with child participants:

Each child participant interacted with the experimenter in a quiet and child-friendly room. The experimenter presented four cardboard houses to the child sequentially as follows: "The people in this house are feeling really [scared because they looked out their front window and they saw a bear]; happy [because their parents said they get to go out for ice cream]; calm, [they are sitting on the couch and having a quiet time]; mad [because someone made a mess but they both got in trouble for it]".

(Bayet et al., 2018)

It is up to you to decide what level of detail is important. In this example, you can see the authors have included the words that they spoke to the children in the experiment. This is because what the experimenter said to the children was important to the categorization task that followed. If your instructions are not particularly important to your study design (e.g. you are just instructing participants to press a key to begin a computer program) then you don't need to include them but could put them in an appendix if you wanted to.

Handy Hint

The methods section is a very large section, something I wasn't fully aware of before writing. The best thing to consider is starting big and working down the details. Start with participants, the procedure, the materials you used, and what the overall design was. You can then go deeper into each section and include details such as how many participants had to be excluded regarding a particular criterion or how both a questionnaire and experiment was used. Make sure you consider the very fine details and remember that the methods section should make your study replicable! Is there a big procedural element you've forgotten as it seems like common sense or how you gathered the particular participants?

Student, Royal Holloway University of London

7.1.5 Qualitative Studies

For qualitative studies, the method section may be a little different. Common headers used in qualitative research papers are:

Participants (including selection criteria)

Materials/survey/interview

Procedure/data collection

You can see that some of the headers described may not be used, such as 'Design'; however, you should still fully describe your method in a way so that it is clear to the reader what you have done. You may have additional headings (see, for example, sections on 'Researcher reflexivity', 'Data', and 'Researcher–participant relationship').

Here is an example of how some authors have written about their interview protocol. Specific details have been excluded for brevity, but you can see the structure of the information that has been provided.

The first author conducted three in-depth interviews with each participant that employed Seidman's (2006) protocol. The first interview . . . . The second interview . . . . The third and final interview . . . . Central topics included . . . . Each interview lasted between 60 and 90 min and was conducted in a private office on campus. Whereas the interviewer began each interview with a general guiding question that framed its focus, the interview protocol was flexible and followed the participant's topics and emphases to allow the participant to develop a meaningful personal narrative (Creswell, 2008).

(O'Shea & Kaplan, 2018)

Researcher reflexivity

Reflexivity can help researchers improve the rigour in their research because it involves thinking about and reporting your decisions about how you conducted your research (Barrett et al., 2020). Qualitative reports may contain a section on this that explains the perspectives of the researchers. For example:

> The other members of the research team included a second-generation Korean American female doctoral student, a transracial Korean female adoptee doctoral student, a Black and Japanese biracial female doctoral student, a Black and Nicaraguan biracial female doctoral student, a second-generation Dominican female doctoral student, and a White male doctoral student in counseling psychology. We discussed our expectations about the data and our internal reactions to the data throughout the analysis. Because the research team was comprised of seven people with differing sociocultural identities, various perspectives were brought to bear in the analysis of the data, which allowed for a robust discussion about biases that were checked by members of the team. The interpretation of the data involved discussing differences and reaching consensus across multiple perspectives.
>
> (Lee et al., 2022)

Data

If you are analysing existing data sources (secondary data), then you should describe those and provide information about how you accessed the data and where it is stored.

Researcher–participant relationship

If relevant to the research process, describe the relationship and interactions between you and any other researchers, and the participants. For example, did you know the participants before the research and if so, were there any ethical considerations needed because of this?

7.1.6 Analytic Strategy (Data Analysis)

This section is quite common in research papers and an analysis plan is an important part of a registered report (see Box 7.2). In this section, you describe your plan for analysing your data.

Here is an extract of a description relating to statistical analysis from a study looking at cats' perception of an illusion:

> For the analyses of individuals' performance, binomial tests were conducted on the proportion of choices for the larger quantity of food (control trials) and for the proportion of choices for the

---

BOX 7.2 Transparency in Analysis

The Transparency and Openness Promotion (TOP) guidelines (Nosek et al., 2015) encourage the use of preregistering analysis plans to make the distinction clear between confirmatory analysis (testing hypotheses that were created in advance of data collection, sometimes called 'hypothesis-testing research') and exploratory analysis (analysis of the data once it has been collected, sometimes called 'hypothesis generating research' because it could be used to create hypotheses). Both types of research are needed. As a student researcher, you need to be clear from the start which you are doing.

portion of food presented on the smaller plate (illusion trials). Population-level values were analyzed using parametric statistics, as they were normally distributed (Shapiro–Wilk test, $p > .05$; Shapiro & Wilk, 1965). To assess whether the cats could discriminate between the two quantities in the two control conditions and select one plate more often than expected by chance in the illusion condition, we performed one-sample Student's t tests (two-tailed with chance level = .50) on the proportion of choices for the larger quantity of food in control trials and the proportion of choices for the food presented on the smaller plate in the illusion trials. Cohen's d values (Cohen, 1988) were calculated to estimate effect sizes.

(Szenczi et al., 2019)

For qualitative studies

It is important to inform the reader of the epistemological standpoint you have applied in your study. State the method of analysis, describe the methodological procedure used for analysis, and how themes were identified in the data. For example, if you have used thematic analysis (Braun & Clarke, 2006), report whether you have adopted an inductive or deductive approach and whether you have identified themes at the latent or the semantic level. The rationale behind these decisions needs to be evident to the reader.

Here is an example from a study about experiences of infertility.

Messages were analysed using the inductive thematic analysis procedure described by Braun and Clarke (2006). First, the data were read carefully to identify and code interesting features of the messages. Second, the different codes generated were sorted into potential themes and all data relevant to each potential theme were collated. Third, the data were systematically reviewed to ensure that a name and clear definition for each theme were identified and that these themes worked in relation to the coded extracts. In total, quotations taken from 28 unique sender names were reported in the analysis, these sender names were anonymised to ensure confidentiality.

(Malik & Coulson, 2008)

Secondary data research (quantitative or qualitative)

You may be analysing a dataset that has been collected by an organization or other researchers. You need to make this clear in your report, but otherwise reporting is similar to if you had collected the data yourself. The participants section will be a little different as you should report which data you have selected to analyse (i.e. which participants), describe when this was collected and what data set it is from.

7.1.7 Results

The results section is where you report the analysis of your data. The results section should include enough detail that someone else could analyse your data following the same process. It is important to be transparent about your analysis so readers can judge whether your conclusions are sound.

Qualitative studies

The results section is where you report the findings of your analysis. Following the method outlined in Chapter 4 ('Choosing Your Method'), if you have analysed your data using thematic analysis, the results section is where you will present the themes you developed, constructing a narrative of the ideas (or codes) within those themes and how your themes relate to your research question.

You can begin your results section with a brief description of your theme structure, followed by a discussion for each of your themes in turn. Your results should not read like a list of your codes. It is important to discuss the different ideas within your themes and the relationship between them. This will provide your reader with justification for why you grouped those codes together into a theme.

It is important to present some supporting evidence for your themes in terms of how each theme manifests in the data. This will be in the form of quotations (data extracts) from participants' responses, which demonstrate evidence of the ideas or codes within a theme. When selecting a quotation to include in your results, try and select one which captures a few different codes within a theme, where possible and relevant. You may also want to present quotations from different participants in your results section to show the prevalence of your themes across your dataset. When writing up your themes it is important to avoid using passive voice, such as 'two themes emerging from the analysis' (Braun & Clarke, 2006). Developing your thematic map is an active process; as such, the active voice is encouraged (e.g. use phrases like 'identified the theme' rather than 'themes emerged').

Depending on your findings, you could also include a figure, in the form of a thematic map, in your results section. A figure would not normally be necessary if you have a simple theme structure, as it wouldn't aid interpretation beyond the text description of your results section.

For example, here is an extract from the results section of a study that used interpretive phenomenological analysis (IPA).

Loneliness as a type of vulnerability

A theme of loneliness being a type of vulnerability was evident in many of the interviews. Some participants spoke about the physical vulnerability they felt in response to questions they were asked about their levels of loneliness. Participants appeared to interpret loneliness in this case as being synonymous with aloneness, since they spoke about being vulnerable in the house alone. They spoke of break-ins and crime in a manner that suggested these were the most salient threats to their safety. Harriet spoke about feeling lonely and scared for her safety in relation to break-ins:

"I'd be lonely at times, certainly, at night, there is this old lady up here who was broken into and during the day, at dinner time . . . . I was scared going to bed that night . . . no, I wouldn't be lonely really like that, there's places being broken into, you know, that would be the most thing I would be [scared of]".

(McHugh Power et al., 2017)

Here, the bold text 'Loneliness as a type of vulnerability' is the title of the theme. This is followed by a summary of participants' thoughts and a quote from an interview to demonstrate the summary. The rest of the section of that particular theme goes on to discuss particular quotes from other participants and ends with a summary of the theme. Notice that in this example, the authors have shortened the quotation by using an ellipsis (represented by '. . .'). This can be useful to cut unnecessary words as long as you don't lose important information.

The next example is from a study exploring women's experiences of smoking and quitting smoking. Again, the bold text refers to the theme identified by the authors and quotes are used as examples.

Addiction as a social and psychological 'habit'

In their accounts of quitting, participants challenged the idea that their addiction was only physiological by emphasising the habitual aspects of their smoking. As Sarah (smoker) explained, "I'm addicted to the habit rather than the craving I think." In their accounts of smoking being a habit, participants positioned their smoking as 'mental', 'psychological', and 'subconscious'. For example, Courtney (ex-smoker) took a photograph of a cup of tea (Fig. 3), which she described as a 'trigger'.

(Triandafilidis et al., 2018)

In these examples, you can see that there is a balance to be made between the author's summary of the participants' data and the use of supporting quotes. Make sure that your results section contains both of these things and not only one or the other.

Handy Hint

It is vital to read and reread your data multiple times as to avoid missing out any important points that can be used when writing out your analysis. Identifying similar themes or patterns within the data and grouping them together can also assist in the organization of your data especially if you're working with large amounts of data, which will make the process less overwhelming. Another tip is to make sure you fully understand your methodology in terms of your analytic approach as this will allow the data analysis process and the writing of your results section to run more smoothly.

Student, University of Roehampton

Quantitative studies

For quantitative studies, you should note any missing data in terms of frequency or percentage and describe methods for addressing missing data. You should report anything related to statistical assumptions that you have found and explain any steps you have taken related to these. For example, sometimes researchers remove outliers or use transformations on the data or corrections on the statistical tests. You should report violations of statistical tests as they might impact on your ability to interpret the results of the tests. For information about testing assumptions, see notes from your statistics courses or a statistics textbook.

Your results section may consists of two types of statistics: descriptive statistics and inferential statistics (if applicable).

- Descriptives (describe your data)

Report descriptive statistics for every group that you have ended up with. For example, if you have a 2×2 between-subjects design then you will need to report statistics relating to all four groups. You should report the number of cases, a measure of central tendency, a measure of spread, and any other relevant measures. These results are often presented in a table or a graph (see sections on Presenting data: figures and Presenting data: tables).

- Inferential statistics

Report the type of analysis you performed and all results of inferential tests. When reporting the type of analysis, remember to include specific details about it. For example, was it a repeated-measures analysis of variance (ANOVA) or between-subjects, was it one-way or two-way? If a regression is being reported, remember to state the type used. For example, perhaps a multiple linear regression was used. State the entry method such as forced or stepwise. If you have used null-hypothesis statistical testing, then you need to report exact p values reported to three decimal places (if your p is lower than .001 then you report '$p < .001$'). You should report sufficient information to allow a reader to fully understand your results. For example, for analysis of variance you need to report the degrees of freedom (df) as well as reporting the F ratio and the p value. You should also report effect sizes (e.g. partial eta square, Cohen's d) and confidence intervals. See Table 7.1 for a summary of how to report statistical tests in text.

Here is an example of an ANOVA being reported. Notice that the authors here have put information about the test in the method section and the results in the results section. Notice too that they report a Bayesian analysis alongside the ANOVA (which you may not do but is becoming more common). JOLs are judgements of learning.

> [From the analysis section in the method section]. For all experiments reported in this paper, we used a 2 (typeface, manipulated within-subjects) × 2 (test expectancy, manipulated between-subjects) mixed ANOVA.
>
> [From the results section]. Using the same model as above, participants in the high test expectancy group gave higher JOLs than those in the low test expectancy group, $M_{diff} = 5.91$, $F(1, 229) = 13.57, p < .001, \eta^2_g = .028$. Arial elicited higher JOLs than Sans Forgetica, $M_{diff} = 15.15$, $F(1, 229) = 87.05, p < .001, \eta^2_g = .161$. There was an interaction between test expectancy and typeface, $F(1, 229) = 13.65, p < .001, \eta^2_g, .029$. A Bayesian analysis revealed that the interaction model was strongly preferred to the main effects-only model ($BF > 100$). Planned comparisons revealed that the JOL effect was larger in the low test expectancy group ($d_{avg} = 1.65, 95\%$ CI $[1.37, 1.93]$) than in the high test expectancy group ($d_{avg} = .72, 95\%$ CI $[.51, .92]$).
>
> (Geller & Peterson, 2021)

Notice that the authors report the results for each main effect (test expectancy and typeface) and when doing so indicate the direction of the effect (e.g. '... higher JOLs than ...'). They then report the interaction effect and comparison tests.

For complex analyses such as factor analysis and hierarchical linear models, you should report details of the model, the associated variance (the covariance or correlation matrix), and you should mention what software package was used to run the analyses.

You should conduct and report the analysis as you had planned to do and do not worry if you don't find significant p-values (see following Smart Solution). You may have noticed from your research of the literature that most published studies have significant findings, but

Table 7.1 Reporting Format for Common Statistical Tests

Name of test	Reporting format	Don't forget!
t-test	$t(XX) = XX.XX, p = .XXX, d = X.XX, 95\%$ CI $[.XX,.XX]$.	To state the direction
ANOVA	$F(X, XX) = XXX.XX, MSE = XXX.XX\ p = .XXX, \eta^2_p = .XX$	To state the direction
Regression	$R^2 = .XX, \Delta R^2 = .XX, F(X, XX) = XXX.XX, p = .XXX,$ $\beta = XX.XX, 95\%$ CI $[.XX,.XX]$.	Type of regression
Correlation	$r(xx) = .XX, p = .XXX$	Type of correlation
Chi-square	$\chi^2(X) = XX.XX, p = .XXX$	To report the odds ratio

Note. Test statistics are reported to two decimal places and p-values are reported to three decimal places.

this bias is maintained if researchers continue to engage in behaviours such as *p*-hacking to enable them to report significant results (see also Bakker et al., 2012). You can report analyses that you did not plan to do originally but you should make it clear that they were unplanned.

Smart Solution—Dealing With Non-significant Results

We all fear the day that our results come out as non-significant. But don't panic! Non-significant is not 'insignificant'! No matter what your results are, they tell you something. Deviations from previous literature allow you to speculate why you may have ascertained such differences. So don't worry that you haven't got a 'significant difference' and focus on evaluating the significance of your non-significant result.

Student, Durham University

- Presenting data: figures.

It might be the case that you have lots of descriptive statistics that you have calculated. It is common to present such numbers in a table or a graph. You only need to present these results once: there is no need to have a graph, for example, and then repeat the same numbers in the text. The main point about graphs, and figures in general, is that they should be clear and easy to understand. When formatting in APA style, anything that is not a table is called a 'figure'. This includes graphs, diagrams, flowcharts, illustrations and pictures. Here we are going to discuss graphs only, but other figures should be formatted to the same rules.

Figure 7.1 shows an example of a column graph formatted according to APA style rules. We've put labels on to point out some aspects to pay attention to. These data are made up but represent how you would portray descriptive statistics from a 2 × 2 between-subjects design. One IV is group, which has two levels: prime and no prime. This IV is placed on the X axis. A second IV is congruency, which has two levels: congruent and incongruent. This IV is also placed on the X axis and is represented by the different shades of the columns. The DV is represented on the Y axis. When creating the Y axis, make sure that the scale used is appropriate. It can sometimes look as though there is a large effect present if the scale used is small. Figure 7.2 shows an example of a line graph formatted according to APA style rules. As with Figure 7.1, the DV is represented on the Y axis. A measure of time (an IV) is placed on the X axis.

Figures 7.1 and 7.2 have been created in Excel, which is fairly straightforward to use for creating graphs. At this point, hopefully you will be somewhat skilled in your use of Excel and should be able to use it to create a graph. If you need some reminders, there are many guides and videos available on the internet. Other packages, like SPSS, could be used instead.

Graphs, and all figures, should be neat and clear, and should be anchored in the text. This means drawing the reader's attention to the figures in the text of the results section e.g. 'see Figure 1'. You should describe what the figure shows and, if showing a graph, you might also describe the pattern of results shown at the same time, but you do not need to detail actual numbers. Here is an example of what you could write for the line graph (labelled as Figure 1) in Figure 7.2:

> The latency to reach the goal is shown in Figure 1. Participants took longest to reach the goal in the first trial, and this seemed to reduce across trials.

Example of APA Formatted Figure

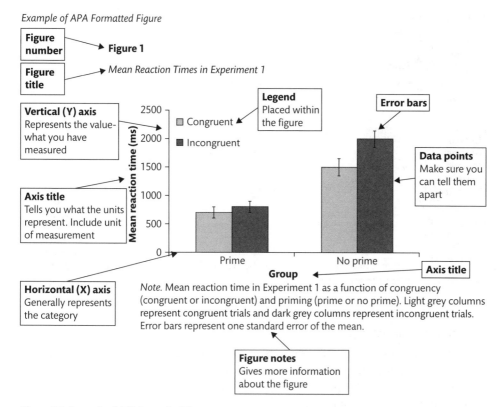

Figure number → **Figure 1**

Figure title → *Mean Reaction Times in Experiment 1*

Vertical (Y) axis
Represents the value-what you have measured

Legend
Placed within the figure

Error bars

Axis title
Tells you what the units represent. Include unit of measurement

Data points
Make sure you can tell them apart

Horizontal (X) axis
Generally represents the category

Axis title

Note. Mean reaction time in Experiment 1 as a function of congruency (congruent or incongruent) and priming (prime or no prime). Light grey columns represent congruent trials and dark grey columns represent incongruent trials. Error bars represent one standard error of the mean.

Figure notes
Gives more information about the figure

Figure 7.1 Example of APA Formatted Figure

Figure 1
Latency to Reach a Hidden Goal

Note. Latency to reach a hidden goal in seconds by trial number. Error bars represent one standard error of the mean.

Figure 7.2 Example of a Line Graph

Table 7.2 Example Table

Table number

Table 1

Table title Brief but clear

Means and Standard Deviations of Reaction Time for Study Variables

		Word		Non-word			Column headings
	Time	M	SD	M	SD		

Decked headings To avoid repeating information

			Reaction Time (ms)			
	1	525	34	675	33	
	2	460	38	660	31	
			Error Rate			
	1	2.4	1.1	4.4	3.1	
	2	3.1	2.2	6.1	3.5	

Stub column Usually an IV

Table spanner Can be used to subdivide the table

Note. Notes might include explanations of formatting (e.g., if you have bolder text) and explanations of abbreviations.

- Presenting data: tables

When you have lots of descriptive statistics and it is important that your reader can see the exact numbers (rather than the pattern of the data) you could use a table to display your statistics. Tables too need to be clear and, again, there are formatting rules you can follow to ensure this. See Table 7.2, which is an example of a table used to report means and standard deviations of two measures: reaction time and error rate. Take note of the formatting details. There are no vertical lines used and italic font is used for the table title but not the table number. In Table 7.2 we have pointed out the main ways you could structure a table to ensure that your table is easy for readers to understand.

To create a table, we find spreadsheet software such as Excel is easy to use as it is easy to manipulate column widths and draw lines (borders) where you want them. Of course, just use whichever software you find easiest; you should be able to create a table formatted according to APA style rules with most software.

A note on reporting if you have used Bayesian techniques

Null hypothesis testing is still the prevalent method of statistical analysis in psychology, but researchers are now starting to use alternatives, such as Bayesian approaches. APA JARS do specify standards for reporting Bayesian techniques (see table 8 of JARS Quant), which you can refer to if you are using only Bayesian techniques. More common at the moment is to report a Bayes factor to further investigate significant or nonsignificant results (Dienes, 2011). A Bayes factor of 0 suggests evidence for the null hypothesis, 1 suggests equal evidence for both hypotheses (the null hypothesis and the alternative hypothesis), and a factor much greater than 1 suggests strong evidence for the alternative hypothesis (Dienes, 2014). Some researchers say that the factor should be greater than three to be considered as strong

(Lee & Wagenmakers, 2014, as cited in Dienes, 2014). Here is an example from a study that used a go/no-go task and reported a Bayesian t-test:

> A Bayesian paired-samples t-test between no-go and no-cue foods gave a Bayes factor (BF) of 0.185, supporting the null hypothesis that no difference occurred between no-go and no-cue stimuli (a BF below 1/3 is considered substantial evidence for the null hypothesis, see Dienes, 2014).
>
> (Chen et al., 2016)

7.1.8 Discussion

Writing the discussion section is your opportunity to reflect on what you found and how that fits with the research area. Think of the discussion as 'describing what your results mean' (Cooper, 2011). This involves writing about how your research fits into context and whether or not there are any factors that may have impacted on your results. The 'funnel' metaphor mentioned in the introduction can be reversed here: the discussion starts narrow where you discuss your findings but then it broadens out to the implications of your research for the topic area.

Handy Hint

When writing the discussion section, it is helpful to produce a plan. The discussion section should consist of an overview of the results section, i.e. what was found, and an elaboration on how these findings are linked to research proposed within the introduction section of the research. To strengthen the discussion section, is it also useful to draw on any new research which support or disagree with the findings, which helps to strengthen your argument. The discussion section should also contain any limitations of the research and discuss how other research similar to your research has combated these limitations. The implications of the research should also be part of the discussion as this draws conclusions of the findings allowing the reader to comprehend why it was important to conduct the research.

Student, University of Roehampton

Place results in context

It can be useful at the beginning of the discussion to reiterate the summary or aim of the research that you are reporting. Whether or not you do this, you should then be specific about whether your results supported or did not support your hypotheses (for quantitative studies). Beware of HARKing (see Box 7.3). In order to put your own results into context and to help explain them, you should compare your results with findings reported by other researchers. This means that, usually, you'll return to the literature you covered in the introduction, but it might be that you include other research too that helps you to explain your results. Explaining your findings is necessary whether you have conducted a quantitative or a qualitative study.

BOX 7.3 HARKing

Hypothesizing After Results are Known (HARKing) is commonly held to be bad practice (Chambers, 2019) because it goes against the hypothetical-deductive approach to research. Discussion in this area is lively as to whether HARKing is harmful, and if it is, how harmful. See e.g. Rubin (2017) and Lishner (2021) for further detail. Rubin (2017) outlines three forms of HARKing:

CHARKing—constructing hypotheses after results are known (i.e. making up the hypotheses to support the results found).

RHARKing—retrieving hypotheses after results are known (i.e. using a hypothesis that has been put forward by someone else).

SHARKing—suppressing hypotheses after results are known (i.e. not including hypotheses because they aren't supported by the results).

Lishner (2021) holds that CHARKing and RHARKing also include the idea that the researcher makes or finds these after the study but presents them as though they were made/found before the study (a priori).

When writing your report, make sure to be as clear as possible in relation to what your hypotheses are and whether or not your results support your hypothesis. In many published papers, the results do match the hypotheses, but it is OK if they do not.

Here are some examples that illustrate how to relate your research to hypotheses/expectations and other research (bold text indicates signposting phrases):

Children's perceptual sensitivity to trustworthiness and cues associated with this trait (emotional expression) have previously been reported to improve with age (Caulfield et al., 2016). Thus, **we anticipated that** relative to younger children, older children (and adults) might show a stronger bias to modulate their investments in line with the emotional expressions of their partners (more tokens for those who look happy, fewer for angry). **Counter to prediction**, however, this appearance-related bias was observed from the youngest ages tested, and its magnitude did not increase with age. Older children invested significantly fewer tokens than the younger children overall, but, crucially, there was no difference in the extent to which their behavior was modulated in line with these powerful trust cues.

(Ewing et al., 2019)

This extract comes from a study on sleep and is an example showing how to broadly link previous research and your own findings:

Studies manipulating various facets of sleep show there is considerable evidence for sleep playing an active role in declarative memory processing (Ellenbogen et al. 2006; Marshall et al. 2006; Rasch et al. 2007; Rudoy et al. 2009; Oudiette et al. 2013; Creery et al. 2014). However, we witnessed no advantage for immediate sleep after 24 h for the relative preservation of restudied information (contrasting 24-h AM versus 24-h PM). These results do not seriously conflict with the idea that sleep plays an active role in memory consolidation, because both wakeful interference and sleep reactivation likely contribute to sleep-related memory benefits. Waking interference may have taken precedent here.

(Antony & Paller, 2018)[1]

This example comes from a study that used thematic analysis:

Despite their desire to be involved, the men in this study frequently described feeling alienated and distant from the infertility treatment procedure. One reason for this may be that, as past literature

---

[1] Note that this article is not published in an APA journal so the style of citing is slightly different.

suggests, the majority of infertility treatments are centred on women, with the man often playing a minimal role (Jordan and Revenson 1999). As a result of this, men in this study exhibited feelings of dissociation, isolation and neglect not only from the actual treatment process but also felt sidelined by medical professionals (e.g. nurses, GPs, consultants, etc.) conducting the treatment.
(Malik & Coulson, 2008)[2]

In an experiment that looked at episodic specificity induction (ESI) in the Deese-Roediger-McDermott (DRM) paradigm, the authors link their findings to a number of other research findings. Here is an example of how they begin discussion about one of these links:

The present findings are consistent with context/content borrowing accounts of false memory (Lampinen et al., 2005; O'Neill & Diana, 2017). In line with these theories, we think that the ESI enhanced the retrieval of episodic details incorrectly linked to critical lure items, thereby increasing the incidence of false memories in the DRM.
(Thakral et al., 2019)

Limitations

When discussing your results, you should be careful not to over-interpret what they mean. For example, if something is close to significance avoid talking about it as though it is significant. It also means that you should be aware of any limitations in your research or anything that might cause your data to be subject to biases. However, it is easy to be tempted to outline everything that might be wrong with your research without justifying what your research still shows. Every piece of research conducted has its limitations and every journal article that you read will mention those limitations, but they do so in a balanced way that still highlights the theoretical value of the research conducted. When reflecting on the limitations of your study, you should consider your methodology, in particular the measures that you used. Think about how well the variables were measured or manipulated. How did you know that you manipulated what you thought you had manipulated (e.g. did you include any manipulation checks)?

You should discuss any aspects of the study that may have impacted on internal validity. For example, think about any potential confounds that may have become apparent in your research and controls that you did/did not implement (counterbalancing or random assignment). These things may mean that you have an alternative explanation for your findings that is based on a technicality of the implementation of your research, rather than your manipulations.

The next example demonstrates a point being made about methodology used in an experiment and how it was different from previous research. Notice how both sides of the argument are considered.

However, one possible methodological problem in the present study, namely, inadvertent cuing by the person holding the cat, could have been an issue because the cats were held by a person (owner) in contrast to previous primate (where the animals were completely separated) or dog (where the animals were on a leash) studies. We cannot exclude the possibility that the handlers may have cued the cats, but as mentioned in Method, we think this is unlikely, as the handlers were blind to the experimental questions and rational of the test design.
(Szenczi et al., 2019)

---

[2] Note that this article is not published in an APA journal so the style of citing is slightly different.

In a study that looks at task performance when listening to music, Gonzalez and Aiello (2019) acknowledged a factor that they did not study:

> . . . despite the central role of attention in our theoretical model, we did not directly examine distraction as a mediator of the effects of music on task performance. Additionally, given that distraction and arousal are closely intertwined in the distraction-conflict theory framework (Baron, 1986), our findings would have been strengthened if we had examined whether either or both of these mechanisms were at work in the current study.
>
> (Gonzalez & Aiello, 2019)

You should discuss any other relevant limitations of your results such as any threats to statistical validity and your sample size and sampling validity. You should think about how reliable your statistics are in order to make a conclusion based on them. Think about the significance value and the effect size obtained and the chances of getting a Type 1 or Type 2 error. You should consider how generalizable your results are. Think about how much your sample represents your target population and any other issues about the context of your research. Don't automatically assume that your sample isn't representative as it depends on what you are interested in studying (the target population) and how far your results can be expected to generalize. For example, if your research question was related to learning techniques of university students then a sample comprised of university students would be appropriate. Similarly, if your research question was related to an aspect of psychophysics that was known to be age-independent then a sample comprised of university students would be equally appropriate.

Here is an example from a research paper that reports a study about visual search that considers the sample used:

> Notably, the gender distribution in the present study was shifted to more females than males in the younger group. Most previous research showed that cognitive sex differences are generally small (Hyde, 2005, 2014), suggesting that our results are largely generalizable across male and female observers. Future studies, however, should aim for larger samples with balanced gender distributions across age groups to control for potential sex differences in performance.
>
> (Wiegand et al., 2019)

Implications

You should discuss any implications of your research: this includes implications for the research area or for applications of the research. You should also comment on any potential future research. Authors sometimes combine limitations and suggestions for future research so consider whether the limitations that you write about could give you ideas for future research.

In Gonzalez and Aiello's (2019) study about music and task performance, some practical implications are described. Here is the first of those:

> First, we offer evidence against the commonly held belief that distractions like music will always harm task performance (e.g., Breuer, 1995; Roper & Juneja, 2008). Instead, we offer a nuanced view of distractions, such that they can either help or hinder performance, depending on the performer and the context. Educators and managers alike may consider a wider variety of factors (e.g., nature of the work, salience of the distraction) when determining whether distractions such as music can benefit or impair their students' and employees' performance on tasks, respectively.
>
> (Gonzalez & Aiello, 2019)

> **FUTURE FOCUS Applying Psychology To The Real World**
>
> The thing which really differentiates psychology graduates from those who have studied other subjects is a knowledge and understanding of human experience and behaviour—the ability to apply psychological theory to real-world scenarios. Whatever you go on to do after your degree, this holds huge value for all facets of your personal and professional life. It is important to showcase this knowledge and its application to graduate employers when you are applying for jobs, so think about whether your project has implications for a particular field or sector. In some cases, the links may be obvious (e.g. if you have conducted research in a school and hope to pursue a career in teaching) but in others they might be more subtle.

Here is an example of a suggestion for future research from a research paper investigating humour of words:

> . . . it is easy to envisage a small step forward to quantitative study of what may be the world's third least funny jokes, word pairs. With humor estimates for the individual words now computed, it is possible to start studying how those values interact with each other and with other measures to affect humor judgments of potentially humorous word pairs such as toothy weasel, muzzy muffin, and fizzy turd. These pairs introduce a small number of manageable complications to the study of simplified humor.
>
> (Westbury & Hollis, 2019)

> **FUTURE FOCUS Postgraduate Research**
>
> Proposing ideas for future research may simply be something you do for the purpose of your project report; however, it might also be the spark of a new research idea you go on to carry out. If you have found interesting results in your project and are keen to pursue postgraduate research, discuss your ideas with your supervisor or another academic to see if they could form part of a proposal or application.

Here is an example from a study that used a qualitative method:

> Findings from this study are relevant to the development of individualized interventions, and important to the evaluation of current public health approaches to smoking. The complexity of these issues calls for a comprehensive approach to young women's smoking, where population-level policies, such as taxation, are delivered alongside local interventions targeted specifically at young women [8]. Interventions targeted at young women need to offer flexibility and variety, allowing women to take control and make their own decisions regarding cessation [91, 92].
>
> (Triandafilidis et al., 2018)[3]

Conclusion

It is helpful to finish the discussion section with a short conclusion that reiterates what the problem was, how you investigated it and what you found, and how it related to previous research.

---

[3] Note that this article is not published in an APA journal so the style of citing is slightly different.

7.1.9 **Citing and Referencing**

Citing and referencing is something that you are hopefully familiar with from your work earlier in your course. The purpose of citing and referencing is to acknowledge other people's work and is vital academic practice. Citing is done in the main text and referencing is done via a list of sources usually at the end of the piece of work. Here, we will provide a reminder of the main points around citing and referencing according to APA format.

Citing

Citing can be done in two ways: with the names in the run of the text and the date immediately following in parentheses or with the whole citation in parentheses at the end of a sentence. For example, citing a source in the text looks like this:

Gabriel and Young (2011) found that when people read chapters from the Harry Potter books they later associated themselves with wizards.

And citing the source in parentheses looks like this:

When people read chapters from the Harry Potter books they later associated themselves with wizards (Gabriel & Young, 2011).

Notice the differences: in text the word 'and' is used whereas in parentheses the symbols '&' is used. In the second example, the names and date are both in parentheses.

It is also important to notice the number of authors named. When there is one author or two authors, you should write the names of the authors in the citation. When there are three or more authors, you should write the name of the first author and "et al." in every citation.

For example,

Crysel et al. (2015) found that on the dimension of agreeableness, people sorted into Hufflepuff scored higher than the average of people in other houses.

Or

On the dimension of agreeableness, people sorted into Hufflepuff scored higher than the average of people in other houses (Crysel et al., 2015).

Notice the punctuation around 'et al.': there should be a full stop after 'al'. The term 'et al.' is Latin for 'and others' and is a standard abbreviation used in writing.

By this stage, you will likely be citing multiple papers in parentheses. The rules are the same as for single citations and you should order citations in alphabetical order of first author and separate each publication by a semi-colon.

For example,

Research (Bird, 2015; Bird & Fox, 2017; Pound, 2012; Singh, 2016; Wolf, 2010) . . . .

For anything more complicated and for exceptions to these rules you should have a look at the latest edition of the APA publication manual (most institutional libraries will have access to a copy) or see http://apastyle.apa.org/.

Referencing

Referencing refers to the full list of sources that you have cited in your work. Note that a reference list is not the same as a bibliography. A bibliography lists sources that you read or used whilst doing the work and may or may not be cited in the work; whereas a reference list only includes those items you have cited.

In a reference list, you need to give details about each source, and which details you include depends on the type of source. Here, we present some of the main types of source you will use and how to reference them in APA format.

- Journal Article

A reference of a journal article should look like this:

Author, A. A., Author, B. B., & Author, C. C. (Year). Title of article. *Title of Journal, volume number* (issue number), page range. https://doi.org/xxxxxxxxxx

Note the reference is made up of:

- the names of the authors;
- the year of publication;
- the title of the article: only the first word and proper nouns (names of people, places, and organizations) in the title are capitalized;
- the title of the journal (italicized with capitalized first letters);
- the volume number (italicized);
- the issue number (if available) (in parentheses, not italicized);
- the page range (not italicized);
- the DOI (not italicized).

For example,

Haselgrove, M., Barnard, M., & Smith, A. D. (2019). Psychology students prefer biscuits that are dunkable. *Psychology of Psychologists, 5*(1), 35–42. https://doi.org/123.45.678.9

Watch out for these common errors!

- Using capital letters in the article title (articles should be in sentence case, that is, not capitalized).
- Not putting the volume number in italics.
- Pasting from the reference given by another system, for example Google Scholar or your library catalogue, and not correcting errors.

- Book

A reference for a book should look like this:

Author, A. A., & Author, B. B. (Year of publication). *Title of work: Subtitle* (Xnd ed.). Publisher. https://doi.org/xxxxxxxxxx

Note the reference is made up of:

- the names of the authors;
- the year of publication;
- the title of the book: only the first word and proper nouns in the title are capitalized (italicized);
- edition number, if applicable;
- the name of the publisher;
- the DOI for electronic books. (You can leave this off if you used a print book.)

For example,

Wynne, C. D., & Udell, M. A. R. (2008). *Animal Cognition: Evolution, Behavior and Cognition* (2nd ed.). https://ebookcentral.proquest.com

● Chapter in an Edited Book

When a book consists of many chapters written by different authors, reference each chapter you used:

Author, A. A., & Author, B. B. (Year). Chapter title. In A. A. Editor, B. B. Editor, & C. C. Editor (Eds.), *Title of the book* (pp. xx–xx). Publisher. https://doi.org/xxxxxxxxxx

For example,

Thompson, W. F. (2013). Intervals and scales. In D. Deutsch (Ed.), *The psychology of music* (3rd ed., pp. 107–140). Academic Press. https://doi.org/10.1016/B978-0-12-381460-9. 00004-3

Reference management software

Lots of students and researchers make use of reference management software to store journal articles and notes and help with citing and referencing. Endnote, Mendeley, and Zotoro are commonly used. Mendeley and Zotoro are free and fairly straightforward to use. They store journal articles and have a plug-in to Microsoft Word which you can then use to insert citations and the reference list. It is still worth knowing the formatting rules around citing and referencing as these types of software are not 100% accurate and you will need to do some editing to make sure the final formatting is correct. However, using this type of software can save you time when it comes to citing and referencing.

7.1.10 Notes on Writing Paragraphs

Using a structure for writing paragraphs can really help to ensure that those paragraphs are focused, that they link to other paragraphs, and that what you are saying is clear to readers. We recommend the point, evidence, explain, link (PEEL) structure (see Figure 7.3).

Point – use the first sentence to introduce the topic of the paragraph (sometimes called a topic sentence).

Evidence – describe the evidence that supports your point, for example an experiment.

Evaluation – comment on the evidence. For example, explain how the evidence fits the point that you are making and say if there is other evidence which supports/contradicts it or highlight any differences.

Link – provide a summary statement of the point you are making. This can help to link to the next paragraph too.

Figure 7.3 PEEL Structure for Paragraphs

7.2 **Language**

It is important when writing that you are aware of any biases that may come through in your language and that you work to reduce these. Here are some to be aware of. The seventh edition of the APA publication manual covers these areas in great detail, so you may wish to refer to that for further clarification. When describing participants, only include details relevant to your study. Think about which characteristics you need to report (e.g. it is unlikely that you'd need to report sexual orientation for a cognitive study).

7.2.1 **Disability**

You may see disability referred to in two ways: person-first and identity-first. In person-first language, you would write, for example 'a person with epilepsy', rather than 'an epileptic'. In identity-first language, you would write, for an example, 'autistic person' as opposed to a 'person with autism'. Identity-first language often reflects an individual or group's own choice and reclamation of a disability (APA, 2020). Use whichever way the group of people you are referring to use themselves.

You need to ensure that the language you are using does not use negative labels (e.g. 'brain damaged') or imply restriction (e.g. 'wheelchair bound') or could be regarded as a slur (e.g. 'invalid', 'alcoholic'). Instead, you would use a person-first approach ('person with traumatic brain injury', 'wheelchair user', 'person with a physical disability', 'person with alcohol use disorder').

7.2.2 **Gender**

You should report genders of participants in a specific way, using the terms that people use themselves. Some terms you could use include: 'cisgender women', 'cisgender men', 'transgender women', 'transgender men', and 'nonbinary'.

Avoid using male or female pronouns when referring to participants from groups of people that may be comprised of a range of genders. There are various alternatives that you could use, for example 'the person', 'they', 'the individual'. Don't use combinations such as 'he or she', instead, use the singular 'they'. If you are writing about individuals, then you can use the pronoun that they have identified (for example: he, she, ze, xe, hir, per, and many others).

If you need to report the gender of your participants, then you may want to get them to self-describe their gender and report what you are told.

7.2.3 **Sexual Orientation**

When describing sexual orientation, use terms such as asexual, bisexual, gay, lesbian, pansexual, polysexual, straight. As with usage of other terms, ask participants to identify terms themselves.

7.2.4 **Racial and Ethnic Identity**

Terms relating to racial and ethnic identity often change and so the guidelines are to use commonly accepted terms and to be specific. Names of groups should be capitalized, e.g. Black, White. Again, it may be advisable to ask participants to describe their identity rather than use a predetermined list.

7.2.5 **Age**

For a person of any age, you can use 'person' or 'individual'. When writing about participants who are younger than 12 years, the terms 'girl', 'boy', 'transgender girl', 'transgender boy' can be used. For participants ages 13 to 17, the terms 'adolescent', 'young person', 'young woman', 'young man' can be used. For people aged 18+, use terms such as 'adult', 'woman', 'man', 'transgender woman', 'transgender man'. The term 'older adults', 'older persons', 'older people', 'persons 65 years and older' are appropriate descriptions for adults aged 65 years and above.

7.2.6 **First-Person Pronouns**

Use of first-person pronouns ('I', 'we') is generally preferred to writing about yourself in the third person. You will likely be writing your research project report on your own so use 'I' and only use 'we' if you have co-authors.

7.3 Improving Your Report

Like with all writing, one of the best things you can do to improve it is to review it after writing it. There are likely two main ways that you can do this. The first is to look at it critically yourself and the second is to use feedback from your supervisor, where available.

7.3.1 **Reviewing Your Own Writing**

Reviewing and editing is a critical step in writing. Always consider that the first time you write something it is unlikely to come out perfectly. This is true for all writers and not just students (ask your tutors about their own experience!). Here are some tips about reviewing your own writing.

- Be objective. It can sometimes be hard to review what you have written, so to make it easier try to detach yourself a little from what you have produced. You are reviewing a piece of work and not criticizing yourself as a person. It can help if you leave a few days between finishing writing and then reviewing it.

- Read aloud. Reading sentences or even paragraphs out loud lets you hear whether or not they make sense and if the length is right or too long (for example if you're running out of breath then your sentence is too long).

- Check paragraph purpose. Go over each paragraph and check PEEL has been used. Can you identify the topic of each paragraph? What is it adding to your argument? Consider making more explicit links if it is not obvious why the paragraph is there. Also don't be afraid to delete sentences or even paragraphs if they serve no purpose.

- Use technology. This can be as simple as using the spelling and grammar check on the word processing software you are using. There are other similar tools available too so have a search round the web or app store. For citing and referencing, reference manager software can be really useful (refer back to 'Citing' and 'Referencing' sections).

- Use the marking scheme or rubric. Read the marking scheme (ideally before writing) so you know what your marker is going to be judging. After you have written your report, read it alongside the marking scheme and mark your report. This may help to identify any areas you could alter before handing it in.

7.3.2 Using Feedback

You may receive some feedback on a draft of your report from your supervisor. If this isn't done as standard in your department then ask your supervisor if they are able to give you some feedback. In some departments it is standard because acting on feedback is one of the most valuable things you can do to improve your work. Make sure to read the comments you get and plan time to work on any necessary changes. Receiving feedback isn't always easy and at first, you may feel frustrated when you receive the comments. A good thing to do is to give yourself some time away from your report and then come back to work on the comments a few days later. Your supervisor is really trying to help you improve your report, so it is important that you work on their suggestions. Do ask your supervisor about any comments they have made if there is something that you do not understand. Do also keep in mind that if there are any particular areas of your work that you yourself are uncertain about then it is OK to be specific with your supervisor about what feedback you particularly need. In fact, your supervisor will probably find this useful in helping to provide feedback that you will understand and be able to use most effectively.

Handy Hint
Get a draft of your dissertation in early to ensure you have plenty of time to act on your feedback.

Student, Durham University

Summary

In this chapter, we have provided some general guidelines on reporting research in psychology. It is important that you follow any guidelines given by your department as they might have specific learning outcomes that they need you to demonstrate. Writing the report is a big task, but by breaking it down into chunks and writing over a period of time, you will be able to complete this lengthy piece of work, good luck!

Table 7.3 Summary of Sections of a Research Report

Title	• Include topic and variables.
	• Mention the population investigated.
Abstract	• What is the main problem being investigated?
	• Describe the participants.
	• Describe the study method.
	• Describe findings.
	• State conclusions.
Introduction	• Introduce the topic and mention the importance of the problem under investigation.
	• Review relevant literature. Make sure to highlight relation to previous research and any differences between the current study and earlier studies.
	• Specify hypotheses, aims and objectives and state how your hypotheses and your design relate to each other.
Method	Participants
	• Sampling method.
	• Inclusion and exclusion criteria.
	• Sample size details.
	• Relevant characteristics.
	Design (if applicable)
	Measures/materials
	• Define all measures.
	• Instruments used (materials).
	Procedure
	• Outline how the study ran (how the data was collected).
	Data analysis
	• Analytic strategy for inferential statistics.
Results	For qualitative studies:
	List themes that were developed and include supporting evidence from data.
	For quantitative studies:
	• Descriptive statistics.
	• Report any problems with statistical assumptions and/or data distributions that may affect the validity of the findings.
	• Results of all inferential tests conducted.
	• Report any other analyses performed, indicating whether planned or unplanned.
Discussion	• Provide a statement of support/nonsupport for all hypotheses.
	• Discuss similarities and differences between reported results and work of others.
	• Provide an interpretation of the results (including potential limitations).
	• Implications for future research, programme, or policy.

Note. Adapted from APA Style JARS-Quant General Principles table https://apastyle.apa.org/jars/quant-table-2.pdf

---

FUTURE FOCUS Professional Writing

Completing your project report is a real achievement and provides great evidence of your capabilities in producing an extended piece of professional writing. To do this successfully, you will have demonstrated skills in synthesizing multiple sources of information and perspectives, building a convincing line of argument, and explaining complex scientific ideas. You will also have shown effective project management, evidence-based decision-making, data-handling and analysis, and an array of other skills. Being able to convey this concisely and comprehensively, and in accordance with a set of writing standards or guidelines, demonstrates abilities which will appeal to many graduate employers; make sure you reflect on the diverse capabilities you've developed during your project, and be ready to highlight what you can do!

 Go online to access further resources for the text: www.oup.com/he/whittle.

References

Antony, J. W., & Paller, K. A. (2018). Retrieval and sleep both counteract the forgetting of spatial information. *Learning and Memory*, *25*(6), 258–263. https://doi.org/10.1101/lm.046268.117

American Psychological Association. (2020). *Publication manual of the American Psychological Association* (7th ed.). https://doi.org/10.1037/0000165-000

Bakker, M., van Dijk, A., & Wicherts, J. M. (2012). The rules of the game called psychological science. *Perspectives on Psychological Science*, *7*(6), 543–554. https://doi.org/10.1177/1745691612459060

Barrett, A., Kajamaa, A., & Johnston, J. (2020). How to . . . be reflexive when conducting qualitative research. *The Clinical Teacher*, *17*(1), 9–12. https://doi.org/10.1111/tct.13133

Bauer, B., Jolicoeur, P., & Cowan, W. B. (1996). Visual search for colour targets that are or are not linearly separable from distractors. *Vision Research*, *36*(10), 1439–1466. https://doi.org/10.1016/0042-6989(95)00207-3

Bayet, L., Behrendt, H. F., Cataldo, J. K., Westerlund, A., & Nelson, C. A. (2018). Recognition of facial emotions of varying intensities by three-year-olds. *Developmental Psychology*, *54*(12), 2240–2247. https://doi.org/10.1037/dev0000588

Braun, V., & Clarke, V. (2006). Using thematic analysis in psychology. *Qualitative Research in Psychology, 3*(2), 77–101. https://doi.org/10.1191/1478088706qp063oa

Chambers, C. (2019). *The 7 Deadly Sins of Psychology: A Manifesto for Reforming the Culture of Scientific Practice*. Princeton University Press.

Chen, Z., Veling, H., Dijksterhuis, A., & Holland, R. W. (2016). How does not responding to appetitive stimuli cause devaluation: Evaluative conditioning or response inhibition? *Journal of Experimental Psychology: General*, *145*(12), 1687–1701. https://doi.org/10.1037/xge0000236

Clark, V., Tuffin, K., Frewin, K., & Bowker, N. (2018). Housemate desirability and understanding the social dynamics of shared living. *Qualitative Psychology*, *5*(1), 26–40. https://doi.org/10.1037/qup0000091

Cooper, H. (2011). *Reporting Research in Psychology: How to Meet Journal Article Reporting Standards*. American Psychological Society.

Crysel, L. C., Cook, C. L., Schember, T. O., & Webster, G. D. (2015). Harry Potter and the measures of personality: Extraverted Gryffindors, agreeable Hufflepuffs, clever Ravenclaws, and manipulative Slytherins. *Personality and Individual Differences*. https://doi.org/10.1016/j.paid.2015.04.016

Dienes, Z. (2011). Bayesian versus orthodox statistics: Which side are you on? *Perspectives on Psychological Science*, *6*(3), 274–290. https://doi.org/10.1177/1745691611406920

Dienes, Z. (2014). Using Bayes to get the most out of non-significant results. *Frontiers in Psychology*, *5*(July), 1–17. https://doi.org/10.3389/fpsyg.2014.00781

Evans, J. B., Slaughter, J. E., Ellis, A. P. J., & Rivin, J. M. (2019). Gender and the evaluation of humor at work. *Journal of Applied Psychology*, *104*(8), 1077–1087. https://doi.org/10.1037/apl0000395

Ewing, L., Sutherland, C. A. M., & Willis, M. L. (2019). Children show adult-like facial appearance biases when trusting others. *Developmental Psychology*, *55*(8), 1694–1701. https://doi.org/10.1037/dev0000747

Gabriel, S., & Young, A. F. (2011). Becoming a vampire without being bitten: The narrative collective-assimilation hypothesis. *Psychological Science*, *22*(8), 990–994. https://doi.org/10.1177/0956797611415541

Geller, J., & Peterson, D. (2021). Is this going to be on the test? Test expectancy moderates the disfluency effect with sans forgetica. *Journal of Experimental Psychology: Learning, Memory, and Cognition*, *47*(12), 1924–1938. https://doi.org/10.1037/xlm0001042

Gilmore, C., Keeble, S., Richardson, S., & Cragg, L. (2017). The interaction of procedural skill, conceptual understanding and working memory in early mathematics achievement. *Journal of Numerical Cognition*, *3*(2), 400–416. https://doi.org/10.5964/jnc.v3i2.51

Gonthier, C., & Roulin, J.-L. (2019). Intraindividual strategy shifts in Raven's matrices, and their dependence on working memory capacity and need for cognition. *Journal of Experimental Psychology: General, 149*(3), 564–579. https://doi.org/10.1037/xge0000660

Gonzalez, M. F., & Aiello, J. R. (2019). More than meets the ear: Investigating how music affects cognitive task rerformance. *Journal of Experimental Psychology: Applied, 25*(3), 431–444. https://doi.org/10.1037/xap0000202

Hirst, R. J., Kicks, E. C., Allen, H. A., & Cragg, L. (2019). Cross-modal interference-control is reduced in childhood but maintained in aging: A cohort study of stimulus- and response-interference in cross-modal and unimodal Stroop tasks. *Journal of Experimental Psychology: Human Perception and Performance, 45*(5), 553–572. https://doi.org/10.1037/xhp0000608

Lee, J., Jung, K., & Han, S. W. (2021). Serial, self-terminating search can be distinguished from others: Evidence from multi-target search data. *Cognition, 212* (July 2021), 104736. https://doi.org/10.1016/j.cognition.2021.104736

Lee, M., Kim-Martin, K., Molfetto, K., Castillo, K., Elliott, J. L., Rodriguez, Y., & Thompson, C. M. (2022). Bicultural Asian American women's experience of gender roles across cultural contexts: A narrative inquiry. *Qualitative Psychology, 9*(1), 62–80. https://doi.org/10.1037/qup0000214

Lishner, D. A. (2021). HARKing: Conceptualizations, harms, and two fundamental remedies. *Journal of Theoretical and Philosophical Psychology, 41*(4), 248–263. https://doi.org/10.1037/teo0000182

Malik, S. M., & Coulson, N. (2008). The male experience of infertility: A thematic analysis of an online infertility support group bulletin board. *Journal of Reproductive and Infant Psychology, 26*(1), 18–30. https://doi.org/10.1080/02646830701759777

McHugh Power, J. E., Hannigan, C., Carney, S., & Lawlor, B. A. (2017). Exploring the meaning of loneliness among socially isolated older adults in rural Ireland: A qualitative investigation. *Qualitative Research in Psychology, 14*(4), 394–414. https://doi.org/10.1080/14780887.2017.1329363

Meltzer, M. A., & Bartlett, J. C. (2019). Holistic processing and unitization in face recognition memory. *Journal of Experimental Psychology: General, 148*(8), 1386–1406. https://doi.org/10.1037/xge0000640

Nosek, B.A., Alter, G., Banks, G.C., Borsboom, D., Bowman, S.D., Breckler, S.J., Buck, S., Chambers, C.D., Chin, G., Christensen, G., & Contestabile, M. (2015). Promoting an open research culture. *Science, 348*(6242), 1422–1425. https://doi.org/10.1126/science.aab2374

Nuzzo, R. (2014). Statistical errors. *Nature, 506*(7487), 150–152. https://doi.org/10.1038/506150a

O'Shea, A., & Kaplan, A. (2018). Disability identity and use of services among college students with psychiatric disabilities. *Qualitative Psychology, 5*(3), 358–379. https://doi.org/10.1037/qup0000099

Rubin, M. (2017). When does HARKing hurt? Identifying when different types of undisclosed post hoc hypothesizing harm scientific progress. *Review of General Psychology, 21*(4), 308–320. https://doi.org/10.1037/gpr0000128

Saltzman, J. A., Musaad, S., Bost, K. K., McBride, B. A., & Fiese, B. H. (2019). Associations between father availability, mealtime distractions and routines, and maternal feeding responsiveness: An observational study. *Journal of Family Psychology, 33*(4), 465–475. https://doi.org/10.1037/fam0000519

Simmons, J. P., Nelson, L. D., & Simonsohn, U. (2012). A 21 Word Solution. *SSRN.* https://ssrn.com/abstract=2160588

Simmons, J. P., Nelson, L. D., & Simonsohn, U. (2011). False-positive psychology: Undisclosed flexibility in data collection and analysis allows presenting anything as significant. *Psychological Science, 22*(11), 1359–1366. https://doi.org/10.1177/0956797611417632

Szenczi, P., Velázquez-López, Z. I., Urrutia, A., Hudson, R., & Bánszegi, O. (2019). Perception of the Delboeuf illusion by the adult domestic cat (Felis silvestris catus) in comparison with other mammals. *Journal of Comparative Psychology, 133*(2), 223–232. https://doi.org/10.1037/com0000152

Thakral, P. P., Madore, K. P., Devitt, A. L., & Schacter, D. L. (2019). Adaptive constructive processes: An episodic specificity induction impacts false recall in the Deese-Roediger- McDermott paradigm. *Journal of Experimental Psychology: General, 148*(9), 1480–1493. https://doi.org/10.1037/xge0000577

Triandafilidis, Z., Ussher, J. M., Perz, J., & Huppatz, K. (2018). Young Australian women's accounts of smoking and quitting: A qualitative study using visual methods. *BMC Women's Health, 18*(1), 5. https://doi.org/10.1186/s12905-017-0500-1

Weber, C., Quintus, M., Egloff, B., Luong, G., Riediger, M., & Wrzus, C. (2020). Same old, same old? Age differences in the diversity of daily life. *Psychology and Aging, 35*(3), 434–448. https://doi.org/10.1037/pag0000407

Westbury, C., & Hollis, G. (2019). Wriggly, squiffy, lummox, and boobs: What makes some words funny? *Journal of Experimental Psychology: General, 148*(1), 97–123. https://doi.org/10.1037/xge0000467

Wiegand, I., Seidel, C., & Wolfe, J. (2019). Hybrid foraging search in younger and older age. *Psychology and Aging, 34*(6), 805–820. https://doi.org/10.1037/pag0000387

8 Presenting Your Project

You will find at university it is often common practice for researchers to disseminate, or share, information about the scientific work they have conducted and the results they have found to other academics in the field or to the general population. Dissemination is important to ensure that the research has a purpose: this can be to advance knowledge of other researchers but also to have an impact in areas of society or on people where there could be a benefit (known as stakeholders). Dissemination of academic work can be achieved through presentations at conferences or to colleagues in one's own institution for example, and at public engagement events to inform a general audience of the research undertaken and subsequent findings; researchers also publish their work in scientific journals and may even present a summary of their research in a blog. Dissemination of academic work is an important aspect of the research process, and how you communicate this work to your target audience is an important skill to develop during the course of your degree.

8.1 Oral Presentations

As part of your final year research project module, you may be required to present your work to a group of individuals either face-to-face or virtually, through an online meeting or event. This group could comprise your supervisor and/or other members of staff, as well as other students who may also be presenting their project work. Some institutions may require students to submit a video or audio copy of their presentation, with supporting materials, rather than to give a live presentation. You may also have the opportunity to present the work you have done for your research project at a conference. Giving a presentation is a really good opportunity to showcase all the work you have been doing on your project.

8.1.1 Think about Your Audience

It is useful to consider who your audience is from the outset, as this will impact how you will structure your presentation, the content that you will include, as well as how you present this information.

Prior to giving your presentation, you may be given information on who your audience is going to be. This is likely to be your supervisor, or other members of staff, along with your peers who may also be presenting their work. If you are presenting at a conference, the audience is likely to be bigger with diverse knowledge and research backgrounds. Although people in your audience may be knowledgeable about the general research area relating to your presentation, you are likely to know a lot more about your research project than anyone else in your audience. If you are using technical terms that may not be familiar to everyone, explaining those terms and the general context of your research can help your audience gain a better understanding of your topic and project.

Smart Solution—Overcoming Presentation Nerves

In the days leading up to my research presentation I was so nervous and kept having this recurring thought that I didn't know anything, and that someone would catch me out. Thankfully my supervisor had some great advice at this point. They reminded me that the people watching the presentation hadn't spent months reading the material I had, and that I was the expert of my specific research project. This really eased a lot of my worries as it is true—at that time, I knew more about my topic than the vast majority of people I was presenting to! They also reminded me that it is a dissertation presentation, and we aren't expected to know everything in the field... and it's ok to admit you don't know something or haven't read something!

Student, Bangor University

8.1.2 What Should I Include in my Presentation?

You will need to be selective in the information you want to convey to your audience. It is likely that you have an allocated time slot, and during that time there is only so much you can say. Decide what the important aspects of your research project are and focus on these when designing your presentation.

Your presentation can model the structure of your research report, incorporating some key points for each section. You can also find an example PowerPoint presentation in the additional online resources accompanying this textbook. Here are some key points to convey to your audience:

- You can begin by telling your audience the topic of your research project. You may want to spend some time discussing the significance of this topic and what has been done in the field. Focusing on key information, such as key theories and the most recent relevant literature can really set the scene for your audience. This is usually a brief overview of relevant literature rather than a lengthy literature review, as your audience would be most interested to find out what you have done in your project, so it may be better to keep this section of your presentation quite brief.

- Outline the rationale of your research project and what your research question(s) and hypotheses are, where relevant.

- You can then present your project: what you have done, how you have investigated this, what you found. A detailed description of your methods will generally not be needed in your presentation. Instead, focus on key aspects of your methodology that are important to convey to your audience.

- Once you have presented your findings, you can then inform your audience what these findings mean, their significance and implications, and how they fit in within the relevant literature.
- You may also briefly want to point out some limitations of your study and avenues for future research.
- It is often good practice to include an Acknowledgments section in your presentation (e.g. on the final slide) where you thank your supervisor and collaborators for their part in your project.

Consider what the important points are, and which points might be worth exploring in more detail.

8.1.3 How should I put my Presentation Together?

When giving a presentation, people often use some visual aids, such as slides shown on a projector, to support their narrative. A common way of preparing your presentation is through specialist presentation software, such as PowerPoint, Keynote, or Adobe. These visual aids should complement and support what you will be saying in your presentation. It is, therefore, important that you spend some time planning how best to present this information.

Here are some common pitfalls and helpful tips on how to avoid these:

- *Too Much Text on Slides*. Often, less is better. You want people to listen to what you have to say during your presentation rather than being busy reading through your slides. Aim for a few points on each slide and try and elaborate on each point that you are presenting. Including too much text on your slides can take away from the message you are trying to convey, and you may come across as merely reading through the slides. Aim for about three to four points on each slide. Depending on the size of those points you may decide to include fewer. Consider using the presenter notes to include information that you may want to say in your presentation but don't have space for on the slides. You should also give each slide a unique title which captures the content of that slide.

- *Use of Animations*. If you are using slides to support your presentation, you may want to consider presenting each point you are referring to in sequence, rather than presenting all points in one go, using the animations feature in your chosen software. This will make it easier for your audience to follow what you are saying and stop them reading ahead of what you are talking about. Using simple animations are often encouraged to support your delivery of the content, however, it is best to avoid more animated transitions between the different points on your slides, as these can be distracting to the audience.

- *Too Many Slides*. Try and be selective in the information you include in your presentation as you want to ensure that key points are featured and that you allocate appropriate time to explain and expand on each point presented. Having too many slides may mean that you don't have enough time within your allocated time slot to cover all the information, meaning that key points may be left out.

- As a general rule of thumb, the amount of content you could cover in your presentation should reflect what you can say in the allocated time at a pace of speech that is slightly slower than how you would normally speak with other individuals. If you find that you have to speed up your pace of delivery to stop you from going over the allocated time, then it is likely that you are including too much information on your presentation slides that will be delivered at too quick a pace for the audience to really follow what you are saying.

- *Font.* When giving a face-to-face presentation, you should consider whether everyone in the room will be able to see what you have written on your slides. Try and avoid using font size less than point 24, as this may make it difficult to read. You may want to think about including a larger font for headings or the main points you want to present, and perhaps a slightly smaller font size for other information. In terms of style, your department or institution may suggest a standard style of font to use in your presentation. Alternatively, try and choose a font style that is generally easy to read. A few examples of such font styles include Times New Roman, Verdana, Arial, or Calibri. It is also important to consider the color of font you choose in your presentation. If you are using a white or other light coloured background on your slides, a darker colour of font would be preferable as this would make it easier for your audience to see what you have written. Once you have prepared your presentation you may wish to show this to a family member or friend for some feedback on whether the information presented on your slides is easy to read.

- *Images.* You can use figures or images in your presentation, ensuring that you are citing the source of these appropriately and have permission to use them if you have not created them yourself. The use of images or figures can be particularly useful for illustrating key concepts of processes, without the need for wordy explanations on a slide. Often incorporating fewer words on a slide can make it easier for your audience to follow your presentation and the information that you are narrating. Depending on the nature of your topic, try to achieve the appropriate balance between images or figures and words as this can help to illustrate the points you wish to convey effectively. Your department may include some recommendations in their guidance about use of images or figures, including the minimum and maximum number that may be included in your presentation.

  If you are using an image in your presentation that is of contextual importance, such as a theoretical model or a graph illustrating the findings of your study, be sure to talk through this when delivering your presentation. This will probably be the first time your audience will have seen this image and it may, therefore, require some description. For example, if you are showing a graph you can talk through what the x and y axes show and explain any bars or lines featured in the graph. You may also want to draw your audience's attention to the point that shows the effect you describe, using a pointer or the mouse cursor of the computer you are using during your presentation.

See also Poster Presentations section on Design and Layout for further information on the use of images.

When creating presentations, it is important that these are designed so that they are accessible to your audience. This means that your presentation can be accessed by individuals with disabilities and specific learning difficulties. One way to help enhance the accessibility of your presentation is through the in-built Accessibility Checker in Microsoft PowerPoint. By using the Accessibility Checker (through the Review tab if you are using Microsoft Office 365) you will receive some guidance on whether your presentation contains any accessibility issues (e.g. colour contrast), and how you can fix these issues. Your department may have some guidance around enhancing accessibility of your presentation which you may want to have a look at.

8.1.4 Preparing for Your Presentation

Handy Hint
Presentations can be nerve jolting experiences. The best advice is to try to know your project inside and out. Discuss your project with friends and family, get immersed in the related research and have knowledge of the details of your design. If you know your project this well, presenting it should be a walk in the park! Also, if you are required to present your project, it is always a good idea to practise presenting it to your friends and family first!

Student, Durham University

Good preparation is crucial for a good presentation. Know your topic well and most importantly practise, practise, practise. It is really important to keep to the timing of your presentation. Practising your talk will give you an indication of whether or not you have the right amount of information and whether or not you can deliver that information within the specified time. You should stick to the time allocated and not go over that limit. When presenting at a conference, the person chairing the presentation session may indicate how much time you have left and ask you to stop presenting when your time is up. This is to allow all individuals to present their work at the specified times.

People often find that practising their presentation out loud rather than merely reading through their notes can provide a good indication of how long it may take to articulate all the information they want to convey. Practising in front of others, such as family members or friends, can also give you some confidence and provide the opportunity for you to get some feedback on your presentation.

Using notes when presenting is generally acceptable. Try and keep your notes brief rather than long pieces of text. Notes often provide some further detail on the points you present on your slides, and these can act as reminder cues during your presentation to help you expand on the topics covered in your slides. Save a copy of your presentation and try and find some time before your talk to upload your presentation on the available device, so that this is ready to go when it is time for your talk. Your supervisor or conference organizers will usually provide some guidance on how to upload any visual aids you may be using in preparation for your talk. If you are sharing your presentation with other individuals, ensure that this is labelled clearly and in accordance with any guidelines provided. For example, you could name your file as your surname and a shortened version of your title so that the file you are sharing is transparent and interpretable to others.

8.1.5 Delivering Your Presentation

Giving a presentation face-to-face, especially for the first time, can be nerve wracking. But remember, you have spent a substantial amount of time working on this project. Your audience may be knowledgeable in the general topic of your research project, but you are the expert on your project, and you are likely to know more about this than a number of individuals you will be presenting to.

It is important to try and deliver a presentation that captures your audience, that is impactful, and memorable, whether this is done face-to-face or online. Maintaining eye contact with members of the audience, or looking in their direction, is more engaging than focusing too much on the slides or any notes you may have. Adopting an appropriate pace for your delivery and pausing before moving on to the next point can help others follow the information you are providing. Rushing through the points you want to present may mean that you are not elaborating on each point sufficiently. You want to ensure that you provide sufficient explanation for your audience to gain an understanding of the information you are trying to convey.

When giving a live face-to-face or virtual presentation, it is important to speak clearly and at the appropriate volume. Often people disengage if they cannot hear the speaker clearly. You can begin by asking the audience whether they are able to hear you clearly, especially if you are using a microphone.

You can use any notes you may have prepared to accompany your presentation to remind yourself of the key points you want to convey to your audience; however, it is important that you look at the audience to avoid giving the impression that you are reading from your notes. Often practising your presentation may mean that you have to rely less on your notes. You may find it helpful to read through any sections of your report which you may have written up to the point of your presentation, and other notes you may have, ahead of your presentation as a reminder of the work you have done on your research project.

> **Handy Hint**
> I used to think that presentations were something to 'get over with' or 'get through' but after chatting with my supervisor I learnt that it's actually a really exciting opportunity. It's a chance to teach others about your research area, pretend to be a hot shot researcher, and also show off what you've been working really hard on! So jazz up your slides, pop on a smart shirt, and have fun with it!
>
> Student, Bangor University

8.1.6 Dealing with Questions

After you have given a presentation, it is quite common to have a question and answer (Q&A) session. Members of the audience are likely to want to find out more about certain aspects of your research. They may also offer some suggestions on further points you could think about in relation to your research project. If your presentation precedes the submission of your written report, these suggestions could also help you in writing up your project.

The Q&A part of the presentation is often what most people feel apprehensive about. You want to be prepared for your presentation as much as possible and to really know your topic. However, sometimes people do get questions that they are not sure how to answer. Take some time to think about the question and reflect on what you have done and know about the topic. It is ok to reply to a question saying that you have not thought about the specific point raised and that it serves as a good suggestion to consider in the future. You are expected to know your topic, but you are certainly not expected to know *everything* there is to know about the topic. You may find it helpful to think of some questions the audience could ask ahead of your presentation and think of some answers to those questions. Similarly, you could also ask some friends to ask you some questions on your presentation which you can verbally answer as a way of practising.

Think of presentations as a really good opportunity not only to showcase all the work you have done over the course of your research project, but also as an opportunity to develop and practise a key transferable skill that you may need in the future. Many graduate jobs will require you to give presentations and communicate about your work to a general audience. Students often agree that it is positive to gain experience of presenting in a supportive environment with the opportunity to get some constructive feedback.

FUTURE FOCUS Building Your Confidence With Oral Presentations

Having to deliver an oral presentation is something which takes many students out of their comfort zone; however, it is a great chance to practise and build your confidence in this important skill. Being able to present effectively to an audience can be a deciding factor in securing a job and is something that is expected across a wide range of professional environments. Although it may seem scary at first, take advantage of this opportunity during your project and use any feedback you get to help you perfect your public speaking!

8.2 Poster Presentations

A poster may initially seem like a strange way to present your project; however, the medium of posters is as common as oral presentations at research conferences. Conferences are places where a large number of researchers will come together and share their findings, challenge each other, and build networks.

Figure 8.1 shows a poster presentation session in progress at the 2009 Society for Neuroscience conference. The image shows a snapsnot of a room set up for poster presentations.

Posters are a good way to transmit information in a way that can be easily understandable for the reader and is concise. There is only so much that can be included on a poster so choosing that information is key, as is presenting it well. Good posters can be like pieces of artwork, while bad posters would generally be passed by (at a conference at least).

Because posters can be used to assess a range of learning outcomes, they may be part of the assessment for your research project module. This section will guide you through constructing a good poster.

Figure 8.1 A Poster Session at the Society for Neuroscience Conference. From Pascal Wallish. Pascal's Pensées. https://pensees.pascallisch.net/?p=257

8.2.1 **Content**

On a poster, you are limited physically with the amount of information you can include. This means you really need to think about the key points related to your research and select those that a reader will need in order to understand your research.

You will definitely need to include:

- Title
- Background info (introduction)
- Method
- Results
- Conclusions (discussion)
- References

You can see that these suggestions tie in directly with the format of the written report. Generally, you will need to include something from each area of the report on the poster. Avoid just copy-pasting text from your report on to the poster. This could be classed as self-plagiarism and might be academic misconduct, depending on your institution's guidelines. Principally, posters are a different way of presenting information to a report, and you need to adapt the text to be suitable.

Title

This is probably the same title as you have in your report, but you could use a different title if you needed to make it shorter. For example, the title of a report could be 'effects of number of shared features between targets and distractors on visual search' but for your poster you might go for a shorter title such as 'visual search and shared features between items'. The title is likely the first thing people would look at, so it is appreciated if it is easy to read quickly.

Background information

This is where you will need to be really selective. After a few months of searching the literature, you will have many articles, book chapters, books, and so on that have formed the basis of your literature review. The main point to get across here is why you conducted your study. What does the literature say? Is there a gap in knowledge? Was a replication needed? Perhaps you could choose two or three core research papers that have been the inspiration for your research and cite those. Some departments may specify a maximum number of references you can use.

Include your research question, aim, or hypotheses. Try to make a very clear statement about what your question, aim, or experimental hypotheses was/were.

Method

In this section, you could be a little more creative than you might be when writing a report. Maybe it would be easier to represent the stimuli and/or procedure with a diagram rather than by writing it out. If you have many stimuli, then just choose one or two images that represent the others. If you include a measure that has been published or has restrictions around use, then you should gain permission before adding it to your poster. You should write this section in enough detail that a reader can understand what you did.

Results

Unless you need to represent your results in number format then a graph is probably the best way to present results on a poster. Make sure that you follow formatting rules here so that a reader can understand what your graph represents. Triple check that you have labelled your axes and legend correctly.

Summarize any analyses concisely. If you have done lots of analyses, then choose the ones that show results in relation to the hypotheses you have identified in the introduction section. If you have lots of results to report, think about dedicating more space on your poster to results than other sections. Readers will be most interested in what you found compared to other sections of the poster.

Conclusions/discussion

State what you found in relation to your hypotheses and summarize if this generally fits in with current theories or literature.

References

Remember to include your list of references. Check your department's guidelines on how to format references as you might be able to use numeric referencing. This is where instead of citing an author and a date you insert a number where this would go and then number your reference list. This style of referencing saves words and space.

Handy Hint

Always think of the narrative and order in the poster itself, as well as the work as a whole. What are you doing, why, how did you answer these important questions? Can you illustrate this graphically and refer to it as you present? Can you concisely summarize the material (if not, do you understand it sufficiently)?

Student, King's College London

8.2.2 Formatting

As with your report, it is important that your poster is neatly presented. Try to follow formatting guidelines (e.g. American Psychological Association (APA)) when including figures and tables. A well-presented piece of work shows that you have attention to detail and take a level of pride in your work.

Text

Like slides, for an oral presentation, posters need to be readable from a distance. Generally, the title is positioned at the top of the poster and should be readable from 2 metres. For the title you could use 140-point font on A0 size paper and use size 96-point font on A1 paper. Any sub headers should be readable from 1 metre away. Avoid using a font size less than 28 point for text. Use the same font across the whole poster.

Avoid very long sentences and try to keep your writing concise and clear. Remember to spell out any acronyms you use as your reader will not necessarily know them. You could use bullet points to present text.

Figures

When presenting the poster, you will probably find the most useful sections on your poster are the method and results section and you'll use the figures you have there to help explain what you did and found. Unless you are told otherwise, format your figures in APA style (see Chapter 7). Make sure the text is large and clear enough and make sure that any graphs are clear and accurate.

You may need to include logos of your institution and department along with any labs, institutions, or funding bodies you have worked with. Make sure these are clear and readable and used in line with any guidance in terms of their use.

> **Handy Hint**
> When creating a good poster presentation, it is helpful to have a proficiency with MS Office and other graphic tools, an understanding of the basics of colour theory—palettes, content organizing into columns or rows, or at the very least sections. Is it legible? Is it clear? Is there sufficient—but not too much—contrast?
>
> Student, King's College London

Design and layout

You may be able to choose the design and layout of your poster. If so, you can position your poster to be portrait or landscape. Either way is likely to be fine, but you should check any requirements set by your department. Some departments may also specify what the poster size should be and what font size to use and some may have a template you can use. Figure 8.2 shows some examples of how you could lay out the sections of your poster. Don't feel limited by these though, you can be creative as long as you present all the important details about your study.

We find it easiest to create posters in PowerPoint (or other similar presentation software). Presentation software is good for creating posters because you can change the size (choose Custom Slide Size in the Design tab) of the page to fit the poster size needed. To set up an A0 poster, set the size to 84.1 cm x 118.9 cm and for A1 set the size to 59.4 cm x 84.1 cm. Presentation software is also much more flexible in terms of laying out text, diagrams and other figures. Make sure to schedule in time for formatting of a poster as sometimes this can take as long as the actual writing of the content.

Try to avoid filling every space on the poster with text. It is very tempting to try and get as much text on a poster as possible but that is not really the idea of a poster. When you are laying out text and figures try to be precise as this can really improve the overall look of a poster. Make sure that any margins are equal around all sides of the poster. You'll likely have a few text boxes so make sure they line up. Most editing software has some useful tools you can use to help this, such as aligning objects to each other or the page. Using the gridlines on the software can also be useful for lining up and spacing objects. For example, any lines drawn as borders could be placed over gridlines, and the gridlines can help you create objects of similar sizes and align objects. There is a tool on most software called 'snap-to grid' which can also help with this. Other things that can improve the look of a poster are being consistent in use of font size; so, using the same size for all section headers on the poster and using the same size font for paragraph text.

You will need to think about colour choices if you are printing your poster in colour. Generally, it is best to have the background a light colour with a darker colour for the text. You might want to use colour to highlight certain aspects of your poster, for example figures in the method and on graphs. Be aware of what colours you choose and don't rely on colour for making distinctions (e.g. between data lines on a graph) as some people won't be able to see the difference. There are various colour combinations that you could use. A simple combination is colours that are opposite on the colour wheel (for example blue and orange). Another

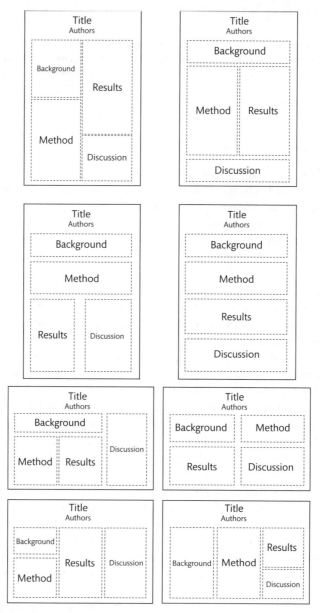

Figure 8.2 Examples of Layout for a Poster

combination to try is colours that sit next to each other on the colour wheel (for example purple and blue). For more detail and examples of colour combinations see this page from Canva https://www.canva.com/learn/100-color-combinations/ (Kliever, 2022).

You could use pictures or photographs on your poster to make it more appealing. However, make sure to choose these carefully so that they add something to the communication of your message. Avoid sticking in random pictures for decoration and check guidelines from your department as they might have specified a maximum number. Make sure that you have permissions if you are using images that belong to someone else. Using your own photographs or creating your own images might be the easiest thing to do if you can't get permissions. You can use Google image search to find pictures you are able to use; filter the search using the 'Tools' to 'Creative commons licenses' (but make sure to double check the licence before using a picture as you may still need to provide some attribution). There are also free image websites like unsplash.com, pexels.com, and burst.shopify.com that you could get images from.

Printing

You may be required to print your poster on large-scale paper, which you won't be able to do with a standard printer. Usually, your institution will offer printing services which can do this for you for a charge.

> **FUTURE FOCUS Creating Digital Content**
>
> Graduate employers often look for applicants who are proficient in working with technology in creative and innovative ways. Making a poster or materials for a presentation gives you an excellent opportunity to hone your skills in creating digital content. Whether this is creating effective visuals that capture and engage a passing audience, embedding multimedia content to accentuate your slides, or producing a video to showcase your presentation, you are demonstrating an ability to use software effectively to communicate complex information.

8.2.3 Presenting Your Poster

At conferences, the author of the poster stands next to their poster to engage people and talk to them about their research. You may or may not have to do this depending on what your department requires you to do. Instead of presenting in person, you may be required to submit an audio file in which you present your poster.

In live sessions where you present your poster, it is quite common for people's first question or comment to be something like "tell me about your research". This could be off-putting unless you have prepared something to say, so prepare a short summary of your research. Outline the general topic area and say what your aims were, mention your hypotheses, say how your study was conducted, and finish up by saying what you found and what you think it means. You could prepare summaries of different lengths (e.g. 2 mins, 5 mins) to practise adapting your communication to different audiences. Be aware that the person may interrupt you during your talk and ask questions. You could take along A4 copies of your poster and hand them to anyone who is interested in your work.

8.3 Coping with Nerves

Presentations, whether they are given as a longer oral talk or as a poster, can be situations that make people feel nervous. If you feel trepidation about giving a presentation, the first thing to be aware of is that you are not the only person who feels like this, and it is possible to control the situation to reduce your nerves. Preparation is key (as you will have read from some of our Handy Hints). There are different thoughts around preparation, some people say it is best to practise everything that you are going to say, and other people say you should practise only the beginning and have a general idea of what you want to say in the middle. Go with whatever makes you feel most comfortable. It is the run-up to the presentation that can be most nerve-wracking. In this time, try practising your presentation out loud. Speaking out loud feels really different to going through what you are going to say in your head. You could ask a friend or a family member to listen to you practise your presentation. They will generally be very supportive so it could be a real confidence boost too.

In an oral presentation, remember that your experience sometimes feels different to the one the audience has. As a speaker, you might feel nervous and sometimes feel like there are dozens of thoughts going around your head as well at the same time as trying to give your planned speech. Things like pauses seem to last a long time to you but will not be noticeable to the audience. Audiences are forgiving, they will not mind if you forget something (and since you are the only person who knows what you wanted to say they probably won't even know!) or if you need to pause. There is some interesting research from psychology that give us more tips about presentations (Box 8.1).

BOX 8.1 Tips from Psychology Research About Giving Presentations

Here are a couple of resources based on psychology research about dealing with anxiety when speaking in public.

15-step tutorial on public speaking—Patrick Friman (https://doi.org/10.1007/s40614-014-0009-y)
Patrick is a clinical psychologist and holds the view that fear is a natural aspect of speaking in public and we should learn to speak whilst being afraid. This guide includes:

- Prepare, prepare, prepare
- Stand up straight and smile
- Use slides—do not let them use you

How to stand out: proven tactics for getting noticed—Rob Yeung
Rob is a psychologist who uses findings from psychology research to help other people improve their performance. A couple of ideas from his book include:

- Reappraising anxiety as excitement

  Tell yourself you are excited to give a presentation. This may help you give a good presentation (see Brooks, 2014).

- Remind yourself of the illusion of transparency

Presenters think the audience can tell how nervous they are, but this is not true. Research shows that reminding yourself of this illusion is beneficial to your presentation (see Savitsky & Gilovich, 2003).

References

Brooks, A. W. (2014). Get excited: Reappraising pre-performance anxiety as excitement. *Journal of Experimental Psychology: General, 143*(3), 1144. https://doi.org/10.1037/a0035325

Savitsky, K., & Gilovich, T. (2003). The illusion of transparency and the alleviation of speech anxiety. *Journal of Experimental Social Psychology, 39*(6), 618–625. https://doi.org/10.1016/S0022-1031(03)00056-8

Yeung, R. (2015). *How to Stand Out: Proven Tactics for Getting Noticed.* John Wiley & Sons.

Some people find poster presentations a little less nerve-wracking than conventional oral presentations because they are unlikely to be speaking to a lot of people at one time. However, others may find that speaking in some detail with only one or two people is still a daunting experience. One advantage of speaking with only one or two people at a time is that if you don't understand their questions or comments then you can ask them to elaborate or explain a little further. You can ask them what their thoughts are about your study and whether they would have come to the same conclusion as you.

8.4 Communicating Your Research to the Public

As part of your research project, you may be asked to write a piece in which you describe your research to the public. Public engagement with science is becoming ever more important and commonplace. Researchers in universities now publish their articles with open access, which means that anyone should be able to access and read the article without having to pay for it. While this is a great practice, writing shorter pieces especially for the non-scientific community is valuable as it may be that such pieces are more likely to be read and can be distributed and accessed easily. Writing for different purposes gives you a new skill and shows that your writing skills are adaptable, that you can communicate in many ways, and helps your own understanding and gives you the opportunity to think critically about the research.

8.4.1 **Jargon**

Writing for a non-science (lay) audience is essentially about cutting jargon. Jargon is all the words that have a particular meaning in psychology or science but may mean something else (or nothing at all!) to someone not studying psychology. Removing jargon might be harder than it initially seems. This is to some extent because you now understand what the jargon means, and it has become part of your day-to-day language. For example, consider the word 'stimulus'. The *Oxford English Dictionary* (2000) defines this as 'stimulating property, action, or effect'. However, the Oxford *Dictionary of Psychology* (Colman, 2009) has seven definitions specific to psychology. One of these being 'any event, agent, or influence, internal or external, that excites or is capable of exciting a sensory receptor and of causing a response in an organism'. The point is that someone not studying psychology or science will have a different idea from you about what you are referring to when you talk or write about stimuli. Another word commonly used in science with a very specific meaning is 'significant'. Often, in research papers we will use this to mean that a value or finding is statistically significant. Using 'significant' in another way, such as meaning 'important', in a research report can be confusing. Because of this potential confusion surrounding the use of 'significant', we would advise you to avoid using it at all, particularly in short pieces of writing.

8.4.2 **Style**

Writing for a non-psychology audience doesn't mean that you can abandon scientific writing practices completely as you should still be careful in your wording and be precise in writing and make sure you have chosen the correct words for what you are trying to convey. Avoid making generalizations and overstatements when trying to summarize your research; a reader should be able to understand your findings if you explain them properly.

Some other useful tips include:

- Making sure your writing is straightforward/simple. Don't use words that are used infrequently in day-to-day conversation. Instead, try to use the simplest word you can think of.
- Using short sentences to enhance readability.
- Providing definitions. Sometimes you may need to include specific terms and if so, you should explain any terms you need to use.
- Using active rather than passive language. For example, 'we used an eye tracker to measure where people looked' rather than 'an eye tracker was used'. This may feel odd at first as you are probably more used to writing in the third person or in a passive way; however, it is important to scrutinize your writing for such phrases as they may make your reader feel distant.

Smart Solution—Writing For Non-experts

One element I found particularly difficult when writing for a public audience was ensuring I was clear and explained the variables and terminology in enough detail for understanding but not so much it took away from my research and became boring. The best advice to overcome this is use your friends and family! Ask them to read your definition or explanation of your work and see if they are unclear/unsure about what you're talking about or about anything you haven't explained. Working with psychology terminology for over three years and with professionals in the field means there is a tendency to gloss over certain phrases or words. I had to explain to my mum that 'DV' meant 'Dependent Variable' and what it meant throughout my work!

Student, Royal Holloway University of London

8.4.3 Types

There are different pieces that may constitute writing for the public. Here we will go through some, but you may come across others at your own institution or see others in the public domain. Each piece may have a particular audience in mind, but they all are writing for people who are not experts in the topic that is being written about.

Lay abstract

One type of piece that you may be asked to write is a lay abstract. The idea of this is the same as an abstract that you would write for your report but with any scientific jargon stripped out. It should contain the key ideas related to your research: a relevant statement of the background of the research, your aims or predictions, a statement of the methodology that was used and the participants, an overview of the main results and a conclusion to explain what the results mean. If your abstract is successful, then anyone should be able to read it and gain an understanding of what you did. To test this, you could try giving your abstract to friends on different courses or to your family to read and see if they can understand it.

Consider the following abstract from a published paper by Whitt and Robinson (2013) about how spacing learning trials can help memory:

Rodents' biased exploration of a novel object over a familiar object is taken as an indication of recognition memory. According to a general associative model of memory, the biased exploration is a consequence of reduced processing of the familiar object. A component of the reduction of stimulus processing is the result of the operation of Arena --> Object associations that are best formed during widely spaced presentations of the stimulus. Results of extant experiments support this prediction but so, too, do accounts based on the effects of handling cues. We report an experiment in which handling cues are matched across stimulus-spacing treatments but that retain improved recognition memory with widely spaced stimulus presentation.

The ideas behind this experiment are fairly straightforward, but this may not be obvious from the abstract that has been written for the journal readers. Here is the abstract rewritten for a lay audience.

Recognition memory in rodents is often studied by comparing the amount of time the animal spends exploring a familiar and a new object. We find that rodents generally spend more time exploring the new, or novel, object compared to the object that is familiar. We can explain this bias using processes that are outlined in a model of memory. The model outlines the idea that the attention paid by the animal to the familiar object is less than that paid to the novel object. This difference in attention could in part be due to an association or connection that has been made between the environment and the familiar object. This association is best created when the animals are placed in the environment with the objects multiple times with a gap in time between the placements, known as spaced presentation.

In other studies that have investigated this with rodents, the researchers have picked up (handled) the animals a different number of times depending on whether the animal was shown objects in a massed fashion or a spaced fashion. Handling may affect how the animals processed the objects they saw. In the study we report here, we have made sure that all the animals were picked up (handled) the same amount of times. We found that memory was better when objects had been presented spaced out rather than massed together.

The main points to note are that the version for the lay audience contains a greater amount of active language and words and phrases have been simplified and explained in more detail.

Blog

Blog posts are becoming more common as a method of assessment across many modules and not just research projects. A blog post is a short opinion or summary piece that is published online. Blogs should be short, easy to read, and direct. Blogs often have a title, but this will be much shorter than a title that you would use for a report. An example of good blog-style writing is the British Psychological Society (BPS) *Research Digest*. You can read the posts online (https://digest.bps.org.uk/) and you can sign up to have a newsletter emailed to you every week. Generally, posts focus on one research article and summarize the research as well as providing some critical thoughts about the research (which is why it is good for a general read as well as for an example of a blog post). You could see if your department or institution has a research blog, and if so you might even be able to see your supervisor's work there.

The tips we have given for the lay abstract apply when you are writing a blog post too. Blog posts are generally a little longer which gives you the chance to provide more detail and explanation about a topic. With longer pieces of writing you may have to incorporate techniques for keeping your reader interested, such as using pictures and separating the writing into sections.

Press release

Another piece that students are sometimes required to produce are press releases. Press releases are generally written by a company's external relations department to announce news or ground-breaking research (in the case of universities). They are generally focused on one research finding or article and provide a bit more detail than you would see in an abstract. They may also contain quotes from the researcher. Press releases will generally be very positive about the research they are reporting. Try searching for the press releases from your institution to see some examples.

Tweet

Twitter is a social media platform where people can post very short pieces of writing called tweets. Tweets are very short statements, so if you are tasked to write a tweet about your research then you will need to really think about what you want to say. Research is generally

Figure 8.3 Tweet from News from Science (2019)

all about your findings and what you have contributed to the research area so an informative tweet might provide a clear statement of findings that is written without jargon. See Figure 8.3 for an example of a tweet that summarizes some research findings.

An advantage of the online methods of communicating research is that you can attach a picture or link to another website to your piece. This can help to capture the attention of possible readers and make your piece more interesting. You just would need to make sure that you have the correct permissions for using the picture or image. Using your own photos is an easy way to ensure you are allowed to use them.

Summary

Communicating your research to an audience is an important part of the research process and oral and poster presentations are very common events for researchers. Presentations give you the opportunity to be excited about your research, engage other people with it, and show what you have done. They are a great way to evidence the fact that you can speak in public. Practising really helps, and overall try to enjoy it!

 Go online to access further resources for the text:
www.oup.com/he/whitt1e.

References

Colman, A. (2009). *A Dictionary of Psychology* (3rd edn). https://doi.org/10.1093/acref/9780199534067.001.0001

Kliever, J. (2022). *100 Color Combinations and How to Apply them to Your Designs.* Canva. https://www.canva.com/learn/100-color-combinations/

News from Science. (2019, June, 12). It's no secret that dogs are sensitive to human emotions. But new research suggests that if an owner is chronically stressed, it can rub off on their dog as well. [Tweet].

Twitter. https://twitter.com/NewsfromScience/status/1138846820505989120?s=20

Oxford University Press. (2000). *Oxford English Dictionary.* https://www.oed.com/

Whitt, E., & Robinson, J. (2013). Improved spontaneous object recognition following spaced preexposure trials: Evidence for an associative account of recognition memory. *Journal of Experimental Psychology: Animal Behavior Processes, 39*(2), 174–179. https://doi.org/10.1037/a0031344

9 Employability and Your Project

Your research project is likely a substantial component of your degree programme. It is often a piece of work which students feel very invested in and one in which they are keen to achieve a high mark. What you may not have thought about in depth, though, is the positive impact your project can have on your employability. In fact, your research project is one of the key things that sets you, as a psychology graduate, apart from graduates of other disciplines. It is critical that you understand the ways in which your project enhances your employability to allow you to make the best use of it. Whatever stage you are at with your career planning and your project, there are steps you can take to work towards this.

This chapter will help you to identify competences you have developed through your research project, and to think about how you can apply these in a professional environment to be successful in a graduate role. It will highlight the importance of taking the time to reflect on your project experiences and will provide practical tips on presenting your skills to a prospective employer to help you secure a graduate role of your choice.

9.1 What is Employability?

'Employability' is a term you have probably heard of, and one which has come to be frequently used in the context of higher education. Lots of different ideas of what employability should refer to have been suggested; despite what many students often assume, employability is about more than simply your ability to get a job (although this is clearly an important component). In the context of the current chapter, a useful proposal of how we might think of 'employability' has been put forward by Professor Mantz Yorke (2006, p. 8) as:

> . . . a set of achievements—skills, understandings, and personal attributes—that make graduates more likely to gain employment and be successful in their chosen occupation, which benefits themselves, the workforce, the community, and the economy.

While you might see other definitions of employability that differ from this one (with more recent approaches arguably taking a broader perspective), Yorke's is useful as it

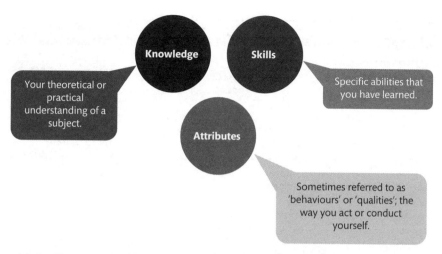

Figure 9.1 Key Elements of 'Employability', All of Which Might be Demonstrated Through Your Project

focuses on one of the most commonly agreed-upon aspects—namely, that employability comprises **competences** (skills, knowledge, and attributes; Figure 9.1) which are valuable in a professional context. The vast potential to develop and demonstrate a range of competences while doing your research project makes this aspect of your degree crucial to your employability.

Yorke's approach also highlights that the competences which are important are those which support you to gain employment and be successful in your chosen career. This tells us two key things, which will be the focus of the current chapter: (1) it is vital that you are able to identify the competences that you have developed through your research project, and (2) you must have a good understanding of how your project competences are applicable in a professional environment and how to articulate them to a prospective employer.

9.1.1 Career Options for Psychology Graduates

One of the most exciting things about studying psychology is the array of career paths open to you when you graduate; having a brief insight into the possibilities can be helpful when it comes to thinking about your relevant project skills. A very brief summary of some popular career directions, along with suggestions of how to find out more, is given in Box 9.1. Whatever stage you are at with your career planning, a brilliant place to discuss your next steps is with your institution's careers/employability service. They are there to support you on your journey towards your future career and will likely offer a range of services that can help you make the best use of your project experiences (e.g. through reflecting on the skills and knowledge you have gained, discussing how these might apply in a professional environment, and advising on how best to demonstrate these when applying for a job).

BOX 9.1 Popular Career Directions

Careers within professional psychology:

These are careers for which you typically need to be a Chartered Member of the British Psychological Society (BPS) in order to practise. They include 'traditional' applied psychology professions such as Educational Psychology, Clinical Psychology, Occupational Psychology, and Forensic Psychology, as well as newer areas such as Counselling Psychology. Many roles within academia, research and teaching also fall into this category. To pursue a professional psychology career, you will need to hold Graduate Basis for Chartered Membership (GBC) which can be achieved by completing a degree or conversion course accredited by the BPS. You will also usually need to complete further study at postgraduate level in an area of specialism.

Careers 'allied' or related to psychology:

These are roles within or directly related to psychology, which may or may not require a psychology degree qualification. Unlike the professional psychology careers mentioned previously, these do not require chartered status but will often involve working with Chartered Psychologists. Among the most popular with psychology graduates include those within health and social care, for example, Psychological Wellbeing Practitioners (PWPs), High-Intensity Therapists, Education Mental Health Practitioners, and other roles relating to mental wellbeing. Many graduates are also interested in Assistant Psychologist roles, which are typically offered in the healthcare sector (in the UK) but also exist in other fields such as education and forensic settings. In some cases, graduates choose these types of jobs as a pathway into a professional psychology career (for instance, Clinical Psychology) while others will pursue them as careers in themselves. Roles such as these can be quite competitive and will usually require some degree of work-related experience and/or postgraduate training or qualifications. There are also opportunities in newer areas of psychology such as Environmental Psychology and Coaching Psychology.

Careers outside of psychology (but where you can put psychology to good use):

These are careers that are not based in psychology in a traditional sense; however, they still allow you to make excellent use of your subject knowledge and expertise and may be strongly influenced by psychology. Interestingly, it is often reported that around 60% of graduate job opportunities do not specify a particular degree subject as a requirement. In addition, the portfolio of skills developed by psychology graduates is appealing to employers. Together, this means that if a psychology-focused career isn't for you, there are many other options available! Indeed, it has been calculated that only 15–20% of psychology graduates go on to become professional psychologists, with the remaining 75–80% pursuing other career paths (Quality Assurance Agency (QAA), 2010). According to the Prospects website (https://www.prospects.ac.uk) some of the major employers of psychology graduates include:

- marketing companies
- human resources departments
- schools and colleges
- local and national government
- social research organizations
- police forces, the National Probation Service and prisons

- commercial and industrial companies
- the media
- financial organizations
- social services
- legal firms and organizations providing advice
- the National Health Service (NHS)

Further study options:

If you're interested in pursuing a professional psychology route, you will need to do a further postgraduate (PG) qualification after your degree programme. Many graduates choose to start with a Masters' programme, which is then sometimes followed by a PG research degree (a PhD) or an applied doctoral-level programme (for example in Forensic, Clinical, Educational, or Occupational Psychology). Which course you choose to apply for will depend on your specific aspirations. In order to allow you to practise as a professional psychologist after your studies, make sure that you search for accredited PG programmes when making your applications. Of course, there are many reasons you may consider doing further study in psychology, whether you have plans to become a professional psychologist or not. You may wish to develop your knowledge and skills in a particular area as a stepping-stone to a career outside of professional psychology or simply because you have a passion for that area and are eager to learn more!

Find out more:

- The BPS website has a useful section on professional psychology career paths, including information on career options, finding accredited courses, and how to get started: https://www.bps.org.uk/find-your-career-psychology

- The Advance HE Psychology Student Employability Guide (Lantz, 2011) also gives some helpful coverage of career options for psychology graduates, as well as suggestions on career planning and decision-making.

- There are a number of valuable resources on the Prospects website which can help with your career planning whether you are interested in a route related to psychology or not. In particular, the career and job match tools available at: https://www.prospects.ac.uk/planner are helpful in exploring the types of roles which might suit you.

9.2 Identifying Competences Demonstrated through Your Project

Of all the modules in your degree programme, your research project arguably offers the best opportunity to develop valuable skills. Nonetheless, students often struggle to recognize the competences demonstrated through their project and the relevance of these to their future career. In particular, this can feel tricky for students who either intend to pursue a career outside of psychology or are unsure of their career plans: it is fairly straightforward to see the relevance of your project if you hope to become a psychology researcher; the same may not be true if your aspirations are in business or teaching or if you are yet to decide on a career direction. However, whatever your career plans—even if you have none so far—your valuable project skills should not be overlooked!

To some extent, it is true that the particular knowledge, skills, and attributes that are relevant for you will depend on your own individual aspirations. A great many competences, though, are widely applicable—that is, they will be valuable in almost any sector and role you might choose. This applies to the vast majority of skills and knowledge you develop throughout your research project. It is really worth keeping this in mind as it means that you do not need to wait until you have concrete career plans to start thinking about your skills development (indeed, it is never too early to get started). Whatever stage you are at in your career planning, your research project presents an excellent opportunity for you to develop and demonstrate a whole range of competences which are key to your employability. The important thing is that you take the time to identify your own skills and to understand their value in a professional environment. If you are coming to the end of your project or have finished already, then it is perfectly possible to do this retrospectively. However, there are many benefits to thinking about your personal and professional development early. If you are reading this chapter before embarking on your project or whilst you are doing it, then now is an ideal time to start.

Smart Solution—Moving Past Disappointment

If you are allocated a project that isn't your first choice of topic, then it can be disappointing. You may be left wondering how valuable your project will be if you cannot see a clear link between the subject area and your future career interests. Be reassured that the competences you can gain go far beyond developing a subject expertise. From project management and data analysis to team-working and resilience, your project will equip you with the skillset to take on a career of your choice!

9.2.1 Competences Valued by Graduate Employers

If you already have an idea of the type of role you might like to pursue, a good place to begin is by looking at job descriptions and person specifications of advertised roles (your institution's careers/employability service should be able to offer advice on where to search for these if you are uncertain). Doing this can be helpful as it should quickly highlight your areas of strength as well as potential areas for development. One of the biggest benefits of thinking about your skills development early is that it gives you the chance to cultivate skills before you start looking for graduate employment. It may be possible to 'fill some gaps' by making particular choices with your research project if you know what direction you would like to take after your degree. If you don't yet have firm ideas of your future career plans, then it is still extremely useful to understand what is valued by graduate employers more generally. A quick internet search on the topic will return a vast array of desirable competences, which can sometimes feel a little overwhelming. One way to simplify the task is to focus on broader 'categories' of skills which are typically highlighted by employers as important. Doing this, you might notice broad themes emerging which are sometimes expressed in terms of your ability to manage certain areas of work; specifically, employers are interested in your ability to manage: yourself, other people, information, and a task (Figure 9.2).

Hopefully, the overlap between these important areas of management and the previous chapters in this book is immediately apparent; if not, an indication of which chapters relate most closely to each area is shown in Figure 9.3. This overlap demonstrates just how applicable your project experience is to your employability. It is difficult to imagine many graduate roles where these broad skills areas would not be important to an employer. Importantly, by considering which management area your project skills fit into you should start to see how these are applicable beyond your research project and their value in a professional graduate role. Some examples of project tasks and related professional competencies that fall under each area are shown in Figure 9.3. The exact competences you have developed will vary depending on the nature of your research project and there are likely to be many others you can think of, so spend a little time thinking about your own.

Most traditional lists of what employers look for focus on the *skills* required from employees; however, recently the importance of particular personal *attributes* has also been emphasized (as mentioned in Mantz Yorke's definition of employability earlier in the chapter). Once again, your research project provides an excellent opportunity for you to demonstrate some of these attributes that employers are most keen to see, for example:

- resilience
- a positive 'can-do' attitude
- flexibility
- integrity and ethical values
- adaptability/ability to cope with change
- empathy

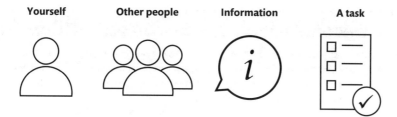

Yourself **Other people** **Information** **A task**

Figure 9.2 Areas of Management that are Likely to be Broadly Valued by Many Graduate Employers

---

Managing Yourself

e.g. creating a project action plan

[planning, self-motivation]; juggling

competing demands on your time

[prioritising workload]; looking after your

wellbeing [self-awareness, resilience].

See especially Chapter 2

Managing Other People

e.g. building a professional relationship

with your supervisor [communication,

negotiation, proactivity]; working as part

of a diverse student team [team working,

leadership]; communicating sensitively

with participants [communication,

empathy].

See especially Chapters 2, 3, 6

Managing Information

e.g. effective literature searching

[systematic approach, attention to

detail]; evaluating and thinking critically

about research [decision-making, critical

approach]; working with datasets

[analytical]; presenting information

[communication, report-writing];

ensuring confidentiality [integrity; legal

requirements].

See especially Chapters 1, 4-8

Managing a Task

e.g. defining the nature of your research

[problem formulation, creativity];

developing a design plan,

troubleshooting [problem-solving];

thinking and planning ahead [project

management]; considering ethical risks

[integrity, professional judgement].

See especially Chapters 1, 5

Figure 9.3 Examples of Tasks Carried out Through Your Project and Associated Competences

FUTURE FOCUS Identifying Your Competences

There are a whole host of skills you learn throughout the project, and many are good, transferable skills employers look for. Some of these include organization, negotiation, diligence, critical thinking, independence, communication, flexibility (for all the times something did not go quite right!) as well as professional skills such as refined statistical analysis and a development of professional interaction.

Student, Royal Holloway University of London

9.2.2 Competences Developed through Studying Psychology

So far, we have considered general competences likely to be valuable across many graduate roles and where you might find these demonstrated in your research project. This is a useful way of identifying examples of important 'generic' skills that you possess. However, equally important (and often more so) is knowing what sets you apart as a psychology graduate. If you look at Figure 9.3, you might reasonably expect a graduate from any discipline to be able to demonstrate a selection of skills from the important management areas listed (e.g. literature searching, prioritizing tasks, effective communication, and so on). In contrast, there are other competences that are more specific to a psychology degree. When thinking about your own knowledge base and skillset in relation to your employability, it is important to demonstrate valuable 'generic' competences but also critical to showcase your psychology-specific contributions. This is particularly the case for students interested in pursuing careers outside of professional psychology because employers often aren't aware of what psychology graduates can offer or what differentiates them from graduates of other subjects (Hugh-Jones & Sutherland, 2007). An effective way of identifying these subject-specific competences in your research project is to learn what knowledge and skills are expected of you as a psychology graduate and which of these are demonstrated through your project work. You can then start to think about the applicability of these competences in a professional environment.

Taking this approach, a handy resource you can refer to is the QAA *Subject Benchmark Statement for Psychology* (2019) which defines what a psychology graduate should know, understand, and be able to do by the end of their degree programme—in other words, what an employer should be able to expect of you having completed a psychology degree. Usefully, these competences are divided into 'generic' and 'subject-specific' lists so you can easily recognize those which are more likely to set you apart from non-psychology graduates. Importantly, the thing which is unique to you as a psychology graduate is an enhanced understanding of human behaviour and the ability to apply psychological theory to real-world scenarios. This can be used to great effect in a range of professional environments, whether the role is a psychology-related one or not. In addition, it has been argued that the competences developed through training as a researcher overlap a great deal with those which are sought by employers (Knight, 2004, as cited in Akhurst, 2005).

To make clearer the competences developed through your research project and their applicability in a professional role, Table 9.1 is adapted from the QAA *Subject Benchmark Statement for Psychology*. It should be immediately apparent from both the subject-specific and generic competences that these are all areas which are likely to be developed in depth as part of your project. For the subject-specific competences, indications of how these might be applicable in psychology-relevant careers and roles outside of psychology are given in the second column:

Table 9.1 Subject-Specific and Generic Competences Expected of a Psychology Graduate (Adapted from the *QAA Subject Benchmark Statement for Psychology*, 2019)

	A psychology graduate should be able to:	Example workplace application(s):
Subject-specific Knowledge/Skills	Apply psychological knowledge to real-world problems Identify and evaluate patterns in behaviour	Using psychological knowledge to interpret and manage behaviour in a work-based context (this knowledge could come from the findings of your research project or from your literature review). For example: factors affecting how children learn; interventions for wellbeing; influences on decision-making; working under stress; inclusivity experiences of working online
	Formulate and test hypotheses and research questions Use evidence-based reasoning Apply multiple perspectives to psychological issues, and integrate ideas and findings across perspectives Critically evaluate theory and research	Roles and tasks that require skills in analysing, synthesizing, and critically evaluating information and sources. For example: problem definition; business decision-making; advising policymakers/stakeholders; preparing briefs and commissioning research; writing and reviewing policy; ability to evaluate own performance and reflect
	Analyse, present, and evaluate data and research findings	Roles or tasks that require research skills in relation to aspects of human behaviour. For example: assessing the impact of business strategies; evaluating the value of interventions on wellbeing/effectiveness/productivity; monitoring and evaluating treatment outcomes; data collection, storage, and confidentiality; project dissemination, communicating complex information
	Conduct empirical studies using wide-ranging methods of data collection	
	Use specialist psychological tools, software, and equipment Conduct extensive piece of research	These skills are likely to be especially applicable to professional psychology/psychology-related roles; however, being able to demonstrate your ability to learn and use specialist tools is a skill which will be of much broader appeal to employers. For example: carrying out assessments of wellbeing, needs, behaviour, or abilities; conducting risk assessments; running statistical analyses; using bespoke in-house software In addition to the research skills indicated above, any tasks which require you to run or oversee extended pieces of work. For example: project management; planning ahead; working with a supervisor; managing work-life balance
Generic Skills	Communicate effectively Demonstrate numerical reasoning Be computer literate Retrieve and organize information effectively Recognize what is important for effective teamwork Take responsibility for own learning	

9.3 Reflecting on Your Project

It is hopefully evident that your research project provides you with the chance to develop an impressive range of competences that enhance your employability. Your project is likely to be a particularly good source of skills development in comparison with other modules you study because of the wide variety of experiences your project offers. In a typical lecture-based module, there are certainly important skills that you will develop, but the range of different experiences you might expect are relatively limited: for example, you might participate in lectures, do some reading, and perhaps plan a short piece of coursework, or prepare for an exam. Your research project, in comparison, will likely comprise a real diversity of experiences. These allow you to build up a repertoire of skills and knowledge that is attractive to an employer and will support your successful performance in a work setting. However, simply having an experience is not enough to gain benefit from it. Rather, in order to learn from an experience that you have, you need to think back on it in an analytical way that allows you to 'make sense' of what happened. This is sometimes referred to as 'reflection'. In his book, *Learning by Doing*, Graham Gibbs (1988, p. 14) explains that:

> *Without reflecting on [an] experience it may quickly be forgotten or its learning potential lost. It is from the feelings and thoughts emerging from this reflection that generalisations or concepts can be generated. And it is generalisations which enable new situations to be tackled effectively.*

This is important because it tells you that, to make use of the experiences you have whilst working on your research project, you must engage in some form of **reflection.**

In its simplest form, reflection entails thinking critically about a past experience in a way that brings meaning to it. It involves not only your thoughts about the experience but also your feelings and other people's perspectives. Reflecting allows you to pull out what you have learned from an experience, to evaluate it, and to apply your learning to future events and situations: for example, in a workplace. It should come as no surprise, then, that the ability to effectively reflect on your own experiences is a competence highly sought-after by graduate employers. Reflecting regularly on your project experiences is an important habit to get into, and one which has marked benefits not only for your academic performance but also for your employability (see Box 9.2).

FUTURE FOCUS The Value Of Reflection

Reflecting on my project has impacted my professional behaviour by emphasizing how important it is for me to start tasks early, and to break up larger projects into smaller tasks and deadlines.

Student, Royal Holloway University of London

9.3.1 **When to Reflect and on What?**

An important question is how often you should choose to reflect on your project experiences and which aspects you should choose as your focus. It is worth bearing in mind that there is no right or wrong way to engage in reflection; rather, it is a case of finding a process which works well for you. One way to approach the task might be to think about the different 'phases' or 'tasks' of your research project, and to reflect on an experience in each of these.

> **BOX 9.2 Benefits of Reflecting on Your Project**
>
> For some students, reflecting on their research project may make up part of the formal assessment for the module. Even where this isn't the case, your project offers an excellent opportunity to make use of a reflective approach. Importantly, engaging in reflection about your project experiences can have a very positive impact on your employability in a number of ways, which include:
>
> ● Graduate employers from all fields are keen to recruit individuals who can reflect on their own performance. Being able to show that you have consistently taken a reflective approach to your project work (whether your course specifically requires this or not) demonstrates this clearly and may help to set you apart from other candidates.
>
> ● **Reflective practice** is a central skill in many professional psychology roles (e.g. Clinical Psychology, Educational Psychology), as well as in some careers related to psychology (e.g. mental health roles) and others outside of psychology (e.g. school teaching). If you are interested in pursuing roles such as these, you will be expected to engage in reflective practice as a key part of your day-to-day work.
>
> ● One of the reasons employers are so interested in reflective abilities is that these are related to enhanced **self-awareness** (e.g. Boud et al., 1985). This is a key component in emotional intelligence, which you may also see listed as a valuable employability skill. Reflecting on your project experiences allows you to identify skills you have used and consider where your strengths and weaknesses lie. In turn, this enables you to make action plans to continually improve your performance (and, in the workplace, your professional practice). Whilst doing your research project, this can help you to learn from your experiences and enhance your ways of working. In a professional context, a similar approach can be critical to meeting important business objectives. Good self-awareness is also key to understanding the type of roles which may suit you and when it is time to move roles or career paths, all of which will support you to make informed career decisions.

This can be helpful as it is likely to result in you reflecting on experiences that cover a range of potential competences. Using the earlier chapters of this book (or their titles) could be a good starting point if you are unsure. For example, you might consider reflecting on:

● your literature review process

● an initial meeting with your student project group

● your project management (e.g. meeting a deadline)

● an early meeting with your project supervisor

● a testing/data collection session with participants

● your first efforts at data analysis

● an oral presentation of your project

You could use a Gantt chart (see Chapter 1 and additional online resources) to pencil in some suggested points to reflect. Because reflection is so beneficial in enhancing your performance over time, choosing early instances of repeated events to reflect on (e.g. one of the *first* meetings with your supervisor or research project team; an *initial* data collection session; and so on) means you can put what you have learned into practice throughout your project itself. Of course, you do not have to reflect on all the suggestions above, and there may be other events that you think would be valuable to you as well or instead. Try spending some time thinking about the experiences that you would benefit from reflecting on and note these down.

Another way of selecting experiences to reflect on is by using the notion of 'critical incidents' (Tripp, 1993). In this context, critical incidents are not necessarily those which are serious or risky; instead, 'critical' refers to the important or relevant nature of the situation arising. These experiences are selected for reflection retrospectively (i.e. you are unlikely to be able to plan for them) because of their unforeseen nature. Deciding what experiences constitute critical incidents is a personal decision; however, these are usually events which have unexpected elements, or differ markedly from your expectations, and which change your way of thinking or working in a significant manner. It is possible to reflect on experiences that have positive or negative outcomes, and employers will often be interested to know that you are able to do both. Some examples from a research project context that you might consider as critical incidents are:

- an early meeting with your project supervisor where you negotiated your research project topic
- setting yourself an over-ambitious project timeline so that you have to stay up late every night in the run-up to your deadline to get everything done
- finding that one member of your project group repeatedly fails to contribute in group meetings and does not complete the work you have all agreed on
- your supervisor unexpectedly having to take time off work during your project
- an oral presentation that goes very well despite your nerves in advance

Reflecting on incidents such as those listed above is useful because the potential for learning and skills development is high. Importantly, by systematically thinking about experiences such as these, plans can be made to apply learning to future situations to improve your performance. As already noted, this is a skill that will help you in any career you choose, and one which employers are keen to see. While there is no set timeframe for reflecting, it is useful to do an initial reflection soon after an event while the details are still fresh in your mind. You can then revisit this episode later to see if your thoughts and feelings on it have changed with some additional distance.

9.3.2 Reflective Writing

The idea of reflection can feel rather alien to students as it is sometimes seen as being different from other forms of academic thinking and writing that you might be more used to. However, even if you have not purposefully set out to reflect on your experiences in the past, you will probably find that you reflect informally fairly often. If you think back to a situation in which the outcome was unexpected or a problem arose which had no immediate resolution, the chances are that you reflected on it in some informal way (Moon, 2007). More formal reflection brings together thoughts, feelings, and ideas from multiple perspectives and sometimes across multiple timepoints; as such, it is often helpful to write these reflections down to help you identify themes which emerge and draw appropriate conclusions. Using some form of structure or 'framework' to guide your thoughts can make the process more straightforward. Many of these exist but one commonly used example is Gibbs' Reflective Cycle (Gibbs, 1988; see Figure 9.4).

Gibbs' Cycle comprises six steps which, together, encourage you to work through an experience in a way that helps you to learn for the future. Table 9.2 takes each stage of the cycle in more depth to show how you might develop a piece of reflective writing.

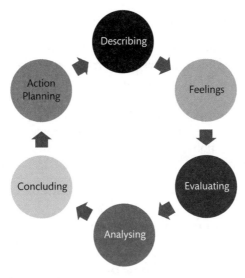

Figure 9.4 Gibbs' (1988) Reflective Cycle

Table 9.2 An Overview of the Stages of Reflection Based on Gibbs' (1988) Cycle

Description	Your reflection will typically start with a brief description of the event that occurred. Avoid reporting superfluous information and stick to a concise outline of the relevant and important details.
Feelings	Next, consider your thoughts and feelings before, during, and after the event, and how you reacted afterwards. At this point, you are still just attempting to give a description of what these were, without any further analysis.
Evaluating	Here, you can outline what went well and what went badly within the experience. Again, this is a descriptive stage where you should aim to note down positive and negative aspects without making an interpretation.
Analysing	At this point in your reflection, you will move away from pure descriptions and start trying to interpret the experience. This stage is very important as it is where you attempt to make sense of what happened and consider the causes of positive or negative aspects, i.e. what it was that led to things going well or badly. Here, you should aim to integrate perspectives from other sources and time points. For example, consider the thoughts and reactions of other individuals involved, and whether these differ from your own. You might also draw on your own feelings at multiple times after the event and think about how these have changed. If you can, this is also an excellent opportunity to use your knowledge of psychological theory to interpret the situation and factors which may have contributed to it.
Concluding	Here, you think back over your analysis and focus on what you have learned. Importantly, you should identify any new skills you developed as a result of the experience, any ways in which you might act differently in the future, and areas in which you feel there are skills you need to develop.
Action Planning	In the final stage, you draw on your analysis and conclusions to think ahead and consider what you need to do to enhance your performance in the future. Importantly for your employability, you can think here about what situations you might apply your new learning to in the future. You might also note down specific actions you will take to develop skills that will help you improve.

9.3.2.1 Using Reflective Journals and Logs to Reflect on Your Research Project

Students sometimes worry that recording their project reflections will be time-consuming; however, this does not need to be the case. Brief reflective journals or logs are an effective tool which should not take up too much time, and the benefits of reflection for your own development and employability make this a highly worthwhile investment. Writing down your reflections not only helps you engage thoroughly with the process, but also allows you to return to these at a later time. This is helpful when you come to applying for jobs, as you can refer back to your reflections in preparation for interviews and when completing application forms (more on this in the next section) to provide evidence of your competences.

Handy Hint

You will gain a wealth of valuable knowledge, skills, and experiences whilst doing your project, as well as having the chance to develop and showcase important personal attributes. These are all things which can enhance your employability and will be of interest to a future employer, but it is easy to lose track of them unless you make a record. Setting aside small amounts of time to reflect frequently across the course of your project should allow you to make the most of your experiences and could save you a lot of time in the long run when it comes to preparing for the recruitment process!

Just as there are many models of reflection and effective ways to reflect, there are also a variety of ways you could approach a reflective journal or log. Box 9.3 shows a straightforward template with headings and prompt questions based on Gibbs' Cycle, filled in with an example reflection based on a project experience. You could choose to complete your journal entries using pen and paper or as a digital version, or even publish your reflections online in the form of a blog.

BOX 9.3 Example Reflective Log Template based on Gibbs' (1988) Cycle with Reflection on a Project Experience

Date:

Description

- **What happened? When and where did it take place? Who was there?**

For my project, I've been working in a team of 4 students for the past 3 months and have been really enjoying it. We work well together as a group and had made good progress on the early stages of our project. Unfortunately, just before we were due to start data collection, a member of our team got in touch to say they need to withdraw from the project. Without their contribution, we wouldn't have enough data to effectively carry out the research we'd planned. As the remaining students on the project, we had to get together to come up with a new plan. We arranged an emergency meeting as soon as we'd heard the news and tried to brainstorm some ideas of what we could do to adapt our plans. We very quickly settled on a new approach and set out to get started the following week. However, in the intervening days it became clear that our new strategy wasn't going to work. We met as a group again after doing some research, spent a little more time discussing our options, and arranged a meeting with our supervisor to run through our new idea. We've managed to reshape our project design so that we can continue as a group of 3 and still address our research questions.

Feelings

● **What were you feeling before, during, and after the situation? How do you think other people were feeling? What were you thinking at the time of the situation? What did you think about the situation afterwards? What impact did your beliefs and feelings have?**

At the start of the project, I had been really happy with the way we were progressing and felt that we worked together very well as a group. However, when our team-mate got in touch I initially panicked! After getting in touch with the other students, I could tell that they felt the same and we were very stressed about how we could continue. I was thinking that this would have a big impact on the quality of our project and would stop us from getting such a good mark. In our emergency meeting, emotions were running very high, and it felt like we jumped to a decision without really considering all of the possibilities. I think we all just wanted to get on with things as quickly as possible as we were under so much pressure. When it became clear to me that we'd made a mistake, I was worried the others might not want to make more changes; luckily, they could see where I was coming from, and this made it easier to rethink our plans. Looking back, I'm really pleased we put in the extra time and effort and am grateful to have had such a good group to work with. In the end, our redesigned project looks to be even better than our original one!

Evaluating

● **What was good and bad about the experience? What went well and what went less well? Were your own contributions positive or negative? Were any challenges resolved?**

The main thing which went well was our ability to work together as a team, and to adapt to an unexpected situation. Obviously, losing one of our team members was challenging, and our initial response to this wasn't as good as it could have been. However, I think that ultimately, my contribution was positive. I initiated the change in direction after realizing our new plans wouldn't work, and I contributed to the redesigned project. All 3 of us in the group made sure that we looked out for each other and checked we were all happy with the way the team was working.

Analysing

● **Why did things go well/badly? How can I make sense of the situation? What knowledge/research/ theory can help to make sense of this? How does my own experience compare with the literature?**

I think our initial attempt at adapting to the change in situation went badly because we all felt that we were under so much pressure. It was clear that all 3 of us were very worried and stressed when we met, and I think this clouded our judgement. I searched for some literature on the subject and came across a review of decision-making under stress (Starcke & Brand, 2012) which helped me to understand what had happened. Some researchers (e.g. Janis & Mann, 1977) have suggested that stress can lead to 'premature closure' which is where a decision is reached before all alternatives are properly considered and weighed up. This certainly seems to be consistent with what happened in our emergency meeting. Stress also appears to be linked, in some circumstances, to decreased performance and more disadvantageous choices which might help to explain why the approach we came up with first didn't work out. In hindsight, meeting up when we were all in such a high state of worry may not have been the most effective thing to do.

However, I was really pleased with how well we bounced back from this challenge, and still feel that we worked together as a group extremely well. With the exception of the few days around where our team mate left, our progress stayed on track throughout the project and all of us very much enjoyed the experience. Our redesigned project was better in a lot of ways than our original one, and I think our success came down to our teamwork. I came across some interesting literature on 'resilient teams' (Stoverink et al., 2020) which suggested the necessary factors for teams to work well. Important contributors that I noticed in our team were a shared understanding of our team's goals and our roles within the team ('team mental model'), and a team culture of respect and openness to others' ideas ('psychological safety'). Having these team attributes, I think allowed us to flourish under difficult circumstances.

Conclusion

● **What have I learned from the situation? What can I do better now? What skills would I need to handle a similar situation better? Should I have done anything differently?**

The main thing I have learned from this situation is the importance of team resilience in allowing a group to bounce back from challenging situations. This is definitely something I would try to foster in groups I work with in the future, focusing on the factors identified by Stoverink et al. (2020); I think that this means I am now able to manage a team more effectively than I would have done previously. I have also come to understand some of the difficulties associated with working under pressure and in situations of high stress. Looking back, it would probably have been advantageous to delay our emergency meeting until we had all had time to calm down from hearing the news. This might have led to us making decisions in a calmer state of mind, and thereby encouraged us to evaluate all our options carefully before making a well-justified choice.

Action Plan

● **How can I use my new knowledge/experience? How will I develop the skills I need? What would I do differently if the same situation arose again?**

Next time I work as part of a team to produce a piece of work, I will aim to ensure that we come together as a 'resilient team'. Given the importance of a shared team mental model, I would make sure that the outset of the project included a meeting with all team members in which we agree upon our key goals and the role of each member. I would then aim to meet periodically to allow individuals to share updates on their activities and to reflect on the progress of the team towards our goals.

In instances of unexpected circumstances, I would take more seriously the impact of stress on my own and others' ability to plan and make good choices. If a similar situation arose, I would allow some time for initial emotions to dissipate before trying to make important decisions. Understanding the effects of stress on work-based performance will also be useful more broadly as it can help to explain and predict situations where myself or colleagues might make less than optimal decisions.

Another important factor in good teamwork identified through my literature search was 'team psychological safety'. This allows members of a team to voice their opinions and ideas without the fear of being embarrassed or rejected. I would like to develop my skills further in encouraging this sort of team dynamic, and plan to attend a workshop on 'Developing Interpersonal Skills for Teamwork' which is being run by the Uni Careers Service next month.

9.4 Expressing Your Project Competences to an Employer

The unique combination of competences psychology students develop is very attractive to employers. However, despite having a range of relevant skills, knowledge, and attributes, employers frequently report that these are not articulated well during the recruitment process. It is important to remember that many employers will not have an in-depth understanding of what a psychology degree entails or what you can offer as an applicant; it is down to you to tell them. While it may be obvious to you that psychology students complete an independent research project, the same may not be true for an employer. Carrying out a project of this nature is one of the key things that sets you apart from graduates in other disciplines. Having identified the competences you have developed it is critical that you are also aware of how to articulate these to a prospective employer.

9.4.1 Evidencing Your Project Competences

One of the most important aspects of expressing your project competences well is the ability to draw on relevant **evidence** from your experiences. Just as in an academic essay you provide evidence in support of your statements, during the recruitment process you need to offer evidence of your competences. It is not sufficient to simply say that you have excellent communication skills or are a great team-player; an employer will want to know about specific examples from your past experiences that demonstrate this. Here we can see the benefit of having recorded reflections from your project experiences as you go: these provide an ideal source of specific examples to back up your competences. Your evidence and the way in which you have learned from experiences through reflection is what will persuade an employer that you can perform effectively in the future should they choose to hire you.

Keep in mind that the language used by employers when recruiting for a job (e.g. on a job description or person specification) may be unfamiliar, so don't panic if it initially seems that they are looking for something you haven't demonstrated. Spend some time thinking about your project experiences, and how they might be more broadly conceived of. For example, if you have conducted your research project with a co-supervisor from another department, this might provide evidence of working in multi-disciplinary teams; recruiting participants from a local primary school demonstrates that you can build relationships with external stakeholders. Remember to take advantage of your institution's careers/employability service to help you make the best use of your project experiences.

9.4.2 Expressing Project Competences in Interviews and Application Forms

Different organizations vary in how they recruit candidates for opportunities. The exact process you're required to go through will depend on the nature of the employer and the role. Nonetheless, most jobs you apply for will ask you to fill in an application form and/or attend an interview at some stage. During this stage of the recruitment process, an employer is trying to understand:

- why you want the role
- what makes you the best person for the role
- how well you would fit into the organization

It is down to you to use the questions you are asked to showcase your competences in their best light. As well as having an in-depth knowledge of your own competences, it is critical that you do your research on the organization and role you are applying for. This will allow you to make clear links between your skills and the requirements of the role.

9.4.2.1 Open Questions

Towards the beginning of an application form or interview, employers typically ask fairly open-ended questions, for example:

- *"Why should we hire you for this role?"*
- *"What skills, knowledge, or attributes do you bring?"*

These can feel rather daunting but are an excellent chance to highlight your most relevant project competences, especially those that you might not specifically get asked about otherwise. For many types of role, employers are unlikely to ask questions specific to a particular discipline. It is therefore easy for them to miss what sets you, as a psychology graduate, apart unless you tell them. Open questions are your opportunity to highlight relevant knowledge and skills developed through your research project that an employer might otherwise be unaware of. As we saw earlier in the chapter, what is unique to psychology graduates is an enhanced understanding of human behaviour and an ability to apply psychological theory to real-world contexts. In addition, your project provides you with extensive research training that develops a host of valuable skills. These are elements you will probably want to emphasize in answers to this type of question, drawing on your project where appropriate.

Of course, for some students, the 'match' between the role they are applying for, and the topic of their research project will be much closer than for others. Even when there isn't a strong subject match, the broader skillset your project develops (e.g. working with datasets, presenting complex information, project management, critically evaluating sources) will be invaluable in a professional context. Table 9.3 includes some indications of how you could use your project competences to set yourself apart whether or not your project topic has direct relevance to the job role.

Other open questions you could approach in a similar way include:

- *"Why do you think you will be successful in this role?"*
- *"What can you bring to the role?"*
- *"Why are you the best person for this job?"*

What you are trying to get across in your answer is what you can offer as a psychology graduate that an applicant from another discipline would not be able to offer; your research project is likely to be an important part of that. Keep in mind that answers to this sort of question will likely draw on examples from across your degree programme as well as extra-curricular activities, work experience, and so on in addition to your project. You need to select which of your project competences to discuss in the context of the rest of your answer. Also, remember your audience when explaining details of your project and tailor your language accordingly. If you are applying for a job outside of psychology, the information on presenting your research project to lay audiences (Chapter 8) may be useful to revisit.

9.4.2.2 Competency-Based Questions

Another type of question commonly used in applications forms and interviews are competency-based questions. These are intended to evaluate your skills, knowledge, and attributes directly in relation to the requirements of a given job and are used by employers to determine whether you are likely to be able to perform successfully in the role you are applying for. An example of a competency-based question is:

- *"Give me an example of a time where you solved a problem in a creative way".*

The important thing to be aware of with competency-based questions is that the answer you give should make reference to a *specific* experience you have had and what you have learned from it. As mentioned already, your research project is an excellent source of

Table 9.3 Examples of Project Topics and How to Apply the Knowledge and Skills Developed to Applications/Interviews

Example research project topic	Example job role(s)	Aspect of project to focus on in your answer
The impact of isolation on mental wellbeing.	Mental health research assistant looking at factors contributing to wellbeing; charity officer working to improve the lives of isolated individuals (i.e. a role with a close match to the project topic).	Highlight your **psychological knowledge**. Where the findings of your research project have direct relevance to the role you are applying for, make sure you highlight this. Explain what your project investigated and found, and how your results apply to the real-world context relevant to the role. Emphasize how the new understanding from your findings might enhance your practice/performance at work.
Predictors of job satisfaction amongst teachers.	Human Resources Officer; Office Manager (i.e. a non-psychology role with some overlap with project topic).	Highlight your **psychological knowledge**. Where your research project topic is not directly relevant to the job role you're applying for, you may still have developed valuable knowledge through your literature review. Explain what you learned through your reading of the literature and how you would apply your psychological knowledge within the job role to enhance your practice.
Biases in decision-making	Clinical psychology research assistant; Social researcher; Statistician; Market researcher (i.e. a research role in an area unrelated to the project topic).	Highlight your **psychology-specific research skills.** In particular, what sets you apart as a Psychology graduate, is an ability to investigate and understand human behaviour through conducting research and interpreting data. Outline the research skills you have demonstrated during your research project, and how you might use these in the role you are applying for.
Factors affecting speed of visual search	Digital marketing assistant (i.e. a non-research role in an area unrelated to the project topic).	Highlight your **skills from conducting an extensive piece of work**. Even where it seems that your psychology-specific skills are not directly applicable to the job role, make sure you emphasize skills which graduates from other disciplines may not have. Importantly, not all degree programmes include an extensive independent piece of research, which demands skills in project-management, planning, report-writing, and so on. These are things to be highlighted. In addition, you can draw on more generic skills that you developed in depth as part of your research project (e.g. attention to detail; teamwork; analytical skills, and so on).

examples because of the diverse range of experiences involved and associated skills and knowledge that you develop. To structure your answer to competency-based questions, a useful technique you can apply is the STAR method (see Figure 9.5).

According to this technique, your answer should first start by describing the **situation (S)** or context, followed by explaining the exact **task (T)** involved in your example. Next, you

Figure 9.5 The STAR Method for Answering Competency-Based Questions

need to outline what you did and what steps of **action (A)** you took: this is the key part where you demonstrate your competences to the employer and should make up the bulk (about 70%) of your answer. Finally, you need to describe the outcome or **results (R)** of your actions and discuss your **reflections** on the experience: this is your chance to demonstrate how the experience has set you up to excel in the role you have applied for. The use of this technique is often suggested as it ensures that you cover all of the relevant points that an employer would be interested to see without straying into unnecessary detail. An example answer using the STAR technique in response to a competency-based question is given in Box 9.4.

The similarities of this structure with Gibbs' (1988) Reflective Cycle (Figure 9.4) should hopefully be clear. This overlap emphasizes how valuable recording reflections on your project experiences can be, not only in developing your competences but also in your preparations for the recruitment process. Doing so will provide you with readymade examples of evidence to refer back to which are presented in a very similar format to that required by competency-based questions on an application form or interview. Indeed, even when questions are not phrased to refer to a specific example, it is often still useful to mentally reframe the questions and apply the STAR approach in your answer to ensure that you cover all important elements. For example:

> **Question:** *"How do you prioritize your work?"*
>
> **Reframe as**: *"Give me an example of a situation in which you were required to prioritize competing demands to meet a tight deadline"*.

9.4.3 **Making the Best of Obstacles**

Because of the nature of a research project, you are almost certain to experience bumps in the road at some point or another. While these can feel very challenging at the time, the good news is that experiences such as these are often excellent from an employability perspective! Not only do obstacles offer a great opportunity for skills development (e.g. problem-solving, negotiation, and so on), they are also an ideal chance to demonstrate valuable personal attributes that an employer might be interested in (e.g. adaptability, resilience, positive attitude, integrity/honesty). Although some competency-based questions relate to experiences which may have been largely positive (e.g. *"tell me about a time where you have successfully led a team"*), many incorporate at least some challenging element. The way you have

BOX 9.4 Example Answer to Competency-based Question Using the STAR and Drawing on a Project Experience

Question: *"Tell me about a time when you adapted to a change outside of your control"*.

"In the final year of my degree programme, I carried out a year-long research project investigating the links between personality and donating to charity. The project involved designing a research study, recruiting and testing a sample of student participants, collecting and analysing a large dataset, and writing up a report of the findings in the context of the current literature. To do this, I worked as part of a small team of students. Unfortunately, just before we were due to start collecting data, one of our team was forced to withdraw. Without them, we were not able to run the research in the way we had hoped to."

Situation: here you have the opportunity to give a few relevant details about your research project. Remember that lots of employers will not know what studying psychology entails; this is a chance to highlight key aspects which emphasize your employability.

"The rest of us had to quickly come up with an alternative approach which would still allow us to address our original research questions. Designing the original study is something which had taken months to plan, so we were now under a huge amount of pressure to complete many tasks in a very short timeframe. As the research project is such an important component of our degree programme, it is something that all of us were very invested in and we knew we needed to complete it by the deadline."

Task: here you need to set out the specifics of the task at hand and highlight anything which was your individual responsibility. Make sure you emphasize any particular challenges involved, or goals/targets you needed to work to.

"I called an emergency meeting with the other team members, and we collectively agreed on a new strategy. However, reflecting on our choice later in the week, I could see that we had not fully thought through our options and had selected an approach which would not work. I got in touch with the rest of my team and tactfully voiced my concerns. I was aware that this may not be well-received as we were working to such a tight timeline. Fortunately, I managed to persuade them of my perspective while still maintaining a good team dynamic. I suggested that we all do some more research and then meet again to discuss our options more carefully, and also arranged a meeting with our supervisor to get their thoughts on our new plan. Ultimately, the strategy we decided on was one which had come out of my own research and ideas I put forward to the group."

Action: here, you should explain what you did and what steps you took to achieve your goal. Remember to lay out your *individual* contribution in detail where you were working as part of a group: make it clear what you personally did, rather than just talking about the actions of the group (e.g. 'I initiated a meeting' rather than 'We all met up as a group').

"In the end, our adapted project design worked very well, and all members of the group completed the project in time for the deadline. In fact, the way we changed our project design meant that we were able to address our research questions more thoroughly than would have been possible otherwise, and we found some very interesting results. When we presented our work to staff and students at the end of the project, there was a lot of interest in the novel method I'd proposed, and we're currently working to submit our findings to an academic journal. Through this process, I have learned about the importance of good teamwork in dealing with unexpected challenges, and this is something I think I could put to excellent effect in the current role."

Result/Reflection: here you need to describe the effect of your actions on the outcome, demonstrate your accomplishment, and reflect on what you've learned. Try to be as explicit as possible about any positive results or change (for example, there might be a way to quantify what you've achieved).

Table 9.4 Example Competency-Based Questions and Project Experiences You could Draw On

Competency-based question	Relevant project experience(s) and example competence(s) demonstrated
Tell me about a time when you have overcome adversity/a challenge.	Unexpected equipment failure; difficulty gaining access to schools for data collection [resilience; adaptability; problem-solving].
Give me an example of a time when you have had to deal with conflict within a team.	Students in your project group are unhappy with each other's contributions to the research project [teamwork; conflict management; empathy].
Tell me about a situation where your communication skills made a difference/where you had to explain something complex.	Explaining technical details of your research project to a student in your team who is struggling; presenting complex research findings to staff/students who do not know the topic area [communication].
Tell me about a time where you have sold an idea that represented a challenge.	Persuading your project group to carry out a more complex design; justifying novel research ideas to your supervisor [influencing; negotiation].
Tell me about a situation that tested your integrity/a time where you made a mistake.	You discover an accidental breach of confidentiality; you suspect one of your project team is making up data [integrity/honesty; professionalism].
Give me an example of a time when you had to prioritize demands to obtain a goal.	Planning to complete your research project for a deadline, whilst juggling a part-time job and a commitment to volunteering [organization; time management; self-awareness].

dealt with these challenges, what you have learned from them, and how you would approach a similar situation in the future all give an important insight into your skills and attributes.

Table 9.4 gives some examples of potential competency-based questions you could expect to be asked in an interview or application form along with some ideas of project experiences you may draw on in your answer. In each case, remember to focus your response on what you did and the competences you demonstrated rather than on how unpleasant the scenario was.

The questions you are asked on application forms and in interviews likely share many similarities. The main difference between the two is that you do not typically know the exact questions you will be asked in an interview in advance. As such, it is worth thinking about probable questions and drafting some example answers in the STAR format so that you are well-prepared.

Handy Hint
Your project offers you the chance to demonstrate and develop a wide range of competencies that might be applicable in a professional context. Knowing which to prepare to talk about at interview is important. To help you anticipate which to focus on, do your research—as well as reading the job description and person specification for a role, the organization information and values can give you clues about what they are looking for. Know these well and consider which of your project competencies are most closely aligned.

9.4.4 Expressing Project Competences on a CV

The best way to get comprehensive advice on creating a CV is by speaking with an advisor from your institution's careers/employability service. However, it is worth noting here that different forms of CV exist, and that you should plan to tailor your CV for individual roles rather than using the same CV for all applications. As with interviews and application forms, select a small number of your most relevant project skills to showcase on your CV and provide examples of those skills to evidence them to an employer. While your descriptions will be notably shorter on a CV than in response to a competency-based question, you can use the same basic principles of the STAR technique to present your examples and refer back to your project reflections to choose appropriate ones.

Summary

As a psychology graduate, there are a multitude of career options available to you, and your research project can help you on the way to all of these! Your project provides an excellent source of experiences and opportunities to develop valuable graduate competences; these will be attractive to employers both in psychology-relevant fields and outside of psychology. In order to make the most of your project experiences, it is critical that you take the time to regularly reflect on what you have done and what you have learned. Doing so will help you become more aware of your own skills and, importantly, how your expertise can be applied in a professional environment. This is one of the key things that gradate employers will want to see. Learning how best to articulate your competences will allow you to showcase the benefits of your research project to the full and set yourself apart as a psychology graduate.

 Go online to access further resources for the text:
www.oup.com/he/whitt1e.

References

Akhurst, J. (2005). *Enhancing the Employability of Psychology Graduates.* The Higher Education Academy Psychology Network. https://www.advance-he.ac.uk/knowledge-hub/enhancing-employability-psychology-graduates

Boud, D., Keogh, R. A., and Walker, D. (1985). Promoting reflection in learning: A model. In D. Boud, R. A. Keogh, and D. Walker (eds), *Reflection: Turning Experience into Learning* (pp. 18–40). Routledge.

Gibbs, G. (1988). *Learning by Doing: A Guide to Teaching And Learning Methods.* Oxford Further Education Unit.

Hugh-Jones, S. and Sutherland, E. (2007). *Employability: How to Maximise The Employability of Psychology Graduates.* Advance HE.

Janis, I. L. and Mann, L. (1977). *Decision Making: A Psychological Analysis of Conflict, Choice, And Commitment.* Free Press.

Lantz, C. (2011). *Psychology Student Employability Guide: From University to Career.* Advance HE. https://www.advance-he.ac.uk/knowledge-hub/psychology-student-employability-guide

Moon, J. (2007). Getting the measure of reflection: Considering matters of definition and depth. *Journal of Radiotherapy in Practice,* 6(4), 191–200. https://doi.org/10.1017/S1460396907006188

QAA (2019). *Subject Benchmark Statement for Psychology.* Quality Assurance Agency.

Starcke, K., & Brand, M. (2012). Decision making under stress: A selective review. *Neuroscience & Biobehavioral Reviews, 36*(4), 1228–1248. https://doi.org/10.1016/j.neubiorev.2012.02.003

Stoverink, A. C., Kirkman, B. L., Mistry, S., & Rosen, B. (2020). Bouncing back together: Toward a theoretical model of work team resilience. *Academy of Management Review, 45*(2), 395–422. https://doi.org/10.5465/amr.2017.0005

Tripp, D. (1993). *Critical Incidents in Teaching: Developing Professional Judgement*. Routledge.

Yorke, M. (2006). *Employability in Higher Education: What It Is, What It Is Not* (Vol 1). Higher Education Academy.

Index